The IEA Health and Welfare Unit

Choice in Welfare No 42

Adoption and the Care of Children:
The British and American Experience

Patricia Morgan

IEA Health and Welfare Unit
London

First published March 1998

The IEA Health and Welfare Unit
2 Lord North St
London SW1P 3LB

ISBN 0-255 36434-2
ISSN 1362-9565

Typeset by the IEA Health and Welfare Unit
in Bookman 9.5 point
Printed in Great Britain by
Hartington Fine Arts Ltd, Lancing, West Sussex

Contents

Tables and Figures

The Author

Patricia Morgan, Senior Research Fellow in the family at the IEA Health and Welfare Unit, is a sociologist specialising in criminology and family policy. Her books include *Delinquent Fantasies*, 1978; *Facing Up to Family Income*, 1989; *Families in Dreamland*, 1992; *Farewell to the Family?*, 1995; *Are Families Affordable?*, 1996; and *Who Needs Parents?*, 1996. She has contributed chapters to *Full Circle, Family Portraits, The Loss of Virtue, Tried But Untested, Liberating Women from Modern Feminism* and *Just a Piece of Paper?*, as well as articles for periodicals and national newspapers. Patricia Morgan is a frequent contributor to television and radio programmes and is presently writing a full-length work on the relationship between capitalism and the family.

Foreword

At a time when large parts of the state have been or are being privatised, the family seems to have been nationalised. This was the point forcefully made by Jon Davies in another IEA publication, *The Family: Is It Just Another Lifestyle Choice?*

In recent decades the state and its many agencies have played a significant and fast growing part in family life. The large-scale breakdown of the family based on marriage has, of course, made increasing numbers of parents (usually lone mothers) and their offspring dependent on the state for support. Indeed the cost to the taxpayer of lone parents has exceeded the cost of unemployment since 1995 as the state has become the surrogate father to millions of broken or incomplete families.

However, it is not only in the field of family dysfunction that the state has assumed the parental role. Decisions on the upbringing of children, which used to be regarded as incontrovertibly the prerogative of the parents themselves, now come within the remit of government regulation or, at least, propaganda. For example, the campaign to criminalise smacking has been successful in schools and may soon be extended to the home. Social workers have shown themselves ready to place children on 'at risk' registers, and even remove them from home, on the basis of incidents which would, until recently, have been regarded as questions of parental discretion in discipline.

Unfortunately the state makes a very bad parent. Children who are brought up by its agencies start life with tremendous disadvantages. As Patricia Morgan shows in this book, the outcomes for children who spend all or a large part of their dependent years in the care of their local authority are atrocious. The council-run children's home now has all the allure of the workhouse. Even foster care, on which childcare professionals place such emphasis, is a very poor substitute for a secure upbringing in a stable family, particularly when it is part of a regime that shunts children from one set of carers to another, with periodic returns to the natural parent(s) who abuse or neglect them again. The downstream costs to society of the many thousands of children who are 'graduating' out of the system and onto the welfare rolls, onto the streets and into our prisons, are enormous.

This makes it remarkable—indeed almost incomprehensible—that adoption has been so down-played as to be regarded as the very last option for children who cannot live with their own parents—and an undesirable one at that.

Patricia Morgan shows how the objections to adoption have changed over the years, from fears that it would undermine primogeniture, or encourage immorality by giving unmarried mothers an easy way out, to the more modern obsession with matching racial profiles. In spite of the objections, studies have shown that adoption has extremely good outcomes. Even in the worst cases, involving children who are severely disturbed or disabled, adoption can offer them the stability they need to develop and triumph over adversities. There is no such thing as an unadoptable child.

The many obstacles which are now placed in the way of couples who wish to adopt, and of children who clearly need a substitute family, must be addressed. Patricia Morgan ends her book with the recommendation that local authorities should not act as adoption agencies, but that the whole procedure should be handed back to the voluntary bodies specialising in the field of adoption. The main aim of childcare services should be the integration of children into normal family life, not their upbringing by functionaries of the state.

John Blundell
General Director, IEA

Acknowledgements

It is with great pleasure and appreciation that I acknowledge the help given to me by Jim Richards, Director, Catholic Children's Society. I owe a particular debt to Marcus Carlton, Team Manager, Statistics Division, Department of Health. I also wish to express my gratitude to Michael Brennan, Principal, Adoption Policy, Department of Health; Karen Irving, Director of Parents for Children, Carolyn Fairbairn, Alison Taylor, Richard Whitfield and Joan Woolard, as well as many others, lay and professional, who have helped make this book possible. Finally, special thanks go to Robert Whelan for help above and beyond the call of duty.

Note on Statistics

One of the most remarkable aspects of the issue of adoption in the UK is the scarcity of data. Other 'family' issues, such as births and abortions, marriages and divorces, have their own annual volumes of statistics. However the only information published by the Office of National Statistics about adoption is confined to three tables included (for no obvious reason) at the back of the Marriage and Divorce Statistics. Apart from these, it is possible to glean some figures from statistics of children in care, but there is nothing else on a national basis. Even the data we have is suspect: returns from local authorities may include misclassifications, estimates and incomplete information. Many of the studies on which we rely concern sample groups, so there are problems with extrapolating the data to the whole country. We are ignorant about such basic facts as the length of time which adoption procedures take, and the number of adoptions which are step-adoptions. A well-informed public debate on adoption clearly requires more and better statistics.

Section A
The Obstacle Race of Adoption

Adoption has fallen out of favour. It is presented negatively by the media, by feminists, by childcare professionals and by racial awareness campaigners. Numbers have fallen dramatically, and baby adoptions have become rare events. The unmarried mother is now asked to chose between abortion and lone parenthood, with adoption scarcely mentioned as an option. Whilst the government nominally supports adoption, recent trends in family law, and in particular the Children Act 1989, make it increasingly unlikely that children will ever be declared free to be adopted. As private voluntary bodies have withdrawn from the field, adoption is largely handled by the social services departments of local authorities, which are charged with implementing the provisions of the Children Act. They make few adoption placements, and place all sorts of obstacles in the way of couples wanting to adopt.

Most children who are placed for adoption are already in the care of the local authority—which is also the adoption agency. The procedure to free a child for adoption is complicated and often pursued without much enthusiasm by the authority. It can take years, during which the child will experience multiple placements. If an adoption is contested it can prolong the process by years, causing distress to all concerned. Social services are unwilling to terminate parental responsibilities since they aim for 'family preservation' at almost any cost. Mixed-race children are particularly likely to get 'stuck' in the system owing to the opposition to trans-racial adoption.

The population of children in care has been falling because the 'threshold' of abuse or neglect at which the local authority will take a child into care has been rising. As a result, the children who are in care are likely to be experiencing severe problems, and are often admitted in an emergency. Increasingly, local authority care is seen as a means of giving 'respite' to parents, while they prepare to make another attempt at raising the child. Consequently, children can spend years being shunted between care, foster parents and their own homes. There is little evidence of success for such a policy. On the contrary, problems are exacerbated with every move of the child back and forwards. Children in care are largely from highly disrupted homes. Children either leave care quickly, or they stay for years.

Legal adoption is a recent phenomenon. The first English Adoption Law was not passed until 1926, when it was seen as a means of helping infertile couples. It established a regime known as 'closed stranger adoption' and involved secrecy on both sides, careful attempts to match biological and adopting parents, and dealt only with baby adoptions. Adoptions reached a peak in the late 1960s, but attitudes were still highly restrictive, with children barred on seemingly trivial grounds. No matter how inadequate the birth parents, if they were unwilling to allow children to be adopted, the legal powers to force them to do so were seldom invoked. Children were more likely to be left to languish in care for years—perhaps their whole childhood—because the local authorities were unwilling to intervene positively. Despite legislative changes in Britain and the USA to try to prevent this, the emphasis on 'family preservation' has thwarted attempts to give needy children more permanence in their lives. In terms of 'family preservation', adoption is an undesirable outcome, with childcare professionals bringing into play an ever-growing number of objections to it.

1

What's Wrong with Adoption?

ADOPTION has a long, but chequered, history, whether as a means to perpetuate or add to families, or as a way of dealing with homeless, unwanted or otherwise abandoned children. The question at the heart of this book is whether it is finally becoming unnecessary as a child rearing strategy, or whether it has a vital part to play in safeguarding the welfare of children in the twenty-first century.

Adoption is under attack as a childcare strategy by a powerful alliance of feminists, childcare professionals, racial awareness campaigners and the media. In the words of one critic: 'legal adoption has outlived its time and should be abolished. Since it is not physically or historically possible to wipe out birth connections, why provide an instrument to do this legally?'[1] The objections raised against adoption are legion, and we will be looking at them in detail later. For now it is enough to observe that, for whatever reason or reasons, adoption gives the impression of being a practice in terminal decline.

On the Way Out?

In 1995 there were only 5,797 adoptions in England and Wales—less than a third of the 21,299 of 20 years before—and about half of these were step-parent adoptions, in which one partner (usually the husband) in a marriage formally adopts the other partner's existing children. (Step-parent adoptions are largely irrelevant to considerations of adoption policy, practice or outcomes, so this book is exclusively concerned with non-relative, or stranger, adoptions.)

The number of baby adoptions in 1995 was 322, a relic of the 4,548 for 1975, or even of the 969 for 1990 (out of 6,533 adoptions). The proportional increase in older child adoptions disguises the way that their numbers have been relatively static. Even then, the totals include the small but growing numbers of inter-country adoptions. (See Table 1:1 and Figure 1:1.)

Table 1:1 Adoptions by Age, 1975-1995, England and Wales

Year	All Ages		Under 1 year		1-4 years		5-9 years		10-14 years		15-17 years	
	No.	%	No.	%	No.	%	No.	%	No.	%	No.	%
1975	21,299	100	4,548	21	5,523	26	7,278	34	3,316	16	634	3
1977	12,748	100	2,945	23	3,002	24	4,185	33	2,192	17	424	3
1979	10,870	100	2,649	24	2,183	20	3,572	33	2,013	19	453	4
1981	9,284	100	2,365	25	1,910	21	2,784	30	1,823	20	402	4
1983	9,029	100	1,962	22	2,094	23	2,651	29	1,832	20	490	5
1985*	7,615	100	1,605	21	1,645	22	2,261	30	1,625	21	454	6
1987**	7,201	100	1,333	19	1,694	24	2,164	30	1,462	20	495	7
1989#	7,044	100	1,115	16	1,875	27	2,244	32	1,331	19	458	7
1991	7,171	100	895	12	2,071	29	2,409	34	1,381	19	415	6
1993	6,859	100	465	7	1,894	28	2,543	37	1,570	23	387	6
1995	5,797	100	322	6	1,494	26	2,216	38	1,433	25	332	6

Source: *1994 Marriage and Divorce Statistics*, London, The Stationery Office, 1997.

* Total includes 25 cases where age was not stated.
** Total includes 53 cases where age was not stated.
# Total includes 21 cases where age was not stated.

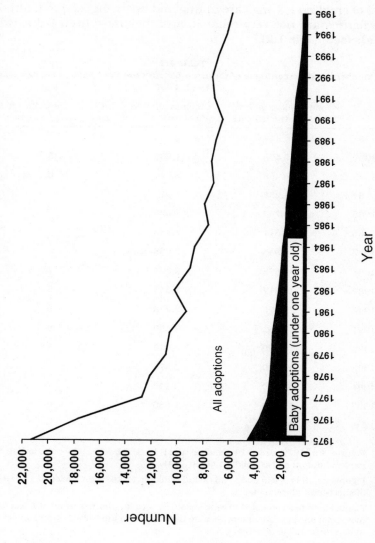

Figure 1:1 Adoptions and baby adoptions 1975 - 1995

Number

Year

All adoptions

Baby adoptions (under one year old)

Source: *1994 Marriage and Divorce Statistics*,
London: The Stationery Office, 1997

Most non-relative adoptions now involve children who have been through the care system, having come from families unable or unwilling to look after them. It seems that around five to eight per cent of children leaving care in England are being adopted, although the figures are not very reliable, and they have been falling in the 1990s (see Table 1:2).

Table 1:2
Numbers and Percentages of Children Leaving the Care System via Adoption
1981 -1996

	Total number of children who left care	Children adopted out of care	% of children who left care through adoption
1981	38,412	1,636	4
1982	37,408	1,828	5
1983	36,409	2,044	6
1984	34,238	1,912	6
1985	32,793	1,920	6
1986	31,611	1,935	6
1987	30,688	2,038	7
1988	30,678	2,301	7
1989	28,917	2,316	8
1990	29,070	2,478	9
1991	28,282	2,439	9
1992*	14,100	1,080	8
1993	32,000	2,370	7
1994	32,100	2,140	7
1995	31,300	1,830	6
1996	31,600	1,710	5

* Figures for 1992 cover 14 October 1991 to 31 March 1992 only, owing to the implementation of the Children Act in 1991.

Figures for 1994, 1995 and 1996 exclude children looked after under an agreed series of short-term placements.

Figures have been adjusted to compensate for local authorities where it is known that more than one per cent of records were missing due to unresolved discrepancies in the data or incomplete returns.

Source: Department of Health.

Taking into consideration the children remaining in the system, it is estimated that about 3.5 per cent of children going through the care system end up adopted.[2] Some areas may have no adoptions,[3] or 'few adoptions, despite a large number of looked-after children... one authority had only three adoption orders and yet had 457 looked-after children'.[4] The low overall level of adoption of children from care, combined with wide local variation, obviously owes more to the practice of local authorities than the children they serve.

Negative Stereotypes of Adoption

Attitudes towards adoption have become increasingly hostile as the numbers have been falling. Along with sexual and reproductive peculiarities, it has become a stock-in-trade of television talk shows, with tormented birth mothers describing their regrets about placing children for adoption years before, and tearful teenagers describing their desperate efforts to locate birth parents.[5] A documentary called 'Forgotten Mothers' focussed on poignant examples of women who might have made good mothers asking: 'How can anyone on this earth make the decision to take a child away from its mother?'[6]

The case against adoption is usually made by invoking the model of 'closed stranger adoption', typical of the 1950s and 1960s. In this stereotype, young, confused and isolated birth mothers are pushed into parting with their babies to unknown couples in a complete and final break, with no prospect of ever knowing anything about their child's whereabouts or fortunes. This tradition is also represented as a 'powerful testimony to the desire of adoptive parents to "own" the child, rather than any realistic assessment of the best interests of the child'.[7]

Women are now more likely to lose their children through the law courts than by signing them away after birth, but the latter is construed as just as bad, if not worse:

> The birth mother's loss is enforced. The relationship between mother and child is ended because other people have decreed it. This increases feelings of anger and helplessness... Parental and professional opinion about what was best for the baby may have brought pressure on the young mother, but the decision to relinquish the child remained hers, even though many felt that in reality they had little choice. The modern-day birth-mother... is officially assessed as unfit to be a parent.[8]

Adoption seems to be an unmitigated woe for all involved. I pick up a leaflet on the Post-Adoption Centre at a local family centre. It aims to provide 'professional post-adoption services for over 3,000 people each year' and is for 'anyone who has been involved in adoption'. The first thing it tells me is that: 'We counsel parents who have adopted and their children, who may be confused, anxious, withdrawn, or angry'. Adopted people come over as a tragic lot in much of the literature, loaded with: 'the feeling of being different and special (chosen), at the same time as being unloved, outcast and forsaken, [which] contributes to a confusion familiar to adopted people of most ages'.[9]

Adoption is portrayed as being anti-child, anti-woman, and anti-black, redistributing children from the poor to the middle class.[10] As the economic system is accused of impoverishing certain groups of people, so the necessity to abandon children 'has been forced upon poor people by Western social welfare practices ever since the first Poor Laws; it is one of the first and longest-lasting Western exports to the countries that come within the orbit of world capitalism'.[11] The adopter only gains a child at the expense of another parent, who has suffered the anguish of giving birth to a child she has to give away, because others are more powerful and richer than she is, making adoption a reflection of society's inequalities and inhumanity. For undeveloped countries it is the relationship to the western capitalist world which produces the drain on resources and the inability to support children, so the children themselves become an export.

At the same time, women are seen as compelled to give up children because of the way in which the male-dominated family is purport-edly supported by the welfare state.[12] In what *Death by Adoption* calls violent, political acts of aggression against women,[13] they are rendered powerless by the narrow-minded stigma attached to illegitimacy and the refusal of society to provide the resources necessary for them to bring up children successfully on their own. 'At every turn in the story' things could have been different:

> Unmarried and unpartnered women who have babies could pass without social comment; their births could be an occasion for joy... Money and a house, community support and friendly help could be given as a matter of course, forestalling the need for the mother even to contemplate giving up her baby.[14]

With professional opinion turning against adoption as a strange, even repellant, practice, it tends to be excluded from the list of possibilities presented to women with problem pregnancies and child-rearing crises. If the mother raises this uncomfortable subject, it may be passed over by telling her to 'have the baby then see how you feel', with the hope that she will be reconciled to keeping the child. In the mid-1980s a University of Illinois study reported that some 40 per cent of those identifying themselves as 'pregnancy counsellors' (in health, family planning, social services, and adoption agencies) did not raise the issue with clients: an additional 40 per cent provided inaccurate or incomplete information.[15] Counsellors do not simply proceed on the assumption that pregnant adolescents have little or no interest in adoption, but provide little or no support for those who might want to explore this.[16]

Thirty years ago there was a stigma attached to having an illegitimate or unwanted child. However, '[a] single woman who brings up a child today may be applauded as independent and strong; the stigma has passed from the unwed mother to the mother who relinquishes her child'. In this hostile climate: 'the revelation that a woman gave birth to a child before marriage is scarcely shocking. It is much more difficult to explain why the baby was adopted'.[17] The result is that: '[w]hereas previously there had been heavy social pressure on unmarried mothers to decide on adoption, they were now more likely to be pressurized in the other direction'.[18] It seems that social workers cannot deal with the idea of women putting a child up for adoption and have difficulty accepting their decisions.[19]

The Race Bar

In the case of trans-racial adoption, the reason to repudiate the practice is: 'exploitation—in that black babies and children, the most valuable resource a community has, have been taken away'.[20]

This has not been the professional view, until fairly recently. The guidelines used by the Child Welfare League of America between 1958-1972 stated that: 'Racial background in itself should not determine the selection of the home for a child. It should not be assumed that difficulties will necessarily arise if adoptive parents and children are of different racial origin'. On the contrary, families 'should be encouraged to consider such a child'.[21] A shortage of white children and black adopters meant that, by 1970, a third of America's 6,500 adopted black children had been placed with white families. However, following the peak year of 1971 for trans-racial adoptions, the solution came to be regarded as a problem. The National Association of Black Social Workers stated that:

> Black children should be placed only with black families whether in foster care or adoption. Black children belong physically, psychologically and culturally in black families... We have committed ourselves to go back to our communities and work to end this particular form of cultural genocide.[22]

With the Child Welfare League now insisting that it was preferable to place children with their own racial group, adoption agencies, as a matter of policy, no longer placed non-white children in white homes. The rate of trans-racial adoptions plummeted: there was a 40 per cent decrease between 1971 and 1972 alone.[23]

The phenomenon spread to Britain, where the National Association of Black Social Workers and Allied Professions claimed in 1982 that putting black children with white families had 'the most devastating consequences for the children and the black community'.[24] In a national sample of children adopted trans-racially in 1995 the majority of local authorities, or 39 out of the 48 surveyed, reported no trans-racial placements.[25] (The adoption of mixed-race children by white parents is defined as a trans-racial placement.)

Few agencies, voluntary or statutory, would admit to imposing an outright ban on trans-racial adoption, but this often exists in practice.[26] *Be My Parent*, the newsletter of the over-arching British Agencies for Adoption and Fostering (BAAF), applies strict racial criteria to its 'advertisements' for children seeking new families. A child who is of African Caribbean, Asian and white English [sic] origins is expected to find a home reflecting his ancestry. Black always predominates, so that a child who is a quarter African-Caribbean has to have at least one black parent.[27] A particular agency's policy may specify that a trans-racial placement cannot be considered until efforts to secure a same-race placement are exhausted; advertisements for foster or adoptive parents may be targeted at blacks only, and children may be removed from foster parents or prospective adopters with whom they have lived for years, to secure a better racial match. This concern can override kin ties; with social workers reported to be looking for separate black and white foster homes for half sisters (one born to her single mother by a black man, and another by a white man).[28]

However, there are still complaints about social workers operating 'in a colour-blind fashion' or 'within an assimilationist/integrationist framework'.[29] There is also speculation that the trans-racial adoptions which unfortunately still get through may be the result of some foster carers adopting children. It is to prevent such cross-race attachments growing up in the first place that there is 'an urgent need to address the short-term placements of minority ethnic children which frequently drift into long term'.[30]

All can be justified with reference to the Children Act 1989. This stresses the need for a local authority to give due consideration to the 'religious persuasion, racial origin and cultural and linguistic background'[31] when making decisions about any child they are looking after. This can be construed to mean that children must be placed with a family of the same race, religion and culture. A circular from the Department of Health in 1992 on the principles governing family placement—speaking of the 'sustained efforts' needed to recruit a sufficient number and range of prospective adopters from ethnic minorities—is taken to mean that children must wait until the right ethnic match comes up.[32]

The Way We Live Now

Prior to the 1960s, a single pregnant woman, particularly if she were young, would be faced with two options: either have the child adopted or marry the father. It has been calculated that, prior to the 1970s, most premaritally conceived births resulted in marriage before the birth of the baby, but if the woman did not marry, there was a less than a 30 per cent chance that the baby would be kept.[33]

However, the social reforms which accompanied the 'sexual revolution' of the 1960s presented a completely different menu of options. Abortion became legal, effectively on demand, in 1968 and provisions for lone parents improved dramatically, particularly after the introduction of 'no-fault' divorce under the 1969 Divorce Law Reform. A comprehensive system of financial support for lone parenthood was put into place[34] so that, by the late 1970s, it was already rare even for pregnant teenagers to consider adoption.[35]

Obviously, the easier it is for women to prevent and terminate pregnancies and the higher the welfare payments for lone parents, the smaller the supply of babies for adoption will be.[36]

Adoption and the Children Act

Adoption as a valid childcare option for children in the welfare system was further undermined by the Children Act 1989. Its aims are understood as keeping children in their birth families whenever possible; reducing the number of children admitted to care through the courts; partnership between parents, courts and social services; and, when children have to go into care, promoting contact, and returning them eventually to their birth families.[37] Foster and residential care are family 'support services', rather than substitutes for home care. Since attempts to terminate parental responsibility—as it is necessary to do in the case of contested adoptions—mean that 'social workers are bound to become involved in disputes' it is understandable that this would make 'it difficult... to sustain the concept of "partnership"... embodied in much recent British childcare legislation'.[38]

The Children Act 1989 and the Children Act (Scotland) 1995 also impose duties on adoption agencies to consider alternatives to adoption, like long-term foster care or residence orders, which might provide a permanent address without severing the connection to the birth family. As such, guardianship in some form has increasingly commanded favour as a replacement for adoption. It is claimed that the 'advantage of residence orders is that they confer parental responsibility without interfering with the child's identity and family relationships'—implying that both are undermined by adoption.[39]

Local Authorities Take the Lead

While adoption was originally something which came within the remit of the voluntary sector, developments over the last couple of decades have passed the responsibility for adoption largely to local authority providers. By the 1980s fewer than half of the 73 independent adoption agencies which had been operating in the 1960s[40] were still working in the field. All of the national placing agencies had gone, along with many of the local ones, and many of the children's diocesan societies run by the churches were concentrating on other social issues and services.

These changes are the result of the 1975 Children Act (with the following Adoption Act 1976) as well as the rapid decline of baby adoptions. At the same time as the number of voluntary societies was shrinking, local authorities were assuming more responsibility for adoptions, especially as these were more likely to involve children who came within the orbit of their social services departments. The Adoption Act 1976 gave this movement a concerted push. This was hardly separable from the Seebohm reorganisation and other developments, which created large 'generic' social work departments out of little groups of welfare specialists and greatly extended the powers and scope of social services. Granting a virtual monopoly on adoption, it required each local authority to have in place, either directly or in co-operation with other agencies, a comprehensive adoption service by January 1988.

In spite of this, the responsibilities laid on local authorities in 1976 are often still not implemented.[41] Arguments for new legislation to facilitate adoption are weakened by evidence that existing law is widely ignored. Most local authorities have not examined whether local services meet current local needs and there are 'clear and unacceptable delays in provision of services'.[42] Most do not have sustained partnerships or agreements with other adoption agencies, whether voluntary bodies or other local authorities. Management information about adoption work is generally very poor. There is a regulatory requirement laid on adoption agencies to review their practice, or adoption policies, procedures and work, not less than every three years. One inspection found that in only one authority was this a developed process, while '[i]n some, it was hard to find any evidence of such reviews being done'.[43]

In theory, the first definitive stage on the route to adoption is when an agency's adoption panel agrees that a child is suitable for adoption and recommends that s/he should be placed or freed for adoption. (Panels also have responsibilities for ensuring the suitability of prospective adopters.) The adoption agency (local authority or voluntary) then carries out a home-finding and matching exercise to find suitable adopters, following which the actual placement is recommended by the adoption panel. While the key task of a local authority's adoption panel is to overlook and ensure consistent quality in adoption work, their role:

> ... was often narrowly-drawn. Some were little involved in promoting children's welfare. They often appeared dominated by local authority interests and insufficiently distinct from authorities' decision making functions.[44]

While the panels are supposedly non-executive bodies—accountable in local authorities to social services committees but not sub-committees of them—they are invariably loaded and chaired by SSD personnel. The ease with which a local authority can create a panel in its own image means that they may be little more than rubber-stamping bodies.

The Adoption Agencies Regulations 1983 require adoption agencies to ensure that staff have adequate experience and qualifications to undertake adoption work. Researchers for the Department of Health and the Law Commission's Review of Adoption Law[45] looked at the proportion of time that social workers 'active' in the adoption area actually spent on this. For a half, adoption took up less than a quarter of their overall work-time, and the data collected by the Social Services Inspectorate also suggests that only a handful of staff spend more than 15 hours a week on adoption, and 71 per cent spend under 10 hours.[46] Schedule II Reports for the courts are a key information resource in the adoption process, yet 27 per cent of social workers had prepared none, 15 per cent just one.[47] While 50 per cent considered their supervisor to have specialist knowledge of adoption, 31 per cent did not. Staff specialising in adoption are rare. The result is diminishing expertise, with decisions being made by people without relevant training or experience, so that social workers feel that they are 'left just to flap in the wind'.[48]

Ironically, local authorities may be least oriented towards placing older children—who are the long-term denizens of their care system.[49] One survey of childcare placements over two years in a sample of English local authorities in the late 1980s found that, despite their tiny numbers, infant adoptions predominated. (These are likely to be straightforward and unproblematic: the child has never had another home and is more likely to be proceeding to its first with the consent of the parent.) Between them, the authorities had placed for adoption only 40 children over five—and 19 of these were placed by one department. The recent study carried out by the Department of Health and the Law Commission reinforced these findings.[50] Two-thirds of its no-relation adoptions going through the courts involved children under the age of five (37 per cent were babies under a year and 30 per cent pre-school children aged one to five).

Suspect Persons?

Jaundiced views of the motivations of adopters may go some way to explain why many people who present themselves as would-be adopters say that they are regarded with suspicion, or treated as social work 'clients' themselves. Local authorities are continually criticised for employing highly restrictive criteria to frustrate adopters. With accusations of bias against 'middle-class' couples, accompanied by a high-profile for 'gay adoptions', it looks almost as if adoption can only be countenanced if it affirms 'alternatives' to the heterosexual nuclear family it is accused of reflecting.

It can reasonably be argued that, as many of the available children may be handicapped or damaged, adoptive parenting may be far more difficult than a lot of people think. The cases that appear in the press are not always easy for outsiders to judge, given that the facts are not in the public domain. Certainly, the prospective adopters may not be as good as they make themselves out to be. Moreover, when the demand for children far outstrips the supply, this means that stringent criteria will be set for adoption, and perfectly suitable families may well be turned down for trivial or obscure reasons. In contrast, foster carers are in demand, so foster care requirements are not so strict as those for adoptive parents. Foster allowances are not means-tested and there is no bar on people on Income Support (as in the USA, where women on public assistance may foster).

However, whatever the veracity of reports that age or 'too-tidy' homes disqualify prospective adopters, the way that they may be made to feel unwanted and inferior is more than newspaper anecdote.[51] Studies of specialist agencies have found that a propor-tion of their successful new parents for special-needs children had approached local authorities only to be discouraged or turned down. Prospective adopters are certainly not encouraged to come forward. Half of the social services departments investigated by the Social

Services Inspectorate did not produce any publicly available information about their adoption service. They were so concerned to maintain a 'low profile' for adoption, rather than promote it 'positively', that those who wanted to know more about the local service 'were not well-served'.[52] Only one authority systematically recruited prospective adopters to hold in readiness for children. Work in family-finding teams was dominated by concerns to recruit and support foster carers. While there is a shortage of foster carers, only 27 per cent of prospective adopters have a child placed with them within one year of being finally approved by an adoption panel, and over 40 per cent are still waiting three or more years later. (Of course, they may be holding out for a baby, but not always.)

Reflecting a hostility or suspicion about the motives of prospective adopters: '[s]taff in several authorities made clear to inspectors that their priority was to find homes for children, not children for would-be adopters'.[53] Yet these are related objectives: children are hardly going to find homes unless people want the children. However, would-be adopters are not easily put off. All SSDs continue to receive approaches from those who want to know about adoption, and to possibly offer themselves as adopters.

2

Getting Adopted

IS adoption being used too much, or too little? Appropriately or inappropriately? We cannot begin to answer these and other questions unless we know more about how, when, and who, is now involved in adoption.

The great majority of children involved in no-relation (or non step-parent adoptions) are in either compulsory or voluntary care, so that a child referred to a local authority adoption service is probably being looked after by the same authority. This accounts for over 80 per cent of those involved in adoption applications.

The Struggle to be Free

Most children with local authorities at any one time are not, and will not, be candidates for adoption. However, small numbers are placed with prospective adoptive parents while in care. There are also children for whom freeing orders have been obtained, but who may or may not be placed for adoption. 'Freeing' is mainly used where there is a care order and dispensation with parental consent is required, to avoid the prospect of difficult, contested adoption hearings.[1] Applications for freeing orders are made by the agency, now usually the local authority, while applications for adoption orders are made to the court by the prospective adoptive parents. The procedure is infrequently used: the legal status of 880 of the 48,800 children up to 18 in care in England on 31 March 1995 was 'freed for adoption'.[2]Investigations in six representative areas of England[3] recorded no freeing applications for Somerset in a two-year sampling period, and only seven for Walsall.

A child might be placed for adoption before, or without, being freed. On the other hand, freed children may not be placed for adoption for a very long while, and may stay in care without being adopted at all —so that the tie to the original family is broken, but nothing is put in its place.[4] In the Department of Health and Law Commission's study[5] only 20 per cent of children involved in freeing applications were already in prospective adoptive homes. Others were with short-term foster parents (43 per cent) and a further 19 per cent were with long-term foster parents. Not only had over half experienced two or more moves since separation from their birth family, but 80 per cent of those with one or more previous placements were being placed again with interim foster parents.

The 'Endemic Nature of Delay'

Applications to free a child for adoption take around six months to get to court from the date the adoption panel formally recommends adoption. Due to the 'endemic nature of delay',[6] only around 30 per cent will have completed by six months, and only 70 per cent by 15 months. Under a half (40 per cent) reach a final order in one hearing and 14 per cent take three or more—although this makes no difference to the outcome.[7] Ironically, 'one of the benefits envisaged when freeing was introduced [was]... expedition of the adoption process'.[8] Afterwards, there is still the adoption application, with about 65 per cent taking at least six months to even reach the courts.

While children in care who are nominally 'placed for adoption' totalled 2,300 out of 48,000 in care in England in 1995,[9] we have no definite figure of how many of these placements are eventually formalised. Numbers leaving care for adoption in England went from 2,301 in 1988 (out of 30,678 leavers) to 1,830 in 1995 (out of 31,300) (see Table 1:2, p. 6).

It is not unusual for the time between making a decision about placement and the actual day of joining the family to take up to two years or more.[10] Recent inspections[11] showed how the time between referral to the adoption service and adoptive placement was two to three years for 11 per cent of the children involved and over three years for 22 per cent. Delays in framing clear plans for children's adoption, the absence of vigour in pursuing these, and the frequent lack of direct work with children were reasons why 50 per cent of six-to ten-year-olds waited over three years, along with 36 per cent of 11-to 15-year-olds. Decisions may be delayed for long periods as yet another effort is made to solve the birth parent's problems or new staff became familiar with the case. Twenty-eight per cent of children who had not yet been placed had been waiting over three years, and a further 19 per cent had waited two to three years.

In addition, there is also the time spent in care *before* any decisions are made about whether a child should, or should not, be placed (or freed) for adoption. In the British Agencies for Adoption and Fostering (BAAF) study of placements for adoption which broke down (or 'disrupted'), 27 of the 40 children involved had spent a total of five years or more, and another six more than two years, in care prior to placement.[12] Astonishingly, eight had spent seven to ten years in care, and a further four had been in care for ten to fifteen years. These children may have been waiting an untypically long time. However, a similar story is told by John Triseliotis and M. Hill about 103 children in care in Scotland in the mid 1980s[13] waiting for permanent placement. Over a quarter had been in care for at least six years, and a half of these were aged eight to twelve. Ten months later only 38 per cent of the children had been placed.

The situation is not dissimilar to that in the USA, where a child who is freed for adoption typically has been in the system for at least two years and has had a permanency plan for at least one year. However, deadlines for plans often come and go, court dates are postponed and files are lost as children are shuffled among foster families. It may take 15 months to terminate parental rights, another 18 months to be placed for adoption and another seven to finalise adoption. In some states a child could have had an official plan of adoption for more than three years without a petition having been filed. When children become free for adoption, more time is often needed to find families. It has been estimated that in 1996 there were 53,000 children, declared as free to be adopted, waiting in state care.[14] Black children wait two or three times longer than white children for an adoptive home and their odds of adoption are five times less.[15]

Long Waits and Many Moves

In the UK, as in the USA, waiting is likely to be combined with many moves before eventual placement in an adoptive home. In particular, older children tend to have had both previous placements in care, as well as multiple moves within the system after separation from their birth family. In the Department of Health and Law Commission's study, over a half of the children aged between one to five years involved in adoption applications, and the great majority of those aged between five and ten (84 per cent), had experienced two or more placements before being moved to their current home.[16] This is reflected in the snapshot provided in December 1996 by the Catholic Children's Society, which looked at the moves experienced by the last 10 children it placed for adoption from local authority care (all were 10 years or younger at the time of referral). While a baby had been placed direct from hospital and two children had experienced only one move prior to adoption, two had experienced two, one had experienced three, and four had experienced four moves.[17]

Social workers are often more prepared to accept adoption when it evolves out of fostering than precipitate it. If children are placed with long-term foster parents and become attached, then adoption may eventually occur as an accidental or unintended by-product of fostering, rather than as part of a definite plan. In the study for the Department of Health and the Law Commission, short- or long-term fostering was the original purpose of the placement in adoption applications before the courts for 35 per cent of one- to five-year-olds, 43 per cent of five- to ten-year-olds, and 75 per cent of 10- to 18-year-olds. However, a child may be in a foster placement for a very long time before any decision is taken to convert, or recognise, this as a possible adoptive placement.[18]

After placement eventually occurs, there is another interval before adoption is finalised. In one study of permanent family placements[19] for 1,165 special-needs children, just over one-third were adopted within the first year after placement, and 28 per cent were in placement for two years or more before adoption. Indeed, 61 children, including 30 who were under five at placement, were not adopted for three or more years. The Social Services Inspectorate also recently found that around 28 per cent of children waited two years (and 12 per cent over four years) before an adoption order was made: 'It was evident that timescales were rarely monitored or managed'.[20]

Contested adoption applications take far longer after the panel recommendation than uncontested adoptions. The most common ground for dispensing with the parent(s)' consent is that this is being unreasonably withheld, or that there has been a persistent failure to discharge parental duties. It has to be shown that it has been impossible to rehabilitate the child in the family and that the adoption will offer the child 'significantly' better opportunities. When birth families oppose intentions to seek permanent, substitute placements for their children, either at the freeing or adoption application stage, frequent adjournments and interim hearings often ensue. With years before there is a clear outcome, and '...no time limits built into the legislation... it *just goes on and on*'.[21] In one case, according to a social worker:

> The mother changed her mind about five times before we actually got to the court hearing which was supposedly contested, but she didn't turn up. She did want him adopted but she just didn't want to be seen to be agreeing.[22]

Both social workers and the judiciary may be confused about adoption law. While 'freeing' means that birth parents can no longer withhold agreement to the adoption itself, ignorance of this leads to unnecessary duplication of work.[23] In a system which is not geared towards children, delay is money to lawyers, and the inefficient get rewarded.

Prolonged court proceedings can lead to prospective adopters withdrawing under the uncertainty and strain, and social workers back-pedalling on placement work due to the ambiguities of the child's legal status. Uncertainty about likely court outcomes even delays the *referral* of children to the adoption service in half of the areas surveyed by the Social Services Inspectorate.[24] In Northern Ireland, where adoption from care is unusual, this is due in part to the courts demanding a very high threshold of evidence to dispense with parental consent.[25]

The Shibboleth of 'Family Preservation'

Moreover, 'placing with a view to adoption' is not so conclusive as it sounds. It may be combined with continued indecision as to whether the child is really going to move to a new family, as he yo-yos back and forth between prospective adopters and original parent(s). Prospective adopters can end up on the receiving end of ideological disputes, or 'disagreement over policy as to whether adoption or return to an unmarried mother should be encouraged for children in foster care'.[26]

One example involves Donna, whose mother Marcia put her into care after birth. Abandoned by the father, Marcia had problems forming relationships, and was uncertain as to whether she could both look after a baby and pursue her career. Despite poor relations with her relatives, she removed the baby from foster care and sent her to Jamaica. When she subsequently brought the child back, she demanded that social services take Donna away since she did not love, and feared injuring, her. Social work support was provided to keep Donna with Marcia, but she was back in care at three. Marcia toyed with the idea of adoption, while social workers explored means of getting her to take Donna back. Marcia did not visit and wanted to distance herself from the child 'to clarify her feelings for her'. However, on being re-housed, Marcia took the girl home, soon to be resenting her again. Donna returned to her foster carers while Marcia had a psychotic breakdown.

By now Donna was disturbed, did not want to live with her mother, and had experienced ten changes of care by the age of four. With Marcia seemingly set on adoption, Donna was referred to the BAAF Exchange. One family decided not to proceed, and her case was not reactivated for several months. At five Donna joined a prospective adoptive family. The mother was prone to depression, and could not cope with the demands of babies. She wanted a fourth child to round off her family, and thought that this might be achieved by adopting

a school-age child, preferably female and bright. The adoptive family
had no opportunity to speak to former foster carers; they had a poor
understanding of Donna's emotional needs and development, and
little or no information about the sort of behaviour they might
encounter—believing Donna to be a normal, intelligent girl, who just
needed a stable home background. Instead, she shrieked, head-
banged and had severe asthma attacks. A social worker commiser-
ated, but no constructive help was offered. The natural children
demanded more attention, while the resident grandmother was
hostile to the whole enterprise. Exhausted and getting little back due
to Donna's superficiality, the prospective adopters struggled on.
Donna made progress in social skills and in relating to others, and
her problems had generally diminished.

But Marcia still hovered in the background, playing intermittently
with the notion of having her daughter back. To encourage contact,
visits were built up until, again, Marcia demanded that her daughter
be taken away—not least because she was in the way of a new
boyfriend. As conflict escalated with the adopters, they terminated
the placement when Donna was 12 years old. Thus we have a poorly
planned prospective adoption allowed to drag on for seven years. The
adopters start out with unrealistic expectations, and are ambivalent
as they struggle on without specialist help and in the face of
opposition at home, while the fancies of the natural mother about
reunion continue to be encouraged and eventually undermine any
progress. At this sorry point, the chairperson of the disruption
meeting concludes that: 'while she [Marcia] cannot parent her
daughter on a full-time basis she might still have a particular and
valuable role to play in her life'.[27]

Throughout the adoption process the door may be left open to
possible reunification with the original family. Social workers have
become increasingly aware of the need to satisfy the courts that every
effort at restoration has been made. They may feel obliged to go 'a
mile and a mile beyond' trying to get the original parent(s) reunited
with their children. Others may not want to face a court, being well
aware that they have not perhaps been as energetic as they might
have been in trying to solve the parent(s)' problems and maintaining
their contact with children in care. Courts propose repeated initiatives to try and get birth parents involved or interested in their
children, even when these have been in the public care for a significant time. In turn, the durability and irreversibility of the family's
problems have to be demonstrated over a 'lengthy period' in order to
dispense with parental consent to adoption.[28]

One judge saw a 10-year old's 18 month stay with foster parents (who were prospective adopters) as too short to judge its comparative merits... In another case, two small girls had been taken into care as a result of the mother's drinking and immaturity. After... a year, restoration plans were abandoned, but the judge thought that the mother had not been given sufficient time to change, so that her withholding of consent was not unreasonable.[29]

This means that 'some contact arrangements sanctioned or suggested in the course of proceedings will be inconsistent with the perceived need to secure children's futures apart from the birth families'.[30] Planning for children is compromised. The courts cannot restrict—and may be encouraging—contact with birth parents, unless an adoptive placement is firmed up by the social services. However, social workers may not even consider a plan for adoption until the child's legal status has been clarified.

The Social Services Inspectorate has criticised delays due to the length of time taken 'to conclude that retention/rehabilitation in birth families was not in children's best interest'. The consequence of using 'adoption... as an option of last resort' was 'too great a tolerance for unacceptable parenting behaviour'[31] where repeated attempts at rehabilitation were at a cost to the children involved.

The position has been similar in the USA with states unable to obtain funds for foster care and adoption unless they have made 'reasonable efforts' to keep or reunite abused and neglected children with their original parents. 'Nowhere in the federal legislation, state policy, or ensuing legal decisions in state courts were "reasonable efforts" ever clearly defined.' When a mother fails a drug treatment programme, a judge has been apt to insist that she try every drug treatment programme available. Neither was 'the inherent and dangerous contradiction between ensuring safety and attempting to reunite abusive parents with abused children... acknowledged by federal or state officials'.[32]

Even where family rehabilitation or restoration is not possible, adoption may still be jettisoned as not in the child's best interests because there is, or might be, contact of some kind with the original family. A parent might have made it clear that s/he has no intention of having the child back, yet the courts may substitute foster care for adoption—if the social workers have not already done so—rather than have an adoption order with a condition of contact.[33] This includes situations where there is any link with any blood relative. According to one social worker:

I know of a case that has just been turned down because the child wanted to be adopted by her foster parents. She'd been sexually abused by her father but her brother was still living with his parents. Social Services wanted access to continue with her brother... It was decided that adoption wasn't in her best interests because of the residual link with her brother. It's changed into long-term fostering which I think is an awful shame.[34]

Family preservation may also be applied to baby adoptions, where the mother voluntarily relinquishes the child at birth. Local authority social workers may allow many months to go by before proceeding, with staff favouring long-term fostering.[35] Where a mother is persuaded to keep the baby, the child may be several years old by the time she refuses to look after it any more. Social workers will now attempt to 'keep the family together', often with the child in care.

Black or mixed-race children wait longest for adoptive homes.[36] Unsurprisingly, a larger proportion of black children in one prominent study[37] were nine or over by the time they were placed with a family, although there was no difference compared to white children in terms of learning difficulties, physical disability or ill health. However, black children were far more likely to be described as 'institutionalised'. Reflecting the squeamishness over whether they are adoptable or not, 35 per cent of the children who had been placed with 'permanent' foster parents, with no expectation of adoption, were black compared to only nine per cent in the whole sample. Trans-racial placement was a particular bar to adoptive status, with fostering felt to be far more appropriate in these cases.

The numbers of black or mixed-race children in care are disproportionately high,[38] yet the investigation for the British Agencies for Adoption and Fostering records a high of only 25 per cent for ethnic minority children among those adopted from care in London boroughs.[39] Similarly, the 1996 Social Services Inspectorate report revealed very low numbers of minority children amongst adoptions, varying from nil in one metropolitan authority to a high of 27 per cent in an inner London social services department.[40] Overall, white children made up nearly 85 per cent of the total, with Black Caribbean or African children a tiny three per cent. Low adoption rates for black or mixed-race children compared to the numbers in care may reflect greater reluctance to sever ties to the original parents, combined with antagonism to trans-racial placements when black homes are in short supply. Children wait for a considerable period until a black home comes along or the agency eventually turns to a white placement.

3

The Children 'In Care'

WHAT happens to that bulk of children in care at any one time who may neither be placed for adoption, nor become legally eligible for adoption? Under the Children Act 1989 (operational in 1991), they may be being 'looked after' by social services departments because they are either 'accommodated', 'in care', or remanded or detained.

When children are under compulsory care orders, a court has given 'parental responsibility' to the local authority as well as the parents, because the child is suffering or is likely to suffer 'significant harm'. This remains in force until the young person is 18, unless it is revoked. 'Accommodation' is voluntary admission to care, and the parents can take the child out at any time. Just under a half of children in care (45 per cent) are in this position, although nearly three-quarters of those starting or ceasing to be looked after are in voluntary agreements. There is a clear trend away from court orders towards these voluntary arrangements, which are better felt to express the 'partnership' in parenting between the state and the parent(s) inaugurated by the Children Act 1989. Following its implementation, the number of children being looked after at the request of and with the agreement of their parents doubled, while the number of compulsory care order episodes was reduced by more than a half.

However, there has been an overall fall in the number of children in the care system at any one time since the 1970s. The general population of children aged 0-17 declined by ten per cent in the 1980s, but there was still an overall decrease of more than a third in care numbers over the decade. The fall continued into the 1990s from 60,532 in 1990 to 48,800 in 1995 (see Figure 3:1 and Table 3:1). One reason is because care orders in criminal proceedings fell into disuse,[1] and were ostensibly abolished when the Children Act was implemented in 1991. Moreover, the figures for children involved in 'agreed series of short-term placements'—estimated at 6,000 in the year to 31 March 1995—are now no longer included in the care totals.

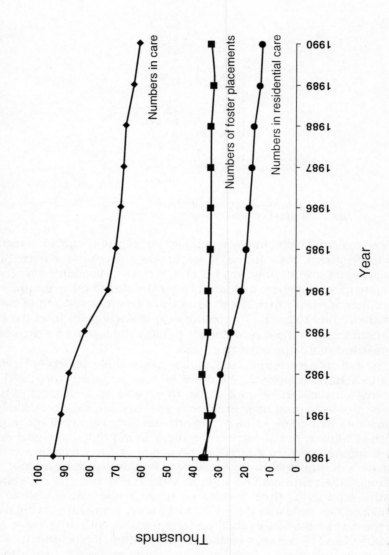

Figure 3:1 Children in care at 31 March 1980 to 1990, England

Numbers in care

Numbers of foster placements

Numbers in residential care

Thousands

Year

Source: *Children in the Public Care*, HMSO, 1991, p.26

Table 3:1
Children in Care/Looked After at 31 March 1980-1995

1980	95,297
1982	88,663
1983	82,165
1984	74,845
1985	69,550
1986	67,326
1987	65,768
1988	64,352
1989	62,148
1990	60,532
1991	59,834
1992	56,200
1993	52,600
1994	49,900
1995	48,800

Source: *Children Looked After by Local Authorities*, Department of Health, various years, and *Children in the Public Care*, HMSO, 1991.

These may mean children going in and out of public care on a regular or intermittent basis for days, weekends or weeks at a time. Such placements still mainly involve children with disabilities receiving respite care. However, they are being extended to other groups as a recommended way to assist parents who, for any reason, find caring for their child difficult. The withdrawal of such cases from the care statistics makes the recent decline in care admissions for the 1990s somewhat more apparent than real.

The fall in care numbers does not mean that children's circumstances have improved. As there is also a higher threshold for admission than there used to be, those who cross it tend to have more problems than their predecessors. They are also more likely to enter care in a crisis.[2] A large recently completed study of the impact of the Children Act on care proceedings found that 'damaging delay in bringing cases to court has been one of the unwanted consequences of implementing a strategy of minimum intervention'.[3]

Once taken into care on interim orders, children enter a state of limbo waiting for their case to go through the courts. Before the Children Act came into force, there had been a general slowing down in the court-case flow in child protection cases, with an average time of 20 weeks (15 per cent took over six months). One of the Act's key objectives was to tackle delay in the court process on 'the general principle that any delay in determining the question is likely to prejudice the welfare of the child'. But one effect of greater legal and administrative safeguards for families was to make this slower than ever before.[4] There may be more thorough case preparation; time-consuming written evidence; more remedies for family dysfunction to explore; more parties, more legal representatives and more experts where, as the number of practitioners involved increases, so the task of liaison becomes more complex and costly. There are more and longer hearings, with more cases moving from magistrates courts to the slower-moving higher courts, where they add to judicial overload. However, the 'more elaborate proceedings become, the greater the financial rewards', with 'virtually no incentives... for practitioners and courts to conduct business more economically and expeditiously'. Except for the child, all of the parties involved have incentives to slow up the proceedings.

> Those who risk losing care of their children have every reason to spin things out... under-resourced local authorities, fearful of getting things wrong, are often slow in preparing their child protection cases once a child has been admitted in an emergency to short-term foster care... The result is that some children... languish for months on end on a series of interim care orders, sometimes being moved from one short-term placement to another, and changing schools several times, regardless of their age and of the psychological damage.[5]

Furthermore, care cases must compete with the great mass of other court business, whether crime and motoring offences in the magistrates' courts or the mass of civil litigation in the county courts. Court administrators have no training in child welfare and, in any case, do not see their role as 'interfering' with the conduct and pace of proceedings.

In Care: For What?

Of the 31,100 children who *entered* public care in England during the year ending 31 March 1995, the most common reason for admission was because the parent(s) needed relief (29 per cent). Other commonly cited reasons were abuse or neglect (18 per cent), parent(s) health (14 per cent) and concern for the child's welfare (10 per cent), followed by the child's behaviour (five per cent) and the request of the child (four per cent) (see Figure 3:2).

The picture changes for the total number *in care* at any one point, as this reflects the accumulation of children over time. For nearly a half of the 34,188 children who had been looked after *continuously* during 1994/5, the child had been abused/neglected, or was considered at risk of abuse/neglect (or 16,070 cases, with a further 1,846 children considered at risk from own behaviour or beyond parental control). The parental health and 'parents needing relief' categories are sharply down (although 2,906 children had been in care for over 12 months because their parents were 'unable to cope').

28

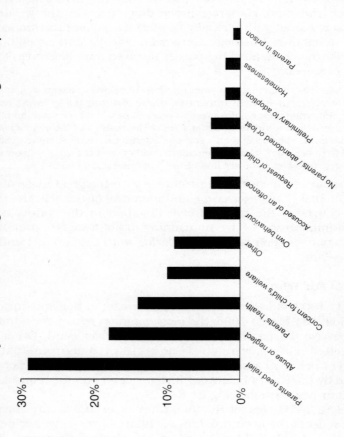

Figure 3:2 Children who started to be looked after during the year ending 31 March 1995 by reason for being looked after, England, percentages. *

Parents need relief
Abuse or neglect
Parents' health
Concern for child's welfare
Other
Own behaviour
Accused of an offence
Request of child
No parents / abandoned or lost
Preliminary to adoption
Homelessness
Parents in prison

* figures may not add due to rounding

Source: *Children Looked After by Local Authorities: Year Ending 31 March 1995*, Department of Health, London: Government Statistical Service

Figure 3:3 Children looked after at 31 March 1995 who had been continuously looked after during the whole of the 1994/5 year, by reason for being looked after (excluding children looked after under an agreed series of short-term placements), England, percentages. *

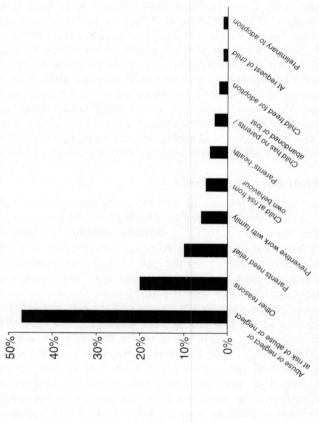

* figures may not add due to rounding

Source: *Children Looked After by Local Authorities: Year Ending 31 March 1995*, Department of Health, London: Government Statistical Service

Furthermore, there are 1,229 children listed as 'abandoned or lost' or who have 'no parents/no-one with parental responsibility' (see Figure 3:3).

Children are likely to be well known to the social services long before they are even considered for care. A study of referrals and admissions on care orders in England in the 1980s[6] found that one in three families had been known for over five years, and around thirty per cent of the children had been in care before. Moreover, almost a third of the children had also come to the attention of the police, and had been the subject of a previous referral to social services, either as offenders or non-offenders who aroused public concern about the protection of themselves and others. Social services do not tend to seek out candidates for intervention: people refer themselves, or are referred by other powerful agencies (as in the US where the fewest referrals come from social work agencies).[7] Behaviour that parents cannot control, or which also involves those outside the family—as well as the child's vulnerability at home—has been likely to push children into the care system.[8]

From What Sort of Homes?

The 'most striking feature of all' about the backgrounds of children going into care is the degree to which the families are 'incomplete, disrupted, or restructured following earlier breakdowns'. The '"normal" family unit of a married couple with children from that and no other union' is 'the exception rather than the rule'.[9]

Three out of four children entering care are from lone-parent families[10]—a proportion which has become more pronounced over time (moving towards the US figure of four out of five). With rising illegitimacy and divorce rates, and tendencies to 're-partner', care children 'magnify... accelerating social trends in a most vivid and exaggerated way'.[11] Jean Packman found that only 28 per cent of children referred for care orders were living with both natural parents, and nine per cent were with neither.[12] Only a half of the children with siblings lived with 'natural' brothers and sisters, rather than a series of half-siblings from a sequence of unions, giving a picture of 'many new family relationships superimposed upon previously fractured marital situations with bewildering effect'.[13] Even a half of the existing marriage relationships were fragile or poor, with generally high rates of heavy drinking and criminality.

Children are particularly likely to go into care following a crisis when the family is 'reconstituting' itself. This is highest for children on care orders for neglect or danger—85 per cent in one prominent study. For those in voluntary care it was 55 per cent, and 48 per cent for those deemed beyond control or in need of education.[14] Not only do the children have to cope with change, but this is often precipitated by, and accompanied by, violence.

Many children who are reunited with their families return to state care. The Dartington Research Unit Study found that previous care spells rose to nearly 50 per cent for 5-10 year olds.[15] In turn, 22 per cent of the children who returned home had to be re-admitted to care within two years[16], and other researchers have found a very similar figure for those discharged from longer-term voluntary care.[17] (A re-admission rate of one third is reported for 'reunited' children in the USA.)

In Care: Where?

The great proportion of children in care are either in foster care (around 65 per cent in England in 1995) or in some sort of community home. A few may be in other residential accommodation, sometimes as handicapped children or as young offenders awaiting hearings, or in voluntary homes, hostels and privately registered children's homes. There are now a number of 'placements with parents'—about 10 per cent—where social services supervise children in their own homes (this may involve 'day fostering' and child minding).

However, around a quarter of placements for those aged ten or over tend to be in residential establishments. The static picture of occupancy on a given day does not convey the extent of movement in and out of 'homes', nor the way that many children in care are likely to have had a residential placement.[18] As care numbers have fallen while as many children as possible have been put in foster families, those with long histories of disturbance, abuse or neglect, and chains of broken relationships, are over-represented in institutions. Just as children in care generally have more problems than in the past, those in homes are far more likely to be there after a final collapse in family relationships, breakdown of foster care, or a crisis of disordered behaviour, with solvent or drug abuse, delinquency, truancy, self-mutilation or suicide attempts—along with other 'long-term casualties' of the care system.[19]

The obverse side of keeping children out of care is the increase in emergency admissions, with more placements made in the context of a shortage of competent foster parents for children who may have already suffered disturbing disruptions.[20] Once the 'easy' children have been boarded out, foster care becomes more difficult to find, and increasingly costly.[21] The unit costs of foster placements doubled during the 1980s (although the costs of placements in community homes rose by 65 per cent)[22] (see Figure 3:4).

In Care: How Long?

Children either leave care fairly fast, or else stay for a long time. Over a half of the children who cease to be looked after in any one year have been looked after for less than six months. Many return home within a few weeks. After that, the flow of discharges slows to a trickle and a substantial minority remain in care indefinitely.[23] Around a quarter of the children being looked after at any one time have entered care five or more years before. A total of 24,900 (out of 48,000 children) had been in care more than two years at 31 March 1995; of which 19,900 had been there over three years and 2,900 more than ten years.[24] Patterns are discernible soon after entry to care. Work on admissions to care over a three month period in Northern Ireland showed how children who remained after six weeks were three times as likely to be there a year later than to have been discharged. By that time, three quarters of those admitted voluntarily had left.[25] Who Needs Care? bears out a six month 'dumping' barrier with voluntary admissions. If children are not re-claimed by then, they are likely to remain in care indefinitely.[26] Long stays tends to rise with age of entry,[27] in contrast to the US where early admission is associated with prolonged care. Otherwise the pattern is virtually identical, with around 50 per cent of US children received into care remaining for six months or less and many leaving within a month, while a quarter or more are still there over two years later.[28]

How Do They Get Out of Care?

On the face of it, the main reasons for leaving care are that the youngster becomes self-supporting or their care is taken over by the parent. However, children come into public care largely because of various deficiencies and difficulties at home or in themselves. When children return to parents, have social services resolved the home problems to their satisfaction or the benefit of the child?

The evidence suggests that it is parents and children themselves who are likely to take the active role in getting out of care, otherwise 'short-term' placement drifts on.[29] It also points to high breakdown rates and continuing abuse for a significant minority of children who return home.

Figure 3:4 Unit cost of children in community homes and foster homes, 1979 - 1990

Index 1979-80=100

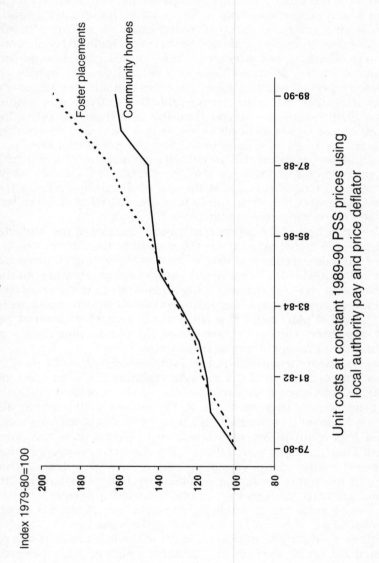

Unit costs at constant 1989-90 PSS prices using local authority pay and price deflator

Source: *Children in the Public Care,*
HMSO, 1991, p.58

A prominent study by Elaine Farmer covered 321 children on care orders who were 'home on trial' in four local authorities in England.[30] These were a *protected* group of young children, in care following abuse, neglect or family breakup. Others were *disaffected* adolescents who were offending, not attending school, or otherwise beyond their parents' control. For only 45 per cent did a panel of parents and childcare experts think that going home was suitable. For 19 per cent it was definitely felt to be detrimental. Sadly, there was nothing 'clearly contributing to success'. Two-thirds of those with offending in their backgrounds went on to re-offend once home. Where there was a failure to go to school, two-thirds did not attend once back home, and almost half of the teenage girls got pregnant. A quarter of the protected children were re-abused or neglected. Overall, 43 per cent were no longer at home at the end of the study period. Other studies have also found that only just over a half of children who returned home were able to stay there.[31]

Well over a half of the adolescents and a quarter of the protected children were 'home on trial' for the second or third time. Nearly a half of the adolescents and over a third of the young children had also experienced three or more substitute care placements, so that 'children who were functioning fairly adequately at the start of their care careers could become increasingly disturbed with each successive change of placement'.[32] A third of the protected children had spent over three years in the care system before returning home, and another third had spent one to three years.

However, the return of children was unplanned for two-thirds of the adolescents and a half of the younger children. Children often just 'graduated' home when they reached the age limit of their particular care placement, or they wanted to go themselves. Children may also go home because parents exert pressure, or because social workers cannot find a substitute placement, even if conditions are unimproved. This happened with a third of the children removed for abuse or neglect. With many young people, it was 'paradoxical that, although not going to school or offending had been [among] the original grounds for removal... these behaviours were not considered... to be sufficient grounds for removing the children a second time'. Social services may not feel that such adolescents are much to do with them, having been pushed to act in the first place: 'it was not unusual for social workers to... breathe a sigh of relief when the parents agreed to resume day-to-day care of their child'.[33]

A half of the adolescent 'at home' placements broke down in the two-year follow-up period, with a quarter moving themselves on to another household, or even a third or fourth household, making it hard for social workers to find out where those for whom they held responsibility actually were. (Under the Children Act 1989, social workers are expected to assess and approve these placements and it is even 'hoped that... local authorities will harness such resources'!)[34] Similarly, most of the young children who were re-abused or neglected stayed with their families as social workers attempted to 'absorb further incidents of concern in preference to removing the child'.[35] Not only were just 57 per cent of the children at home after two or more years, but many of these were living in very unsatisfactory circumstances—similar to other findings for 'at-home-with-parents' children.[36]

As restoration of the child to the family is the aim and criteria of success, its achievement is 'implicitly seen as the end of the road', and social workers are 'likely to develop a high threshold of tolerance for rather marginal standards of childcare'.[37] In the wake of the Children Act 1989, the Social Services Inspectorate referred to 'evidence of overlong and over ambitious attempts to secure adequate parenting of children where the quality of parental commitment was a cause of real concern. In a few cases... the focus on birth parents' needs overrode those of their children'.[38] Attempts to maintain the impetus towards restoration meant there was 'insufficiently clear or over-optimistic assessments of some birth families' parenting skills' combined with confused care plans for children, insufficiently monitored.

What this may mean in practice is illustrated by Gerrilyn Smith, who described a four-year-old girl being strapped screaming into a car to be driven to contact sessions with her parents. 'The child was inconsolable... she had been physically and sexually abused by her parents but the plan was to return her home to their care'.[39] Her case 'is not unusual', and there are children who are compelled to see parents who use meetings to continue their abuse, despite the children being adamant that they do not want contact with anyone from their family. The government White Paper *Adoption: the Future* expressed:

> concern that local authorities may sometimes work to keep a child with an unsatisfactory family for too long when it would be better to apply to the court for an order authorising an alternative family placement with perhaps a view to adoption. There is also some feeling that planning for a child who needs a permanent new family can be more difficult because of the emphasis in the Act on maintaining contact with birth families.[40]

But seeking a long-term, and possibly adoptive, substitute placement is absent, or low on the list of social service possibilities. Cases are more likely to turn out like Brenda's, cited in a National Children's Homes booklet:

> Brenda's parents separated before she was born. When she was three her mother agreed she couldn't care properly for Brenda and she was taken into care. When she was seven Brenda's mother felt she was able to care for her daughter again and she started going home for weekends. 'Almost right away my stepfather started interfering with me. He kept on sexually abusing me and threatening me for the next three years. If I didn't do the things he wanted me to do to him he would hit me, sometimes he would even tie me up and put me in a cupboard. At 10, I'd had enough, but when I told my mother she just beat the living daylights out of me and told me to get out'. Brenda returned to the children's home but could not tell anyone about her sexual abuse. Her behaviour began to deteriorate and she often ran away. She also tried to commit suicide by cutting her wrists.[41]

However, she stayed in the children's home until 17. The 'lesson seems to be that *if placement at home has not worked on a previous occasion, very careful thought needs to be given to trying it for the second time'.*[42] The probability of reunification is greatest immediately following placement. Children are likely to go back to their families where there is an intention to return, and receive, a child within six months of committal to care (and there has been only one substitute placement). This reflects both the family's ability and willingness to resume care, or its rehabilitation prospects, and the social work planning associated with purposeful efforts to secure reunion.[43] Later attempts, however intensive, are likely to be pointless.

A Family to Return to?

Family change has an impact on the capacity, or willingness, to have a child back. Not surprisingly, children from two-parent families are likely to exit the care system at far higher rates than those from lone-parent or 'reconstituted' families. While families of children going into care are disrupted to a quite astonishing degree, transient relationships, or the irregular and frequent arrivals and departures of 'parent figures',[44] are also the most striking feature of the families of children in care.

The younger the child at admission, the more his family is likely to be transformed in his absence. In one study[45] the families of nearly three-quarters of children admitted to care before the age of 11 had changed radically during two years of the child's absence, as had a half of the families of the older age groups. A similar picture emerges from Elaine Farmer's[46] work on 'home-on-trial' children, where fewer than a third of those removed for their own protection found their families unchanged on their return. A third returned to a parent who had separated or was in a new 'partnership'. In 41 per cent of cases the other children were no longer the same, since siblings were in care or new half-siblings had appeared. At least one in ten children went to completely different households from the ones they had known before.[47] As care families change in a remarkably short time, the continuous process of family turbulence means that social workers' judgements and the plans based upon these can become out of date within weeks or months.[48]

Periods in care are short if the parents take the child back, but tend to extend to the chid's maturity if they do not. Even when it is definitely known that a child will not go home, he will often stay in the system. After 18 months it is unlikely that a child will either return to his family or leave care for an alternative permanent home. This figure has an astonishing stability over time and place. The first study to look at the life courses of children in the public care (in nine US communities) appeared in 1959. It concluded that a child who remained in care for more than one-and-a-half years was very likely to grow up in care.[49]

4

A Short History of Adoption

L EGAL adoption, which confers upon the child a status exactly
equal with birth-children, is a relatively recent development in the
modern world, although adoption in various forms has been known
and used in many different societies. It has been secretive and
unusual in some epochs, while being accepted, commonplace and
applauded in others.

In the life of St. Symeon Stylite a man escapes punishment because
of three kind acts during his otherwise wicked life: he gave a monk
clothes, a stranger money and took up an abandoned child.[1] Long
before, the compassion of Pharoah's daughter for the infant Moses
meant his assimilation into her family's household.[2] There was
nothing unusual about this in a society where adoption was an
expected way to ensure family continuity. The scribe Nekhemmut was
berated for his 'inflated ego', and 'in being excessively stingy. You give
no one anything. As for him who has no children, he adopts an
orphan instead [to] bring him up'.[3]

The Kindness of Strangers

In ancient Rome, the care of unwanted and abandoned children,
described by John Boswell as 'the 'kindness of strangers', figured
prominently in writings 'from laws to novels, embodied in the statue
of a kindly wolf suckling two fatefully abandoned human infants'.[4]
Indeed, the adoptive relationship came to appeal to refined sensibili-
ties. Being initially voluntary, it was brought within the moral ambit
of kin relations, to embody their essence: 'Simple devotion went into
making the bonds... and the term *alumnus* became a symbol and
expression for a particular type of selfless and loving relationship in
Roman society and among its Christian heirs'.[5]

The ancient world left the fate of these abandoned children to the
whims of individuals. Exposed in prominent public places, there was
no civic intervention, and no effort to regulate children's treatment or
ensure their well-being. This obviously increased the risk of death,
but children were also likely to be picked up and reared by someone

else. Many households had children 'collected from other families, who may have been permanent or temporary residents, free or servile, exploited or cherished, legally adopted or simply supported'.[6] They might be brought up in slavery, as prostitutes, or as heirs to a rich man. Adopted by someone of greater rank or resources than their parents, they might achieve considerable success in life.[7] In short, they occupied any status open to natural children.

The abandoning of children was not uncommon in pre-industrial society, when many families found their survival threatened by too many children, and when high mortality rates took away the parents of dependent children. As such a convenient source of plots, it is reflected everywhere in early modern culture from Mozart's operas to Spanish picaresque novels to Fielding's *Tom Jones* and George Eliot's *Silas Marner*.[8]

The Great Disjunction

Adoption, meanwhile, had come to be regarded as an inherently troubling and risky concept in western society because of the overwhelming significance attached to lineage and birth in the Middle Ages. The result, for centuries, was that while there might be acceptance of foundlings as servants or second-class members of households, and the orphans of the rich might be cared for by relatives, they were rarely given the same status as the biological children of the couple. Families sometimes reared abandoned children, but usually with the pretence on both sides that the relationship was biological. 'Such deceptions doubtless improved the lot of individuals, but ultimately undermined the status of foundlings as a group by implicitly denying the ancient idea that adoptive parent-child relations were not only as good as, but in some ways better than their biological counterparts.' There was none of the 'much idealised, almost transcendent relationship of *alumnus* with foster parent, so admired in the ancient world'.[9]

With the virtual demise of adoption came what John Boswell calls 'the great disjunction' in the treatment of abandoned children, whose legacy is with us today. Instead of transplanting abandoned children into new families, they were more likely to be separated from the mainstream of social and family life and treated as a class apart. This 'great disjunction' was marked by the rise of foundling hospitals or orphanages in all major European cities:

> ...which neatly gathered all of the troubling and messy aspects of child abandonment away from view, off the streets, under institutional supervision. Behind their walls, paid officials dealt with society's loose ends, and neither the

parents who abandoned them nor their fellow citizens had to devote any further thought or care to the children.[10]

Even the orphanages did not have to care for children for long, since the great majority soon died: mortality rates were still 90 per cent or more in the eighteenth century. Institutionalisation replaced a pattern where, for centuries, child abandonment had resulted in a complex transfer system, which shifted unwanted or burdensome children into situations where they might be useful or valued. Instead, they 'disappeared quietly and efficiently through the revolving doors of state-run foundling homes, out of sight and mind, into social oblivion', where the 'walls afforded little opportunity for *anagnorisis* (recovery by parents), adoption, or triumph over natal adversity'.[11]

Communal care continued to be the accepted way to deal with poor orphans and abandoned children until after the Second World War. There was residential provision attached to workhouses, and voluntary societies like Barnardo's took in the destitute or 'ragged' children of the streets. These children might be apprenticed or contracted out to employers, or sent to the colonies. Indeed, colonisation—by putting a premium upon children and family size—began to encourage the re-allocation of otherwise displaced or unwanted children between households. Legal adoption re-emerged at about the same time in 'frontier' societies like North America, Australia and New Zealand. The first modern adoption law was enacted in Massachusetts in 1851.

> The spectacle of colonial households absorbing 'indigent relatives', let alone totally unrelated children, amazed English visitors; they put it down to an abundant supply of food, but... 'There were few substitutes for human labour on frontier farms', and the extra hands more than paid for the extra mouths... adopters much preferred 'children of "useful" years'—small babies were 'uneconomic'.[12]

The Legalisation of Adoption

It was not until the 1926 Adoption Act that the English adoptee acquired all the rights of a biological child. (*De facto* adoptions occurred before this time and there had been a growth in agencies that placed children). By then adoption had again begun to be seen as a way to build or add to a family; to give an infertile couple the satisfaction that they would get from having a child of their own. By the 1970s it was a way to provide for older children who could not go back to their original parent(s).

However, following the 1926 Adoption Act, only about 4,000 adoption orders were made annually in England up until the Second

World War. The practice was still widely felt to be somewhat dubious, with:

lawyers suspicious of the threat to well-established family law, with implications for legitimacy and inheritance in particular; and many of the general public seeing adoption as an unsavoury if not dangerous development, with overtones of babyfarming, cruel step-parents, and foster-parents on the one hand, and bastardy, 'bad blood', and a threat to decent family life on the other.[13]

Great stress was laid upon keeping the natural and adoptive parents from meeting or even knowing each other's identity. Much effort went into matching the physical and intellectual characteristics and background of the baby and adoptive couple. Notions of a 'complete transplant', together with the effort which went into confidentiality and helping the adoptive parents 'pass off' the child as their own, testify to the continual unease surrounding adoption. The secrecy incorporated into law and practice was felt necessary to protect the unwed mother and her child from excessive stigmatisation, and would-be adopters from the shame of infertility. It was also felt that adoptive parents might not be so willing to come forward if there were any threat of interference from the birth parent(s).[14]

There is now much talk of women having been coerced, bullied or persuaded to part with their babies. However, before the Second World War, adoption was likely to be the response to out-of-wedlock pregnancies only in special cases (the result of an extra-marital affair, or very young pregnancy). If a mother was unable to rear her children, single, married, widowed or deserted, the usual answer was institutional or foster care. Maternity homes encouraged girls to care for their babies, so that they might not neglect or abandon them. Adoption 'apparently allowed the young woman to "wipe the slate clean" and begin again. In some people's eyes, this was its biggest drawback'.[15] Anyway: 'There was very little demand for illegitimate babies... for they were thought to be 'tainted' by the circumstances of their birth'.[16]

A post-war change in approach gave more weight to the welfare of the child. Adoption might not only be best for the child by offering a better start in life with two loving parents, but an advantage to the mother, by allowing her to preserve her educational, occupational and marital prospects. However, the continuing assumption was that families would not offer homes to older children or others who came into special-needs categories. As the Hopkinson Committee reported in 1922: 'cases of clearly marked serious physical or moral defects are generally best provided for in institutions'.[17] Adoption was largely irrelevant to children in the public care.

The End of the Poor Law

The Children Act 1948 finally removed the care of deprived children from the Poor Law, and statutory social services developed on the premise that children would seldom, if ever, need alternative homes.[18] Public care was not endorsed as a way of rearing children in the long term, but neither was providing substitute families a recognised aim for children and adolescents in the system. Instead, the background assumptions, legislation, administrative rules and procedures of child welfare services developed on the understanding that stays in care would be transitory. As in the Home Office Report on the work of the Children's Department 1964-66, reception into care was seen as 'a temporary measure to prevent a final breakdown, or... part of a longer-term plan for the rehabilitation of the whole family'.[19]

An obstacle course often ensured that even children whose parent(s) had readily relinquished them could end up unadopted or unadoptable. In particular, children with imperfections or disabilities were not 'fit for adoption'. Extravagant claims about 'first-class' babies for 'first-class' couples were often defensive responses to the unsavoury connotations of adoption.

> Any characteristic seen by the authorities as an imperfection led to the removal of the child from the adoption list... at this time, mixed race usually debarred a child, while some doctors regarded any deviant behaviour in the mother as a genetic risk.[20]

> [T]he sorts of 'defects' which, in the 1950s and 1960s, could lead doctors to declare a child not suitable for immediate adoption ...included bat ears, an asymmetrical head, minor talipes, minor correctable squint, hernia, frailty and ill-health, feeding problems, and heart murmurs... One social worker commented, 'the number of babies who never went for adoption because of heart murmurs must be legion'.[21]

Babies with any health or developmental problems or difficult family circumstances were referred to the local authority or one of the large children's organisations which had residential nurseries. Many were eventually fostered, sometimes with a view to adoption, if their development was satisfactory. However, once placement was no longer a priority, years could go by while inquiries were made and doctors waited to see if a child turned out to be deaf, epileptic and so forth. By that time, another 'imperfection' may have been spotted: 'one child seemed slow to develop, another had no hair at twelve months, a third had red hair and so "not to everyone's taste"'.[22] As infancy passed, even more reasons could be found for not placing a child who was 'clinging and demanding', or 'shallow' or 'aloof and cool', or 'boisterous'.[23] One child spent his life in an institution because the comment on his record was 'not suitable for adoption because of his background'. When, by 1965, a society 'started placing babies with "slight medical difficulties and several who appeared to have an unpromising start" ...this was seen as a real breakthrough'.[24]

Yet, at the same time, prospective parents 'were going from agency to agency seeking a child'.[25] While local authorities were advertising for long-stay foster homes, prospective adopters were complaining to the Association of British Adoption Agencies that 'when they wrote to agencies expressing interest in an older child they were told that none were available'.[26]

Until the 1970s mixed-race adoptions were also commonly seen as 'very suspect by social workers', with some leading adoption societies not accepting non-white babies. Colour prejudice was mixed with a 'frank incomprehension that anyone could love as their own a child from a very different background, who could not "pass" as their biological child'.[27] The British Adoption Project found that non-white children comprised only three per cent of the 13,122 adoption orders made for agency-placed children in 1966. Yet agencies in the UK knew of another 846 who needed adoptive families, and there was evidence that at least a half as many again would have been put forward if it had been thought that a place might have been found for them.[28]

In Barbara Tizard's study of older adoptees, these children waited between two and seven years for a home. In half of the cases, the mothers relinquished the babies at birth and never saw them again. Delays were due to physical imperfections, or the fact that a relative was epileptic, and it was necessary to find out if the child had inherited this. What was already known about the background was often enough to make the child initially unacceptable for adoption: for example, a parent might have been insane or retarded. Social workers may also have thought there was still a chance that the mother might reclaim a child. It was assumed that every effort should be made to restore a child to his mother, even when there was little or no prospect of her having him back. Lois Raynor mentions the terrible anxiety which 'caused much insecurity and unhappiness' by repeated delays in legalising adoptions, even where children were with prospective adopters. (A number waited five years or more.)[29] They often believed that the agencies concerned had not really wanted them to adopt and had put all obstacles in their way:

[N]atural mothers had been encouraged to 'take a breathing space' in which to consider the pros and cons of bringing up the babies themselves... [but] they seem to have been given very little help in coming to a decision. They continued to waver, sometimes for years or in a few cases until a child was nearly grown up, before deciding to relinquish him for adoption by the foster parents... [who] lived with uncertainty and a constant fear that she would one day reclaim the child they had come to love as their own.[30]

Where the child was the result of an extra-marital affair, the mother may not have given up the child until she left her husband for a further lover. Other women had a number of illegitimate children, and did not relinquish them until they married, went to prison or into hospital. Mothers often hoped to reclaim children when their circumstances improved, although this tended to coincide with final relinquishment. Mothers sometimes disappeared for a number of years, so that the children could not be placed until they were found.

Dispensations Withheld

It was considered inappropriate to place children for adoption against their parents' wishes and contested cases were rare:

> Agencies seldom recommended prospective adopters to resist natural parents who changed their minds and claimed their children back... cases were almost never brought to court.[31]

This was not because grounds for dispensing with agreement did not exist before the 1976 Adoption Act. In the original 1926 legislation parental consent was required except where the parent had abandoned the child, could not be found or was incapable of giving consent. Courts also had power to dispense with the consent of any person 'whose consent ought, in the opinion of the court and in all the circumstances, to be dispensed with', but it was hardly used. In 1949 two new grounds of 'neglect' and 'persistent ill-treatment' were added, and the court could dispense with consent if it were satisfied that this was 'unreasonably withheld'. In 1958 'persistent failure without reasonable cause to discharge the obligations of a parent' was added. The 1976 Act simply brought together and consolidated existing law—adding one additional ground for dispensing with consent where the parent 'has seriously ill-treated the child [and] (because of the ill-treatment or for other reasons) the rehabilitation of the child within the household... is unlikely'.[32]

The use made of the law up to the 1970s would seem to reflect the weight given to parents' rights and the 'blood tie'. Certainly, few parents were 'likely to be so unredeemedly appalling' as to be caught by the stringent interpretation of the grounds for dispensing with parental consent.[33] But the disinclination to pursue adoption in the face of parental opposition was also strengthened by the same popular psychology which made the adoption of a child after infancy seem disastrous to social workers. Taking over from the fear that 'bad blood will out' were beliefs that early 'bonding' was irrevocable and unrepeatable, and that 'early trauma may have caused irreversible personality damage'.[34]

A Neo-Freudian Twist

This 'maternal deprivation' version of psycho-analytic or neo-Freudian theory asserted that separation from the mother, or early lack of mothering, had lasting and far reaching consequences for development, disposing to criminality and crippling the capacity to make relationships—or turning people into affectionless psychopaths. According to John Bowlby 'even good mothering was almost useless if delayed until after the age of 2½ years'.[35] This pointed to the need for adoption in the earliest months of life, and from the mid-1950s this was accepted practice. However, while Bowlby favoured adoption to save babies from the adverse effects of institutionalisation, the damage purportedly done by maternal separation was invoked as a reason why older children were unadoptable. It also reinforced the reticence about removing children from destructive parents—they would be doomed anyway—and encouraged their restoration.

In fact, the notion that adoption violates an unsubstitutable bond between child and birth mother is the most persistent strand in the aversion to adoption. It has recently been given a new lease of life by feminist insistence on the primacy of the rights of the birth mother.

The Reversability of Early Trauma

There were studies which pointed to a considerable degree of reversibility of early trauma, and they involved adoption. These included a British post-war follow up of 56 children with 'inferior histories', adopted in infancy from institutions.[36] It found that favourable development in early childhood continued into adulthood. Another involved 38 foundlings under six, adopted in the USA from Greece and Korea. Nearly all had come from institutions where both attention and food was scarce, and 20 per cent were very disturbed, aggressive, and made excessive demands (which were most severe in children over four). Six years later most of these children were judged average in emotional health, IQ and social competence.[37]

Studies of institutionalised children, describing them as permanently emotionally crippled, often involved subsequent fostering. In the more optimistic accounts, the children were adopted. The great corrective to the effects of institutional care was family living.[38] Parents adopting children showed unusual persistence and commitment, which may neither be expected of, nor given by, foster parents to the same degree.

As the accumulating evidence about multi-disadvantaged children was demonstrating that the effects of early adversity might be more or less reversible, a different model began to replace the determinacy of early experience.[39] In this, there are factors which increase risk over the life course, and others which are protective. Timing may be important and, at particularly points, children may be developmentally more vulnerable. However, cumulative stresses were more important than time-limited events, particularly when they set off chain reactions, where one traumatic event led to, and reinforced, others. Moreover, compensatory experiences do not have to be present at the time of adversity in order to counter any ill effects—they may also be efficacious if available later.

Even if the effects of early problems could not be entirely reversed, this was no argument for adding to these, or not mending where it was possible. What was not altered was the evidence that, the longer the stay in an institution, the greater the chance of intellectual deficits and the more extreme and entrenched any emotional and behavioural disturbances were likely to be.[40]

The Dead Children

In the early 1970s a spate of highly publicised child deaths also helped to discredit policies appealing to the 'once and only relationship' doctrine. Where the mother's plea for her baby to be taken into care had been turned down because of the 'likely effect of parting the child from the mother', the coroner commented that: 'I cannot see the point of leaving a child with its mother merely to let it die of starvation'.[41] Most prominently, Maria Colwell—after spending six years being fostered by her aunt—was returned to her natural mother (who had ten children by four men), and a violent, drunken stepfather. He beat her to death on 6 January 1973.[42]

The Children Act 1975 (and the subsequent 1976 Adoption Act) strengthened the rights of foster parents who, after caring for children for three years, might apply for a guardianship order and, pending the hearing, the natural parent(s) could not 'snatch' them back. They could then make independent application for adoption. By 1984 local authorities could go to court and ask that a child be declared 'free for adoption'. It was envisaged as useful in cases where an agency was unwilling to go ahead and place a child in its care, in case the court refused to dispense with consent at the adoption hearing and the child had to be returned.

Older Children: Adoptees in Waiting

The increasing emphasis on the child's current needs, and the research suggesting that late adoptions could be successful, suggested the possibility of a family for those who would otherwise grow up in care. It would also give couples the choice of adopting a handicapped or older child, and open up the lists to older people, or others who would not usually be considered eligible.

In 1973 Jane Rowe and Lydia Lambert produced the first systematic and major study of the *Children Who Wait* in Britain, on the model of the Henry Maas and Richard Engler study *Children in Need of Parents*, which first documented 'foster care drift' in the US in 1959.[43] While many children in care had little or no prospect of ever returning to family life, social workers insisted that:

> They were seeking for the children not substitute parents, but professional foster care workers who, without usurping the role of the natural parents, would see the children through a period of temporary difficulty and then return them to their own homes.[44]

The great majority of 2,812 children under 11 in the long-term care of a sample of local authorities and voluntary agencies had been there for the greater part of their lives. Half of the five- to seven-year-olds had been in care for four years or more, and half the eight- to ten-year-olds had been in care for at least six years. One in four had moved three or more times, either in or out of care, or from one foster home or children's home to another. Many of the 44 per cent in foster homes were in placements that were not expected to continue. More than 60 per cent of the children were expected to stay in care until they were 18 years old (including nearly 80 per cent of those in long-stay foster care).

Over forty per cent of these children had no parental contact and a further 35 per cent only saw a parent very occasionally. Many had gone into care too young to have any memory of parents or home life. Lone illegitimate children were particularly likely to go into care very young and stay for a very long time, and were seldom reunited with a family. In this discouraging situation family 'rehabilitation' was planned for two per cent of cases. No less than 70 per cent of children had mothers considered to have severely limited capacities for parenthood, due to mental incapacity or illness, or their mode of life.[45]

When asked, the social workers involved estimated that only 22 per cent of the children needed permanent substitute homes. This alone amounted to over 6,000 pre- or primary-school-age children nationally. Even so, very few children were thought to need adoption in comparison with 'permanent' or 'indeterminate' fostering, and adoptive homes were being sought for only 35 of the study children. Otherwise, adoption was only allowed to happen as an exceptional outcome of long-term foster care. Long-term placement, of any kind, was scarcely considered: 'Over and over again... months and years had passed before agencies woke up to the fact that the child was likely to stay in care indefinitely and that a permanent plan must be made'.[46]

The reasons for non-adoption included the fact that the child was too old, maladjusted, had brothers or sisters in care, or there was some link with his parents or grandparents. Some agencies insisted that the rights of biological parents should never be terminated, or that fostering was best even when children had no links with any parent. Among those thought by their social workers not to need a substitute family were a group of 81 children who had no family contact at all.

> Nearly half of this group had severe mental or physical handicaps, requiring specialist care, but almost all the rest could only be described as agency casualties. Most of these children could have been adopted if resources of home, staff and skill had been available at the right times, but their social workers now considered them too emotionally disturbed to be able to accept a substitute family.[47]

Another investigation later in the 1970s revealed much the same pattern.[48] Less than a half of the under-14s who had been in the residential care of Midlands authorities for at least three months were assessed by their social workers as appropriately placed in the long-term. However, only two out of 286 were felt to require a direct adoptive placement. A further 35 were felt to need fostering with a view to adoption, while the main choices were long-term fostering (52 per cent) and residential care (27 per cent). On these figures, only 70 children in the whole region were thought to require an adoptive home.[49]

It seemed that 'social workers had no idea of how to get children out of care', whether restoring them to their families or placing them in another home.[50] The trickle of children into adoption was, initially at least, externally prompted, or stimulated and facilitated by children's advocates and organisations like Parents for Children in the wake of *Children Who Wait*. But in reality the Children Act 1975, which made it possible to obtain a court ruling to free a child for adoption, changed little. Hopes that 'special-needs' adoption would reduce the public care population, or become a mainline childcare option, here or in the US, have been disappointed.

5

New Excuses for Old

IN 1985 the Dartington Project estimated that there must be 7,000 children entering care each year in England and Wales who were destined for a long stay and withering links with any family members. At any one time, at least 18,000 children—a third likely to be under eleven—were without meaningful contact with any relatives, and often in unstable care arrangements.[1] Again, in 1991, at least one in five care children were judged unlikely to return home and in need of stable long-term arrangements.[2]

'Permanency Planning' vs 'Partnership with Parents'

The advent of the 'permanence tendency' for children in care was opposed by social workers on the ground that it seemed to introduce 'a new and more suspicious relationship between the social worker and client'.[3] Because the Children Act 1975 made it easier to dispense with the consent of natural parents in contested adoptions it has been blamed for going too far, and causing 'confrontation' to take the place of 'conciliation'.[4] By making it easier for foster parents to apply to adopt the children in their care—an attempt to prevent a repetition of the Maria Colwell scandal—the 1975 Act was accused of encouraging foster parents to anticipate the transfer of parental rights to themselves, giving them more security than the natural parents of children in long-term care.[5]

Following a series of highly-publicised scandals involving the snatching of children by social workers, sometimes in 'dawn raids', on suspicions of abuse which proved to be unfounded, the Children Act 1989 represented yet another attempt to regulate the situation of children in care or thought to be in need of care. It was a response to disquiet over the power of social workers to short-cut the normal safeguards of the judicial process in the name of welfare. An important aspect of the Children Act 1989 was the application of the principles of due process to care proceedings, with proper examination of the evidence in court, regular procedures, fair hearings and legal representation.

It is now deeply embedded in the culture of social work that the Act introduced the principle of 'partnership with parents', and this in turn is construed as a reaction against the intrusion of a 'permanence' principle into children's services, by strongly re-affirming family preservation, rehabilitation and restoration as the goals of welfare services for children.

In fact, the term 'partnership' does not appear in the Act. Parents now retain parental responsibility when a child is taken into care, even if it is also awarded to the local authority. It is this sharing of parental responsibility—albeit on an unequal basis—under care orders, and its sole possession by parents voluntarily receiving services, which has been translated as a 'partnership' by politicians and civil servants promoting the Act. From here the term has passed into the social work lexicon as a duty to avoid anything which might antagonise the family of origin.

When a court determines any question regarding the upbringing of a child, the Children Act 1989 insists that 'the child's welfare shall be the court's paramount consideration'. On the face of it, this points as much in the direction of adoption as away. The same applies to the general duty of local authorities to 'safeguard and promote the welfare of children within their area who are in need' and '*so far as is consistent with that duty*, to promote the upbringing of such children by their families' (emphasis added).

It would seem that the touchstone of the child's best interests, which is in the Act, has given way to the emphasis on 'partnership with parents', which is not. As a result we are now witnessing the re-emergence of naïve claims that this all somehow makes it possible for nearly all children to remain with their families, or, if they are looked after by the local authority, to return to their families within a short time.

The American Experience

The 1980s saw similar developments in the US. The 1980 Adoption Assistance and Child Welfare Act, widely considered to be the most significant legislation in the history of child welfare, was a response to the feeling that too many children were going into foster care, with too few coming out, and costs rising exponentially. Its 'permanency planning' was 'a revolutionary change in child welfare practices': an attempt to introduce some structure, long-term perspectives and stability, with 'clearly defined pathways and time-frames for children and families'.[6] The aim was prompt and decisive action to keep children at home, restore them to their biological family, or place them for adoption as quickly as possible, thus reducing entrances to foster care and expediting exits. The intention was that children would no longer enter care inappropriately, drift in care or remain in care for years on end. Together with six-monthly reviews of the child's situation, the Act required that, within 18 months of opening a case, a permanent plan must be in place.

Permanency planning was the unifying theme of three 1970s demonstration projects: the Comprehensive Emergency Services Program (Nashville), the Alameda Project and the Oregon Project.[7] They showed how comprehensive improvements to child welfare could be achieved and that it was possible to develop the techniques for substantial reductions in the care population.

In the first, emergency services diverted inappropriate cases away from substitute care. The Alameda Project for children going into care focussed on family problems, and tried to get children home as quickly as possible. Caseworkers developed contracts with parents, spelling out the expectations, procedures and responsibilities of the agency, and what parents must do to get their child back. The restoration rate was 60 per cent in the experimental period—double that of the control group— with a 15 per cent adoption rate (compared to nine per cent in the control).

The Oregon project developed strategies for reducing the backlog of children accumulating in public care. Half of the children under 12 taking part had been in care for more than two years and over two thirds had had multiple placements. The major new weapon was the threat to terminate parental rights if the parents did not sincerely co-operate and work for conditions in which the child might return home—hitherto viewed as a very last resort in the most extreme circumstances. The achievement was 27 per cent of children restored and 52 per cent either adopted or in the process of being adopted. In counties where the project was implemented, the daily care population dropped 31 per cent, compared to four per cent elsewhere. It was estimated to have saved more than a million dollars in foster care payments alone, although it was not initially cost effective.

These successful programmes promised to usher in fundamental reform. However, in every case, 'reasonable efforts' had to be made either to prevent the removal of the child from home, or to make it possible for the child to return home, and planning guidelines became completely subordinated to this end—thus neutralising any real progress towards reform. The 'permanency plan (or "permanency goal") is almost always "return home"... this goal is rarely changed, no matter how unlikely its achievement'.[8] Welfare agencies operate on the assumption that children are always (or nearly always) better off with their biological parents, even in cases of extreme abuse and neglect, with the Child Welfare League of America insisting that 'no-one can truly substitute for the family of origin'.[9]

An initial hope may have been that 'almost every child who could not be permanently reunified with parents would be considered for adoption ... and that many would be adopted. As experience with permanency planning has accumulated... the low likelihood that adoption will occur has become clearer'.[10] One result is that children spend their formative years without attachments while attempts are made to rehabilitate parents who have no desire to change. Another result is that between 30 to 50 per cent of the children killed by parents or caretakers died after being identified as at risk by child welfare agencies, and were either left in their homes or reunified with parents who continued to be abusive.[11] In 1985 29 per cent of children referred to child welfare agencies had previously received help and their cases had been closed: by 1989, this had increased to 40 per cent.[12]

Adoption as a Negative Outcome

In terms of 'family rehabilitation' adoption is a negative outcome, not a positive placement option. At most, it is something to use when all else fails, or a measure of last resort and, as such, a failure in terms of social policy objectives. Its exclusion creates an *impasse*. When attempts at family rehabilitation do not succeed, children continue to suffer, either in the instability of out-of-home care, or in family environments that remain destructive.

> [The social workers] were worrying what to do with an eight-year-old, now in voluntary care, placed there by his mother and stepfather who said they could not manage him. A neighbour... first called in the social workers. The boy had been strapped and hit... The boy's mother admits she never wanted him and hated his father. Now she has married again, has two other children, and no-one wants the first child around. They keep saying to him: 'We don't want you, we don't love you. Why don't you go away? You don't belong in this family'. The boy's behaviour grew worse and worse, and the parents regarded the problem as entirely his. They refused to see that their treatment of him had anything to do with it. The parents had refused to go with him to the child and family psychologist. Is it better to go back to his bad family, or to stay in care?[13]

Yet, when parenting breaks down, neither at or after the time of crisis are mothers asked whether they really want 'to rear the child and whether they thought it likely that they would be able to rear it lovingly and with care'.[14] Instead, the story has been one of parents pushed to keep children, even when they expressly reject them, rather than pressured to make children available for adoption.

A case in point is that of murdered six-year-old Rikki Neave, subjected to endless cruelties during his short life. Nothing was done to remove him from his single mother by social workers persisting 'with a strategy in line with the principles in the Children Act 1989, which was designed to keep the family together'.[15] Ruth Neave, diagnosed as an 'inadequate psychopath', punched, kicked and beat a child she suspended over bridges and choked with his clothing, sending him out at night to collect her drugs. She behaved violently in front of social workers, who ignored her pleas to take Rikki into care: 'I am telling you I want him out. If anything happens to him be it on your heads. Don't say I haven't warned you'.

The case is a close parallel to Richard Gelles' story of David from the US. David was suffocated at 15 months by his mother, after reports that he was being abused. Prior to his birth, his six-week-old sister had suffered injuries which would disable her for the rest of her life. The case plan called for reunification, as mandated by the Adoption Assistance and Child Welfare Act 1980. She spent 18 months in care, with her foster parents wanting to adopt, as social workers tried to reunite her to the parents who had nearly killed her. Despite counselling, parenting classes and parent aides, they 'never were and were not becoming caring, nurturing, concerned or even barely adequate parents'. Yet: 'No one... set a deadline for ending the re-unification efforts. No one took stock of the family and made a determination about whether efforts were likely to succeed'.[16] Social workers only 'gave up' when the mother thrust the crippled child at them and furiously repudiated her parental rights.

'It Won't Work Anyway'

In an area where facts and values intertwine, the present tendency is to see adoptions against the wishes of natural parents as both impermissible—in leading to conflict and the involuntary removal of parental rights—and as unlikely to succeed. Contact with the original parents, however minimal, is seen to both preclude adoption, and to militate against its success. The responsibility for being unavailable for adoption may be attributed to children themselves, as something they do not want. Alternatively, children in the care system may be held to be largely unadoptable because nobody could want, or cope with, such handicapped or difficult children. Moreover, it is also seen as unfair or cruel to expose vulnerable youngsters to the possibility of a placement breakdown.

Such claims often lack credibility. A study of 1,165 special-needs placements found that, far from parental consent being vital for a successful adoption to take place, it was the *contested* adoptions which were more likely to succeed.[17] A significantly *smaller* proportion broke down if the child needed a family to cope with a contested adoption, even given that the children involved were older and had more difficulties. (Twenty five per cent for the over-nines with a contested adoption broke down, compared to 40 per cent where the adoption was not contested.)

It is possible to question the weight attached to contact compared with having a family to live with, or why one should rule out the other. Post-adoption contact need not alter the legal status of the adoptee, or militate against a complete transfer of parental responsibility to the adoptive parents. Older children may be more likely anyway to be in some kind of contact with members of their original family, which would have to taken into consideration in any adoptive placement.[18]

Certainly, when children have contact with someone hostile to adoption, their placements may be more apt to breakup.[19] An 'older sibling who had left the prospective adoptive family... [used] contact visits to unsettle his sister'. A boy was 'unsettled by the birth of a new baby to his birth mother and... was encouraged by her to think he could return home to live'. The middle-class parents of a 'five-year-old boy with severe learning difficulties... undermined the adoption placement because they tended to be overbearing and intrusive and treated the adoptive parents "like servants"'.[20] But should almost 'limitless irresponsibility' be 'tolerated in the natural parents' so that—provided they maintain contact of some kind—they are able to both disturb the child and effectively prevent him from forming any alternative relationships, without taking any responsibility for his care?[21]

There is also a failure to recognise that while: 'There are some immature and disturbed parents who can truthfully be said to "need" their children... these same parents are unable to offer any stability or security'.[22] It might be better to weigh contact against whether or not the birth relatives are supportive of adoption and accept the limited role that is appropriate for themselves.[23] Curiosity and concern on the part of the natural parents are not the child's responsibility, but something to be managed by the new caregivers, who can also hold any material in trust until the appropriate time comes.

Readiness for adoption on an older child's part may be a crucial indicator of probable success. However, ambivalence over the loss of old ties and the formation of other relationships should not be confused with a refusal or incapacity to adjust to the adoptive situation. While it is possible to point to care samples where a half of those unlikely to return home did not want another home—mostly older children removed from their families at a late age—there were just as many who did accept adoption.[24] It is questionable anyway whether a child should be allowed 'a waiver stating he doesn't want to be adopted and that he wants his goal changed to "independent living". This is akin to asking a child to sign his own homelessness warrant'.[25]

What Is So Special About 'Special Needs'?

The use of the term 'special needs' for what is often effectively all children in long-stay care gives the impression that they must be physically or mentally handicapped. In fact it is used far more loosely than that, for children with a religious affiliation, or who need to retain contact with siblings placed elsewhere, or whose adoption will be contested. It is even used for children who are simply over five years, or black, or have a sibling.[26] The term is also applied to children who have had multiple moves in care, are institutionalised, have behavioural or emotional difficulties and are, in effect, casualties of the care system. There is an element of self-fulfilling prophecy here.[27] The length of time children spend in care, or shuttling backwards and forwards between care and abusive or neglectful parents, may be the cause of problems which make the child 'hard to place' or unadoptable.[28] The 'unadoptability' of black children may be nothing to do with the children at all, stemming from opposition to trans-racial placement.

If some children have terrible legacies of abuse and neglect, this is an argument for intervening earlier, for limits to family preservation measures, and for the shortest time in care. A case in point is that of Mark:

> He has nightmares. He urinates in his bedroom. He soils his pants and hides them behind the radiator. He lies about everything, and he steals constantly. He masturbates in public. He makes sexual approaches to younger children. At the table he grabs at food and gorges it, then sometimes vomits it up. He cannot be left alone with small children or animals. Mark is nine years old... [He has] witnessed extensive violence between his mother and stepfather who were often high on solvents and alcohol. He has been hit, locked in cupboards, tortured and forced to participate in the sexual activities of his parents and visitors. Mark never wants to return home.[29]

The Extra Special Needs

There may be children who are so disturbed or dangerous as to be extremely difficult or impossible to put with families, or who require specialist facilities. Unfortunately, it is the impression of adoption workers that, over recent years, children have been coming from more disturbed families or have been kept longer with such families. However, there must be hesitation about describing even a very difficult or handicapped child as unadoptable, when it is 'nearly always possible to find another child with a similar background who has been placed elsewhere, so we must look at evidence of what has worked for these children'.[30] Perhaps it is better to talk of *adoptable children* as any children who can benefit from family life, or any children for whom a home can be found.[31]

It needs to be borne in mind that children may be as or more manageable in the hands of competent parents than in public care. Moreover, a parent's skills can be increased for dealing with children with severe behavioural and emotional problems. It is assumed that public care workers have access to assistance and expertise if they have problems with their charges. Why then, in the worst instances, should families be left to 'struggle alone and unsupported for many years with escalating control battles, often fearing to speak out',[32] coping with children from highly abusive backgrounds? If families are effectively acting as providers of intensive therapeutic services, should not resources be available to them? The parents may have to help the child overcome his history, develop the interpersonal and social skills to live successfully with others, and learn how families function, in what is an entire restructuring of his representations of self, others and relationships.

Take No Chances?

There is a tendency to assume that, since the breakdown of an adoption placement can traumatise an already disadvantaged child, we cannot therefore afford to take any chances unless there is a cast-iron guarantee that a placement will not breakdown. Akin to this is the assumption that it is somehow unwise to proceed where there is not an 'ideal' family. However:

> There is no such thing as an ideal family, any more than there are ideal children. This attitude to family placement has led to an expectation of 100 per cent success that cannot be achieved: it certainly isn't in natural families.[33]

Those who speak of the risks of adoption breakdown sometimes fail to take into consideration the countervailing risks involved in keeping children in long-term care:

Take the most negative scenario in terms of age at placement: a 48 per cent risk of breakdown for a child placed at the age of 12. This can be read alternatively as a 52 per cent possibility of the placement lasting. The more than 50 per cent chance of success... suggests that to exempt older children from permanent schemes, as some agencies have done, is inappropriate.[34]

Moreover: 'It will do the child a great disservice not to look for another family because of our feelings of inadequacy'. If the 'original decision was made on the basis of an accurate assessment of the child's needs, those needs have almost certainly not changed as a result of the disruption'.[35] In the study of 1,165 special-needs placements, 67 per cent of those who had experienced at least one broken permanent placement were successfully placed.[36]

Working Arrangements?

Given the deeply-held reservations about the validity of adoption,[37] it is hardly unexpected that local authorities are often poorly equipped to provide something to which they give such low priority. Successful practice involves the accurate identification of children who would benefit from adoption; selection and preparation of suitable families; matching children and families; arranging and monitoring introductions; supporting the placement and seeing it through. This depends on the quality of training and relevant experience, but we face the limitations of generalised social work qualifying courses, and the lack of in-service training.

The intention of the Seebohm reorganisation of social services in the late 1960s was for the generic social worker to replace the welfare specialist. The report in 1968 failed to explain why services would be improved by creating unitary social services departments. On the contrary, a number of submissions to the committee maintained that any improvements which may have accrued over the years were attributable to the expertise accumulated in specialist departments.[38] Some local authorities, finding the Seebohm vision unworkable, kept or re-introduced their specialists. Without specialisation, the opportunities to acquire experience are clearly limited. This creates a vicious cycle: if childcare workers have little experience of adoption, its volume hardly seems to justify specialist teams.[39]

Adoption work is labour intensive, and the time is difficult to find in the context of 'generic' social work. Even if people want to do this, they 'get torn to shreds by other aspects of departmental responsibilities which get in the way'.[40] The result is that 'enormous gulf between the conditions under which local authority social workers currently undertake this work and the minimum standards which are required to do the job properly'.[41] The pressures can mean that only high-priority, short-term, crisis work gets done. (Similar problems crop up in social work legal departments, where child protection also pushes adoption applications out of the way.) Thus many children remain in care or in a particular placement by default, not because it is decided that this would be the best course of action. As social workers are reactive, rather than proactive, once a child is in foster care the matter is settled unless the family complains:

> [I]n the Midlands [one social worker] said that once a child had been placed in care, *'they were then safe technically'* so social workers could *'pick up the next child abuse referral'*. One of the social workers in the South West with a general case load put the matter this way: 'Something may not be more important than adoption but it may be more immediate. In the scheme of things there may be a case which is less important—perhaps arranging holiday care for elderly people—but it's immediate... Adoption can always wait for another day. I know children who are waiting for adoption—the children who wait syndrome—and they are still there. And that's not a criticism of managers. I've been a team leader in a district office and I've had to say "that adoption will have to wait" '.[42]

Moreover: 'Because they are so final and clear cut, adoption decisions generate considerable anxiety in the professionals involved'.[43] There is often an inability to make executive decisions where the outcome is not absolutely certain and controllable—or where there is the possibility of failure, and thus of potential adverse repercussions for the individual or organisation. This tendency of functionaries to avoid 'making waves' means that for the 'ordinary, generic social worker, understandably paralysed by the enormity of the task, the temptation—perhaps at times the only professionally responsible course of action—is to play safe and do nothing' and leave the child in care.[44] At best, she might 'prefer fostering first because it postpones taking final and often painful and complicated decisions', where there 'may be an element of self-protection alongside the stated aim of protecting the child'.[45]

Children as Cashflow

In the US a prominent reason cited for the failure of government policies to place children in permanent homes is that: 'a public funding scheme ...rewards and extends poor-quality foster care'[46] and gives child-welfare bureaucracies incentives to keep even free-to-be-adopted children in state care. The states have received grants from the federal government based on the number of children in care, but there is no financial incentive to recruit adoptive families. If more children left the system, they would take money with them which supports substitute care. (This is due to change under the Adoption and Safe Families Act 1997 which will give bonuses to states for every child placed in a permanent home, with extra for children with disabilities.) There have been similar rewards for foster parents to keep children in care. Subsidies are tax free, and increase as the children get older.

In the UK, local authorities have not so much a financial incentive to keep children in care as a disincentive to use adoption. Adoption is a marginal extra for the child protection and care system and there are no special or extra resources earmarked for this. Local authorities often do not build up a 'bank' of prospective adopters, from which to choose when a child comes up for placement. (Similarly, in the US, many states do not support a recruitment programme.) If specialist organisations are used to find parents, local authorities must pay an inter-agency fee, instead of absorbing the costs. So they try to recruit parents from scratch for individual children, in between meeting all the other demands on time and resources:

> They may say 'I'd love to refer, but haven't got the money', and we cannot do it for free, we employ highly skilled people. Recently we placed a 13-year-old. The local authority first approached us when she was five, but could not use our services because they could not get the funding. They tried for six years to find a family, and came back when the child was 12. Although she is disabled we would have found an adoptive family easily at five, but now it is only a long-term foster home. She talked at one stage, but she lost her speech in the meantime.[47]

Local authorities use 'in-house' services because they are supposed to be cheap, but they do not really know how much their own adoption service costs and, in reality, these may be more expensive than using specialist agencies.[48] There are suggestions that some children's societies have backed out of adoption due to frustration at the way in which local authorities operate.

Certainly, finance is a commonly cited reason why UK foster carers —who might otherwise adopt—prefer the child to remain indefinitely in care. Significantly, children are sometimes adopted just before reaching 18 years, when the subsidies would come to an end anyway.[49] Where they are available, adoption allowances and residence order allowances are means-tested, so that middle-income families are ineligible (while fostering fees are not means-tested and are payable to those in income support). Where there are children who will need 24 hour close attention, even specialist agencies may recommend fostering in preference to adoption. An advertisement for salaried foster carers for Islington children with difficult behaviour—quoting fostering allowances of £160-190 per week and a fee of

£250 per child in 1996[50]—appeared at the same time as I heard of an offer of 11p a week for the adopters of a similar child.

Similarly, post-adoption support is left to local authorities to provide without extra resources from government, so that they may only fund services for foster parents. (In some cases, post-adoption support is understood only as arrangements for contact with birth families!) Adopters who take on what may be very disturbed or damaged children are engaged in a rehabilitative endeavour in parallel with that of a psychiatric or other therapeutic unit, without the recognition or resources. However, adoption is not recognised as a childcare option on a par with residential or foster placements in the care system, let alone one with remedial possibilities. Local authority budget holders do not balance the savings from adoption against the extraordinary costs for children in care, or the placements for detached adults in hostels, hospitals and prisons.

So much for the philosophical, organisational, and financial constraints in the way of adoption. But can the barriers be justified on the basis of evidence about its outcomes compared with the alternatives? It has been claimed that adopted children are prone to learning disabilities and underachievement; that they often exhibit dependency, fearfulness, and a lack of self-identity, and show a propensity for stealing, running away, and destroying property.

We must now examine the evidence of the outcomes from adoption.

Section B
The Outcomes of Adoption

When measuring the outcomes of adopted children, we should not compare adopted children with natural children in similar homes, since being brought up in stable, two-parent families in not an option for them. We should rather compare them with children in the circumstances they would have been living in, had they not been adopted. The outcomes for adopted children are generally good, not only compared with children brought up by lone parents, but even compared with children in two-parent families. The breakdown rate for adoptions overall is low—at about nine per cent. Baby adoptions are the least likely to break down, but even adoptions of older children with 'special needs' are successful in 80 per cent of cases.

A survey of adopted children as adolescents found that there was good communication and high levels of attachment between parents and children. Adopted adolescents were found to have good mental health and to be less prone to anti-social behaviour involving drugs and crime than adolescents as a whole. Adopted children do better than children living with lone parents on every score, but sometimes not quite so well as the biological children of two-parent families. When surveyed as adults, the majority of adopted people have expressed satisfaction with their upbringing. The most successful adoptions are those in which parents perceive the children as being 'like' them in some ways. In one British study, adopted people at 23 were more highly qualified than non-adopted people.

Even when children are adopted 'late'—i.e. after the age of five—the outcomes are still encouraging, and there is still, in most cases, a high degree of satisfaction on both sides. A study which compared children who had been adopted from care with those who had been returned from care to their parents found that the 'restored' children did badly in every respect compared with the adopted children. Very few of the adoptions broke down, but a high number of the 'restorations' did. Although late-adopted children experience more problems than baby-adoptions, these problems probably have more to do with difficult early experiences prior to adoption than to the adopted status itself.

Research shows that children who are adopted—even when they are 'late' adoptions with multiple problems—fare much better on all measures than children who remain in long-term residential homes or *foster care. Positive adoption experiences can overcome genetic predispositions towards mental disabilities.*

Most adopted people have no problems of self-esteem or self-confidence as a result of being adopted. The few adopted people who are unhappy with their upbringing are often those whose high-achieving adoptive parents wanted to force them into roles they could not carry out. It is sometimes said that adopted children are impeded by a lack of knowledge of and continuity with their past, but this is much more likely to be a problem for children in public care. Adopting parents who are accepting of the child's needs and limitations can overcome initial disadvantages. Despite some celebrity re-unions, most adopted people choose not to contact their birth parents when they are given the chance and, if they do contact them, they do not keep up a relationship. The adoptive parents remain the 'real' parents.

There is no basis in research for the view that children placed for trans-racial adoption are unhappy or unsuccessful. On the contrary, trans-racial adoptions have a high success rate—like other adoptions. Nor do the children lose their sense of racial identity, although they are less likely to form judgements about others based on their racial group than other children. The majority of adoptive parents had the support of their family and friends in making a trans-racial adoption. However no amount of research evidence will shake the implacable hostility towards trans-racial adoption of leading elements in social services, who are reduced to using obscure and undefined concepts such as 'institutional racism' to justify their opposition. There are large numbers of black and mixed-race children in care, as well as a shortage of black or mixed-race couples willing to adopt. Consequently many of these children will never exit the system owing to the objection to trans-racial adoption. The comforting explanation that they have a vast 'extended family' out there ready to take care of them is usually a myth.

6

The Adopted Infant in Childhood

THE most basic measure of adoption success is whether or not the relationship breaks down. The next is whether the adoptive parents and other members of the family are happy with the child, and do not regret the decision, even if the child is difficult or disturbed.

Another measure is whether the adopted child is free of serious behavioural problems, or if development is at least average or 'good enough' by standard measures, and—if they are older—whether it improved after the placement. There is a 'tendency among social workers, and to a lesser extent in the general population, to expect a successful adoption to be perfect and to equate problems with failure'.[1] Unfortunately, when adopted children experience problems there is a tendency to blame these on the fact of the adoption, without considering the many different factors which could be involved, and the fact that children experience problems in all family types.

Points of Comparison

With whom should we compare the adopted child? The obvious answer might be the natural children of parents of the same social class and general background as the adoptive parents. While such a reference point is useful and is employed by longitudinal studies like the National Child Development Study, it may be unrealistic in a number of ways.

For many adopted children, the option of growing up as a natural child in a stable, financially secure, two-parent family was not available. Hence: 'comparing adopted adolescents to non-adopted norm groups is comparing apples and oranges... the only *bona fide* comparison is to youth raised in settings that would have been the destiny of adopted youth had they not been adopted'.[2] The '*bona fide* comparison' here, then, is with children reared in residential care, fostered, or restored to the biological parent(s). The last option often means, in reality, returning the child to a lone mother of low socio-economic status, who is also likely to have complex and multiple problems.

The characteristics of adoptive parents—and adopted children —change over time. While adoption continues to be represented as an overwhelmingly middle-class practice, this may only characterise adoption in a particular era. Certainly, material standards have become less important in the selection of adoptive parents since the 1950s. In turn, as baby adoptions have become uncommon, adopted samples may contain an increasing proportion of more or less physically and mentally handicapped children, or those who have had very adverse early experiences. These children will not be comparable to the biological children of middle-class couples, or even children in the general population. Ideally, adopted and unadopted samples of children chosen for comparison should be matched for genetic as much as for home factors. The technical problems and cost of such a project renders it improbable. Yet, without it, do we rate the following as successes or failures?

> A father now 75 and widowed said convincingly that it had been a happy experience in spite of his daughter being a slow learner and 'mildly epileptic'. It was his opinion that nearly all the good things in life have some cost one way or another and that he and his wife had never regretted taking this child.

> ... Another kind and homely family had taken a little boy who today would be labelled a battered child, and had found great satisfaction in seeing him grow into a less insecure child whom they loved as their own, although he had never been able to achieve much in school. The... mother of another boy, who was so backward that the agency delayed the legal adoption for several years, said the boy was just as a natural son, kind, honest, hard-working, helpful and 'you couldn't ask for a better son'.[3]

What we may be able to discover is if, and to what degree, various traits, deficiencies and pathologies recorded for birth families are perpetuated by their children when these are adopted into very different environments.

When children are adopted after babyhood, there is a significant segment of their lives which has not been shared with their adoptive families, during which they have been shaped by others. It may be possible to see how adopted people fare at different stages of their lives, compared to those from different environments. This will tell us if early difficulties persist, and whether problems emerge later.

Studies looking at adopted children who have received psychiatric treatment have helped to paint a pessimistic view—in which 'adoptees are a high risk population for psychiatric disorder and [where]...

these higher risks may be attributable to problems associated with adoptive families'.[4] Certainly, adopted persons tend to be over-represented in clinical populations. For the USA it is calculated that, while non-related adopted children under the age of 18 make up about two per cent of the population, they comprise about five per cent of the children referred to outpatient mental health clinics, and between 10 and 15 per cent of those in residential psychiatric facilities.[5]

What we really need to know is whether there is a heightened risk of actual problems for adoptees, rather than an increased propensity of parents, teachers and others to recognise and report them. However, it is possible to have both more referrals, and more problems. Also, if 'adopted children are at increased risk for psycho-logical and academic problems in comparison to their non-adopted counterparts',[6] what is the rate at which these problems are likely to occur *for people with similar origins who are not adopted*? Even if we have a raised incidence of psychological disorder in adopted people, this has to be distinguished from whether there are special problems associated with *the status* of adoptee. In other words, any difficulties which adopted people may have cannot be automatically attributed to adoption—there may be other explanations.

Breakdown

The British Agencies for Adoption and Fostering (BAAF) estimates that the breakdown rate of adoptions averages around nine per cent. These include children suffering from major disabilities or multiple problems and school-age children.[7] For those aged under two, the breakdown rate is under five per cent—rising to 12.8 per cent for the six to nine age group and to 14.2 per cent for the over-tens. Not surprisingly, the younger the child at placement, the lower the risk of breakdown.[8]

Babies are, of course, the easiest to place and easiest to parent. More typical of present-day adoptees are the children in the major study of 1,165 'special needs' placements made by voluntary agencies for local authorities in the early 1980s.[9] A small number had one special need, mainly Down's syndrome, while 84 per cent had eight or more, whether being seriously ill, institutionalised, having behavioural or emotional problems, and so forth.

Overall, 21 per cent of their placements had broken down within a period of between 18 months and six-and-a-half years, making 79 per cent successful—being almost identical to the one in five recorded for other prominent studies.[10] Breakdown rose to 34 per cent for children aged nine to eleven at time of placement, and peaked at 48 per cent for 12-year-olds. After this age, it declines again. (It may be more difficult to make a mistaken assessment about a teenager's readiness to accept a new family, and the families may also be clearer about what they are taking on.)

Rates of breakdown were highest for children who had experienced multiple moves in the care system prior to adoption, for children who has been in institutions, and for children who had experienced deprivation or abuse. Children placed for adoption with brothers or sisters were less likely to experience breakdown than those placed singly, surprisingly perhaps in view of the fact that they were more likely to have experienced multiple moves; to have had a history of deprivation or abuse; and to need a family prepared to cope with a contested adoption.

Breakdown was low for children with Down's syndrome (only eight per cent) as it was for physical disability and serious ill-health (13 per cent). Such children may not be difficult to parent. This is underlined by investigations on behalf of the American Office of Health Development Services, where physically and mentally handicapped children were less likely to be involved in breakdowns before adoption was formalised than children with emotional and behavioural problems.[11] The rise in breakdown with both age and with emotional and behavioural problems shows the relevance of the child's experience prior to adoptive placement—a crucial factor for the handicapped as well as the non-handicapped. Just under five per cent of the adoptive placements of children with disabilities made through the Adoption Resources Exchange between 1974 and 1977[12] broke down. Most were babies or toddlers. The least successful placements were for the over-fives, who were also likely to have been in institutions for two years or more.[13]

Despite the preference of social services for fostering with a view to adoption, this seems more likely to break down than direct adoptive placements, or even permanent fostering arrangements.[14] The assumption that adoption can best develop out of fostering may be based on cases in which children have been adopted by the only parents they remember, where there was no threat from natural parents, and no previous placements. For a child with a 'history', it may mean continuing insecurity and uncertainty.[15]

Difficult behaviour in children may precipitate breakdown, particularly where there is a history of physical or sexual abuse. However, the capacities and attributes of adoptive parents also differ. The most comprehensive American study of adoptive breakdown for (mainly older) special-needs children implicated the unrealistic expectations of families and their problems in coping with the children's demands and difficulties.[16] Some 'attachment-disordered' older children who developed coping patterns of 'divide and rule' to survive in their original families or in the welfare system may undermine their adoptive parents' relationship as much as their own placement.[17] Other work has shown that married couples (as opposed to singles), families with prior adoptive experience, and couples where both spouses are equally committed, have fewer breakdowns,[18] although placement with a single woman may be preferable for severely sexually abused children. Family size, age, income, or education do not matter much, and trans-racial adoptions endure as well as same-race adoptions. Having a natural child close in years, and thus in needs, to the adopted child increases the risk of break-down, making childless couples better with sibling groups.

The skills of adoption agencies also affect breakdown rates. Thus, a specialist agency may have 'placed 32 of some of the country's neediest children [over three years]' with 'one disruption, a three per cent failure rate compared with disruption rates for this type of child of 40 to 60 per cent elsewhere'.[19] Families can more successfully parent these children if post-adoptive services are available to help and support parents in managing children who may have severe behavioural difficulties. Adoptive placements are put at greatest risk where parents are not told enough about their child's genetic background or early experiences, and they do not get to understand the effects of abuse on their adopted child.

The Outcome of Early Adoptions: The Adopted Baby as a Child

Most studies of adopted children until the 1980s were of early adoptions.[20] All the children born in a particular week in 1958 in the UK have been subjects for the periodic follow-ups of the National Child Development Study. These included a study of birth status, involving 366 illegitimate children who had not been adopted and 182 illegitimate children who had been adopted, as well as those children born in wedlock.[21] Running on parallel lines, the Christchurch Health and Development Study followed a cohort of 1,265 New Zealand children born in 1977 and has, again, compared adopted and non-adopted children born to single mothers.[22]

In the UK study, adoptive families tended to be well-off in terms of housing and domestic amenities, in not having financial problems, changes of home or school, or a mother in the workforce to any significant degree. (Two in five had manual fathers: but adopted children in working-class families were also likely to be living in financially secure homes with good amenities.) For children in non-manual homes, only one per cent of the adoptive mothers showed 'little or no interest' in their children's education, compared to four per cent of the mothers of children born in wedlock and 21 per cent of those of illegitimate children. (For lower-class families, this was respectively four per cent; 20 per cent and 27 per cent.)

Similarly favourable conditions prevailed in the New Zealand adoptive and biological two-parent families, compared to those of children born illegitimate, who had lower levels of childhood activities and pre-school education, poorer health care, greater residential change, more parental separations and more unresponsive, punitive mothers. The single mothers had low levels of education and qualifications, more difficulties with child rearing, and greater numbers of stressful or negative life events.[23] Overall, children placed in adoptive families had the most advantaged mix of childhood, family and social circumstances and children of single mothers the least.

At age seven, the adopted children in the UK study were doing somewhat better than natural children born within marriage and much better than children born out of wedlock. Educationally, only 16 per cent were graded as 'below average' in terms of general knowledge of the world around them, compared to 28 per cent of those of married parents, and 45 per cent of those born illegitimate. They were better readers than either the legitimate or illegitimate children, being about ten months ahead of the legitimate who, in turn, were 14 months ahead of the illegitimate children. They were as good at arithmetic as the legitimate children and better than the illegitimate. Nearly a half of the illegitimate children fell into the bottom grade of 'poor', compared to 28 per cent of those of married parents, and 18 per cent of adoptees.

When it came to social adjustment, a slightly higher proportion of the adopted (16 per cent), compared to children of married parents (13 per cent), were rated as maladjusted, although a quarter of those born illegitimate were in this category.

At 11 years of age,[24] one in three of the illegitimate children was living with a lone parent or in 'other situations': one in six had been in care and one in three families was receiving public assistance. (One in ten of the legitimate children was no longer living with both natural parents.) The illegitimate children living with both natural parents, as well as with one parent, or a step-parent, also tended to live in poorer circumstances than the legitimate children. In comparison, the adopted children were continuing to live in 'exceptionally favourable circumstances'. Very few had experienced a family break, only four per cent of families received public assistance, and both middle- and working-class adoptive families usually maintained or improved their circumstances over time.[25]

Adopted children were still likely to be better readers, on average, than either legitimate or illegitimate children from the same sex, class and family size. Only when all environmental variables *were considered together* did the differences diminish significantly, as we might expect. Allowing for all background conditions, adopted girls had the highest, and illegitimate girls and adopted boys the worst maths scores for the children's groups. Adopted boys seemed to have made less progress in this area between seven and eleven compared to other groups in similar conditions.

At 11, the born-illegitimate children again showed the poorest social adjustment according to ratings made at school, and the difference with the legitimate was only slightly reduced when allowance was made for environmental factors. However, background factors made a bigger difference for the adopted children, so that these were less well adjusted on average than legitimate children when allowance was made for their relatively more favourable home environment. It seemed that the behaviour of the adopted had deteriorated relative to the other children between seven and eleven. A similar change in behaviour ratings of adoptees between ages five and ten has emerged from reports of another cohort of UK children born in 1970.[26]

Somewhat raised levels of behaviour problems at school have been reported elsewhere for infant adoptees in mid-childhood, as in the Delaware Family Study.[27] In turn, D.M. Brodzinsky and colleagues also found that six- to 11-year-old adoptees showed some rise in behaviour problems compared to matched controls.[28] Others who have reported very similar findings include B.W. Lindholm and J. Touliatos who, using school ratings, reported higher and increasing rates of conduct problems, personality problems, and delinquency in adopted compared with non-adopted children during the primary years, principally affecting boys.[29]

None of these studies record very marked differences in behaviour problems for adoptees compared to non-adopted controls. Others have found little or no appreciable differences in adjustment levels, particularly for youth adopted as infants, and—that in certain areas anyway—adopted persons functioned better.[30]

On the whole, those adopted as babies tend to do well compared with children in general, but not always quite so well as the biological children of families in similar circumstances. Adopted children share the advantages of other children from small, intact, stable and financially secure families. This generally favourable picture is reflected in recent US data from the 1988 National Survey of Child Health.[31] Comparing across four groups—adopted children, children of single mothers, children of intact families and children being raised by grandparents—this shows how adopted children enjoyed health similar to that of those from intact families and superior to that of other groups. They did better in educational attainment than single-parent and grandparent-raised children. When compared to those adopted later, born outside marriage and raised by a single mother, or raised in an intact family, those who were adopted in infancy repeated grades less often than any other group; saw mental health professionals less; and had a better standing in their school classes and fewer behavioural problems than all other groups—except biological children in intact families.

7

The Adopted Infant
at Adolescence and Adulthood

THE Search Institute of Minneapolis undertook the investigation of adoptees in adolescence, using the largest-ever sample of adoptive families in the United States. This involved a total of 881 youngsters, aged 12-18, adopted as babies between 1974 and 1980, their parents, and non-adopted siblings. The research used a plethora of psychological and family measures, many of which were specially developed for the project, and also used a national USA sample of 47,000 adolescents for comparison, and a matched school sample. A third of the adopted adolescents were American Indian, Asian (mostly Korean), African American, or Hispanic. The participation rate was around 50 per cent of the eligible families, obtained from adoption records.[1]

Over a half (54 per cent) of adopted youth were highly attached to both parents, and absence of attachment to both parents characterised less than two per cent.[2] Overall, 70 per cent of adoptive parents reported that their children's attachment to them was strong or very strong. Only eight per cent reported weak or very weak attachment. In turn, 95 per cent of parents felt strongly attached to their adopted child, and 88 per cent reported a high level of emotional closeness. Attachment is promoted when families have a high degree of cohesion, warmth and communication, but also by the child's perception of similarity to parents. For adopted adolescents, the similarities to the adoptive parent on interests, values and personality were nearly as high as those of non-adopted siblings.

The percentage of adopted adolescents reporting high self-esteem (55 per cent) was higher than in the national sample of adolescents (45 per cent), and there were no differences between adopted and non-adopted siblings.

As elsewhere, adopted adolescents were far less likely than adolescents in general to experience parental divorce (or 11 per cent as against 28 per cent), or to live with lone parents (eight per cent compared to 19 per cent).[3] The adoptive families were also marked by higher educational attainment (26 per cent of adoptive fathers were graduates, compared to 13 per cent in the national sample); family income above the national average; and a stronger connection to religious institutions.

There were far higher levels of parent-child communication and parental involvement in schooling for adopted adolescents, compared to the national sample. Indeed, for positive parent-child relationships, warmth, discipline, positive communication and parents as a social resource, the adopted sample exceeded the levels shown generally and more or less matched the levels for non-adopted siblings. In terms of factors important for children's well-being, adoptive families seem to accentuate the positive and minimise the negative factors. This probably demonstrates the effects of agency screening, pre-adoption and post-adoption services, high levels of support from family and friends, as well as competent families, as a formula for successful child rearing.

There was a near unanimous agreement from parents (96 per cent) that adoption has been a rewarding experience, although one out of five said it had created marital stress. Eighty-four per cent reported the impact on family life as 'positive' or 'mostly positive', with only four per cent viewing the experience as 'negative' or 'mostly negative'. There is no comparative poll of how parents of adolescents feel about the experience of raising biological children, and what proportion are satisfied. As the researchers comment:

> Given current realities about family life, tension between parenting and work, and the perils of raising children in a society that is neither family- nor child-friendly, it is quite conceivable that adoptive parents are as, or more positive, as might be found for a parallel study of biological parents.[4]

The Behaviour Question

While there are conflicting reports of levels of adjustment of adoptees as children, compared with the non-adopted raised in similar homes, the results are even more contradictory at adolescence. As in the UK's National Child Development Study, another longitudinal study conducted in Sweden showed that adopted boys at age 11 had a higher incidence of behavioural problems (with an overall disturbance rate of 22 per cent, compared to 12 per cent for controls). The disturbances were more pronounced among children who were restored to their natural mother or reared in foster homes, and these two groups did worse academically.[5] However, at 15, the adopted children were no different from their peers, while those in the two other groups were now worse than before in terms of behaviour and achievement.[6] The results were similar when adopted males were compared with a control group of 18-year-old boys at the time of registration for national service. The adopted youngsters received virtually the same assessments as the control group, while the restored and fostered had more problems and a high drop-out rate for medical and psychiatric reasons.[7]

Given this, the Search Institute paid particular attention to whether their adopted adolescents showed raised rates of difficult behaviour or other problems of adjustment. According to indicators of psycho-social well-being related to the successful navigation of adolescence, the adopted adolescents did at least as well as and often better than youth from a general sample. Of course, the adopted sample had experienced less divorce and separation, had a higher average family income, and higher parental educational attainment. However, adopted youth also did as well as non-adopted siblings in the same families. There was no tendency for well-being to decrease across the teens, although boys in both the adopted and general sample tended to have worse adjustment than girls.

For nearly all high-risk behaviours (covering drug-taking and alcohol consumption, sexual activity, truancy, criminal behaviour and so forth) rates for adoptive adolescents were lower than for the general sample; appreciably so for the overall score. A relatively high percentage of adopted adolescents had received counselling or therapy (34 per cent), although most of these were not in the psychological danger zone (only 27 per cent of those receiving help were in the clinical range). A tendency for adoptees to be referred for treatment at a lower threshold than non-adoptees has been noted by others.[8] While this can clearly lead to an exaggeration of the association between adoptive status and risks of psychiatric disorder, it may not hold outside the US. A UK study of psychiatric referrals for adopted children aged seven to seventeen showed that these did have *more* problems than the biological children who were being referred, particularly regarding difficult behaviour. However, adopted and biological children from similar families who had never obtained mental health services were little different, even if the adoptive parents thought that their children had the most problems.[9]

However, it was on the independent mental health assessment that more of the Search adopted adolescents fell into the clinical and borderline ranges than was the case for the national adolescent sample, particularly for problem behaviours—or 15 per cent compared to 11 per cent (and 28 per cent compared to 19 per cent if we include borderline cases). There may have been underestimations of symptoms in the general population, but the results are in line with other reports of somewhat higher psychiatric disturbance in adopted samples.

It helps to compare these findings for somewhat raised rates of problem behaviours on clinical scales to those from the New Zealand cohort.[10] Adopted children were compared at 14 to 16 years with both children who entered two-parent families at birth and others who remained with their single mothers. Rates of low self-esteem of children born into single-parent homes were twice those of the other groups. The three groups did not differ significantly for mood disorders, anxiety, or suicidal behaviour. However, oppositional and defiant behaviour was marked in 36.7 per cent of adolescents of single mothers; in 21.9 per cent from adoptive families; and in 14.2 per cent of those born into two-parent families. Hyperactivity and attention deficits were present in 15 per cent of adolescents born to single mothers; in 9.4 per cent from adoptive families; and in 5.6 per cent of those born to two parents. Self-reported offending rates were respectively 42.6 per cent, 28.1 per cent and 20.3 per cent.

Adjustment for family and social backgrounds, as well as perinatal history, brought the measures for children born into single-parent homes and those adopted closer together, while children born to two-parent families still had much lower rates of disorder. Thus, the rates of difficult behaviours in adoptees were *higher* than expected given the generally advantaged characteristics of their adoptive families. However, it was *lower* than would be expected given the characteristics of their biological parents. The same pattern is present for achievement and ability scores.[11]

For the parallel British National Child Development Study, the illegitimate 16-year-olds had the highest rates of difficulty overall, according to school ratings, even after allowances were made for material and social factors. While the difficulties of the adopted group fell between the illegitimate and the legitimate, the apparent deterioration in the adjustment of adopted children between seven and eleven did not continue into adolescence. Indeed, difficulties had clearly peaked by late childhood and were much less marked in adolescence. Moreover, while the high overall scores of the illegitimate for disturbed behaviour reflected a wide range of problems, the restless and anti-social scores of the adopted differed little from those of the legitimate, and they mainly showed significantly greater problems in their relationships with peers.

By the mid-teens, the illegitimate children were by far the most likely to have been separated completely from their homes and to have spent time in care. As in earlier studies of the group, they were also most likely to be in families receiving state benefits and 'for many... the picture is one of continuing material disadvantage and an increased likelihood of family instability'.[12]

The Adopted Baby as Adult

Lois Raynor's The Adopted Child Comes of Age looked at the long-term outcomes for adoptees, aged 22- to 27-years-old, who had been born between 1948 and 1951 in England and Wales.[13] The families involved had either fostered a child whom they later adopted, or had adopted directly.[14]

Two-thirds of adoptive parents had found adoption to be very rewarding and an unqualified success, and only 14 per cent thought it had been more or less unsatisfactory. As with the Search Institute's study at adolescence, the factor with the clearest link to parents' satisfaction was the perception that a child was similar to them in some way. (Less than two-thirds were satisfied where the child was seen as different.) For adoptees, 60 per cent were very satisfied with their experience of growing up adopted and around one in five dissatisfied. Again, young adults were much more often satisfied when they were able to perceive or imagine likenesses to their parents, even if '[t]hese were not necessarily thought of as similarities which under other circumstances might have been inherited'.[15]

While adopters and adoptees who saw themselves as alike in some respects were more satisfied with their experience, the converse was also true. Where the child achieved poorly, or had emotional or behavioural problems, parents were less likely to see him as like themselves: 'thus, one suspects, increasing the difficulties. If his achievement, and adjustment were good, parents tended to identify readily with him, thus cementing the bonds'.[16] When Lois Raynor asked what adoptive parents liked least about their child, it was the child's poor academic showing or lack of interest in school work which was most often mentioned, followed by cases where the child was said to have no ambition or no staying power to achieve any skill. When failure to share the family's values extended to other areas of life, parents were always unhappy and dissatisfied. Thus, all but one of the adoptees who felt very much like their adoptive parents were now well adjusted, but only a little over a third were making a good adjustment when they thought they were not at all like them or were uncertain about this.

None of this should distract from the fact that 70 per cent of these adopted adults had made a good or excellent life-adjustment, and something like 34 per cent had acquired higher educational qualifications. There were:

> ...solicitors, doctors, scientists, social workers, nurses, teachers, secretaries, and some less well endowed who, nevertheless, were self-supporting, likeable young adults, most of them still enjoying a close and significant relationship with their adoptive family. Among those who were best adjusted nearly all had made their adoptive parents' way of life their own.[17]

Only six subjects were very badly adjusted, and five of these had not only shown difficult behaviour when growing up, but had been fostered first by their adoptive parents. Virtually none of the adoptive parents who had fostered first saw any advantage in this, and many saw serious disadvantages. They had only done it because they could not adopt directly due to their age or the existence of natural children. In parallel with the accounts in Barbara Tizard's work, these parents' experiences: 'provided many examples of... the "corrosive impact of uncertainty"'.[18] One adopter said that:

> ...the baby's mother had second thoughts ...and 'every time she visited she turned the knife'. As one mother expressed it: 'There is too much strain in fostering the child first. I never want to go through those two years again. We lived on the edge of a precipice'. Another family said the worry and anxiety over this was worse than anything else that had happened to them and they believed that the child, who was nervous and clingy, had sensed their distress. More than one mother spoke of being afraid to answer a knock at the door... A few had already had a child reclaimed... Some people... had felt uncomfortable about the fostering fees. Some even sent fees back to the agency after the adoption had been completed, and one father had written... 'Received payment from Pharaoh for looking after Moses'.[19]

Even the few who felt it was important to have time in which to see whether the child and family were suited to each other usually recommended a far shorter period of fostering than they had experienced. Moreover: 'they nearly always qualified their statement by adding the proviso that they would have to be assured that they definitely would be able to adopt the child at some time, an assurance an agency alone could not give'.[20]

None of the parents who had adopted directly wished they had fostered first, and preferred to take the risk of the child not being 'all right'. Overwhelmingly:

> Their view of fostering was that 'it is neither here nor there, it is insecure for everyone concerned', and they did not want to have anything to do with it. They spoke of being anxious enough during the few months until these direct adoptions were legalised; they would not have been prepared to go through... a longer period of fear and uncertainty. A woman who... was able to complete the adoption in the minimum time under the law said; 'Even so, I shook all the way to the court fearing the natural mother might turn up and take the baby'.[21]

While the former foster children in this study had all been adopted eventually, Lois Raynor wondered:

> what has happened to those... placed at the same time... who were never adopted or restored to their birth parents, but instead remained in the much more nebulous relationship of foster children? [If] they are 'in limbo', if they worry about the future and feel insecure in their most important relationships with adults, they do not flourish.[22]

Certainly, poor or barely adequate adult adjustment appeared to be closely associated with earlier problems. Nine out of ten of the adoptees described them as free of marked difficulties when growing up were well adjusted, whereas nearly half of those who had shown problems earlier on were still having trouble. However, 'this means that half of those who had problems earlier, nevertheless achieved a good adjustment as adults'.[23]

A longitudinal Swedish study showed somewhat curious patterns of adjustment over time.[24] While the adopted children were well-adjusted and did not differ from their control group at 15 or 18 (after having more problems in mid-childhood), by 23 the men were reporting more problems with job stability, employment and relationship breakdowns (although not for the criminality or alcohol problems, which affected ex-foster children significantly more). The problems of children who were initially put up for adoption, but grew up in their biological homes, or were fostered, deepened over the years.

To get a wider picture of the adjustment of adoptive adults compared to non-adopted people, this study was broadened out to include 2,000 adopted people, born between 1930 and 1950, who had been placed before the age of three. They were between 25 and 45 at investigation and their adoptive families were far more socially diverse and representative of a cross section of Swedish families than is typical of smaller scale studies. The majority of these adopted people were upwardly mobile compared to their biological parents and showed the same professional and social distribution as others of their age. For alcoholism and criminality, they did not differ from the general population. However, they tended to have a higher rate of mental problems, personality disturbances and sick leave compared to the non-adopted of the same age. The likely explanation is that there was a predisposition or vulnerability inherited from biological parents, who showed high rates of serious problems, which was not entirely compensated for by the adoptive home.[25]

The message from the UK's National Child Development Study[26] is not substantially different. Its 23-year-old adoptees had done well academically and vocationally; over 80 per cent had some formal qualifications, compared to just over 75 per cent of the legitimate group. The born-illegitimate group fared worse, as it had at every other sweep, where over half of the women and 30 per cent of the men had no formal educational or vocational qualifications at all. Illegitimate women showed the greatest vulnerability to depression and the highest rates of relationship breakdowns. Both sexes in the illegitimate group were more likely to be parents by 23; to have prolonged unemployment spells; and (in the case of the women) to have had a rate of unwed teenage pregnancy around treble that of either the adopted or born-legitimate groups.

Overall, it was illegitimate women who had by far the greatest risk of showing persistent adjustment problems—much worse than their social disadvantages would have predicted. Adopted women, in contrast, had adjustment scores 'exactly comparable with those of legitimate women in all of the areas we have been able to examine, and there were no indications of any elevated rates of difficulties in functioning'.[27] The transition to adulthood was not so smooth for the adopted men, mainly in terms of their elevated risk of job instability and relationship breakdown compared to legitimate men. However, these differences were small, even after allowing for their relatively advantaged social backgrounds. As for the Swedish studies of differences between adopted and non-adopted people as adolescents or adults, the actual proportion of adopted people likely to have significant problems of any kind may be very small in terms of practical importance.[28]

8

Late Adoptions:
New Families for Older Children

CHILDREN who are adopted 'late'—i.e. at five years old or over—can tell us much about the capacity which children have to become members of new families. They can also tell us the extent to which a change of environment can counteract the effects of deprivation, abuse and an unpromising genetic endowment.[1]

The Impact of Abuse

Alfred Kadushin's landmark study in 1970 was a significant part of the challenge to the 'irreversibility of early trauma' dogma. This involved 91 families with children adopted between the ages of five and eleven. The children came from family backgrounds which included alcoholism, psychosis and mental deficiency; they had often been removed from cruel or neglectful parents, and had 'failed' in one or more foster homes.[2] The time it took to get them into adoptive placements meant that they had spent an average of three and a half years in foster care, and a third had three or more placements each. The children had shown an average of three specific, identifiable behaviour problems.

However, the breakdown rate for adoptive placements was nine per cent when, at the same time, another researcher was showing that 78 per cent of children aged five and over when placed in foster homes had to be subsequently removed.[3] After six to ten years, when the average age of the children was nearly 14 years, children with exceptionally unhappy and disturbed early childhoods at least brought more or less satisfaction to around three-quarters of their adoptive parents, as well as having stable and permanent homes. The level of success matched that for infant adoptions. However, the more behavioural disturbances shown by the child, the less likely was the outcome to be favourable.

The question at the time of Kadushin's study had been whether older children could accept and be acceptable to new families. When the answer to this turned out to be yes, so research attention shifted more towards adjustment. The tendency for late-adopted children to have more maladjustment than continuously home-reared biological or adopted children is found in the National Child Development Study's sample of those adopted from care by the age of seven. Double the proportion of adoptees had problem scores at seven, eleven and sixteen, compared with children as a whole.[4]

The Lessons from Overseas Adoptions

Since adoptees tend to experience advantaged patterns of child rearing, whether in terms of parent-child relationships, family stability or family living standards—everywhere associated with good outcomes for children—the reasons hardly lie here. Adopted children with the most severe problems are often those who have endured extreme adversities in early life, as in the Dutch study of 1,538 inter-country adoptees aged 14-18 from countries such as Korea, Indonesia and Colombia.[5] In this study 22 per cent of boys and 18 per cent of girls, compared with 10 per cent of youngsters from the general population, could be regarded as clinically deviant from self-reports (or 28.5 per cent for boys and 17 per cent for girls, according to parents' reports). The problem rates at 14-18 were higher than at 10-15. Not only were there more social problems, including withdrawal, anxiety and depression, but higher rates of aggressive, delinquent and generally socially undesirable behaviours were shown by adopted boys.

The majority, even where there were very poor backgrounds, turned out well. In their native countries, these children may have suffered nutritional deficiencies and abuse, lacked stimulation, affection and opportunities for developing attachments, as well as having learned behaviour patterns necessary for survival in institutions or on the streets.

There are no comparative samples of youngsters who had remained in very deprived conditions in their own countries. The way in which extreme adversity in early life can cause later problems would seem to be borne out by another Dutch study of 116 Thai adoptees aged between seven and eleven.[6] The adopted children did better than the average Dutch child at school and lived in generally more advantaged conditions. Overall, the problem rate was low, but only 55 per cent of those who had been placed at two or older were problem free, compared to 92 per cent of those placed under six months of age. (This did not affect the very high levels of mutual attachment and satisfaction with the adoptions.) It has been noticed in the Swedish longitudinal research how late adoptive placements, or multiple placements prior to settlement in the adoptive home, along with low social class on the part of adoptive parents, increased the later risk of criminality or alcohol abuse—but only among genetically vulnerable individuals.[7]

Severely Deprived Children Adopted in the USA

Adoptive samples from very adverse backgrounds usually involve same-country adoptions. These include Victor Groze's four-year analysis of subsidised adoptions provided by the Iowa Department of Human Services in the 1990s.[8] The children were placed from infancy to eleven (at an average age of nearly five) and had been in their adoptive homes for an average of five and a half years. Over a half were known or suspected to have been sexually abused, and 76 per cent to have been physically abused. A half were in special classes for learning disabilities, and 15 per cent were in schooling for the mentally retarded or behaviourally disordered. A significant proportion had behaviour problems during all four years, with a half of the parents reporting an increase in difficulties. Children with a pre-adoptive history of sexual abuse seem to be particularly traumatized: 40 per cent had attention problems, 50 per cent had social problems, nearly 30 per cent were withdrawn and around a quarter had problems with anxiety/depression or offending.

Yet, over the four years, about 90 per cent of parents claimed to get on fairly well with their adopted children, and 80 per cent each year reported being close, with positive attachment in the majority of families. The 78 per cent who had reported adoption impact to be mostly or very positive in the first year had declined to 69 per cent by the fourth year, but 90 per cent had not thought to end the adoption, and over 60 per cent would recommend adoption to others. No family dissolved the adoption, although eight per cent of children ended up in out-of-home placement, usually with major behavioural problems or developmental difficulties.

Similar results have been found in other recent US studies of adoption outcomes for severely maltreated children, where the majority showed significant behaviour problems, although most families were satisfied with the adoptions.[9] These are samples composed almost exclusively of children from the very worst backgrounds. Many other studies of children adopted from adverse environments show more favourable long-term outcomes. Among these is K.A. Nelson's study[10] of American families who had adopted 257 children with 'special needs', whether mental or physical handicaps, a history of abuse, institutionalisation, or multiple moves. Parental satisfaction was, again, high in 73 per cent of cases, and satisfactory in 20 per cent. Not only had 85 per cent of the children developed a sense of permanence according to the parents, but there were also improvements in regard to school work, health, and ability to relate to others.

How Much Progress Can Be Made?

It cannot be expected that children will be 'cured' after a few years; the question is more one of whether and by how much they have improved. Sometimes the answer is a great deal. A boy 'placed at eight, and thought to have severe learning difficulties, now goes to college at 17 with GCSEs'. Another 'very successfully adopted at 15 by the same family, was a normal baby, but battering left him very disabled' yet, now 'in his mid 20s he is functioning remarkably well'.[11] In a small but long-term study of 21 children placed by the Children's Society,[12] more than half had been abused or neglected before going into care, and 11 were over ten when placed with permanent new adoptive or foster families. After five years, when the children ranged from six to 20, the adjustment of nearly two-thirds was improved or much improved, and only one had lower well being. Indeed, 67 per cent were rated as having at least average or above average well-being. In 15 placements all members of the new family were satisfied or very satisfied and the children were considered attached or fairly well attached. In 81 per cent of cases the children themselves were completely satisfied, or satisfied with reservations, about their new families.

The Adopted and the Restored

Barbara Tizard's studies show what happens to children when they are adopted after infancy compared to being restored to poor environments. Thirty children were adopted from institutions between two and seven years and compared at four and eight years with those returned to their natural mothers. There was a further follow-up at 16. There were also comparison groups of continuously home-reared children from the general population, one primarily middle-class for the adopted children, and another from socially disadvantaged homes for the restored children.[13] One group of 'earlier' adopted or restored children left the institutions between the ages of two and four years, and another group of later adopted, later restored and fostered children left between four and seven and a half years of age.

None of the children were initially considered suitable for adoption, either due to the mother's indecision or because of their own or their relatives' imperfections. All the children were in institutions before four months. A third were of mixed race and all were illegitimate. In the nurseries, the children appeared to be receiving excellent care in small groups from professionally qualified staff, with a physical environment and play facilities superior to that which most parents could offer. However, with students moving from group to group, rotas, time off for studies, holiday and weekend leave, day and night shifts, task specialisation and economies of scale, a child could have been looked after by 24 different people in one week. Close relationships were discouraged: nurses deliberately minimised involvement and children were distracted if they sought attention. This was in case the child might find it difficult to relate to his mother when the time came to leave. As one matron put it: 'It isn't fair to them, it isn't fair to us, to get too fond of the children'. The children were intellectually retarded compared to working-class two-year-olds. They had little imaginative play, were highly competitive and aggressive, fearful of strangers, and clung indiscriminately to any adult to whom they were at all familiar: 'By the age of four, 70 per cent of those still in institutions were said by staff not to care deeply about anyone'.[14]

Where the children were restored, few went to families who would have been considered acceptable as adopters. The parents had few resources, personal or material, and were ambivalent about the child living with them. They did not tolerate immature behaviour or put anything into building a relationship. One child went to a father living with a woman with seven other children. Another became part of a family of five, all disturbed, with periods in care, and living in temporary accommodation, with almost no possessions, because one of the children had burnt the house down. Another in a family of four was looked after by a neighbour and older children while the mother was out from 11 a.m. to 10 p.m. 'At the time of our visit she had a black eye, the consequence of a push from her overwrought mother.'[15]

With five out of 25 restored children, the mothers wanted adoption, but their children were not accepted, because of mixed race, a history of mental illness, or because the child could not be genetically 'cleared' due to inadequate background information. Mothers who felt that they had been pushed into taking the child against their will deeply resented this:

Mother   I didn't want him, I did not want the responsibility of him, I wanted him adopted. The society kept asking me what I was going to do about him. I don't know what one is supposed to feel for a child. I'll be glad when he grows up. Often he irritates me just by being in the room. I used to thump him a lot, but now I can't be bothered, I just try and keep out of his way (child restored at four).

Mother   I feel resentful, because I might meet someone I like, and they won't want me because I've got a child. When I think about this, I think why did it happen to me, and I get in a filthy temper with P. (child restored at three and a half).[16]

Black or mixed-race children were more likely to be restored than adopted, while most of the non-white children stayed in institutional care. At four and a half years, the IQ scores of restored children were slightly lower than those of the children who remained in the institution, while adopted children scored highest. Attachment to a parent and a comparative lack of behavioural problems were associated with better intellectual performance, and these were more likely to be found in adopted children. Restored children were far more difficult to test, given that two-thirds had very poor concentration, or would not co-operate. More restored than adopted children wet the bed, had fears and anxieties, were more demanding (three-quarters were strong attention-seekers) and some were very unhappy.

At eight years the restored children had a reading age behind their chronological age and the adopted children had one in advance. Both groups had more problems than average. More were restless, fidgety, irritable, quarrelsome, disobedient, unable to settle down, solitary, demanding of attention, aggressive, and not much liked by other children. However, less than a quarter of the adopted children were badly affected, compared to nearly a half of restored children. Two-thirds of the restored children, compared to only 15 per cent of the adopted children, had been referred to specialists because of their behaviour.[17]

Children whose mothers would not let them be adopted at all, yet would not take them back, went on to foster care. For a child, fostering was inferior to adoption. Foster parents who wanted a close relationship felt anxious and threatened and wondered whether or not to give the child up. When the child responded with aggressive and disturbed behaviour, this further endangered his security, since both foster parents and social workers might think that the placement had failed and remove him. Other foster mothers tried to fulfil the role which social workers regarded as 'correct'—or tried to maintain distance from the child: 'I keep telling her—her mother comes first—I don't want her to get too attached to me. I don't want to draw her away from her mother—I'm really getting her ready to live with her mother'.[18] Although much social work effort went into maintaining the child's links with his natural parents, it brought to the fore the child's confusion about his position, and sense of rejection. This not only had little to offer the child, but prevented him forming other relationships. Combined with constant uncertainty about the natural parent's intentions, the result was highly disturbed behaviour. This was evident in a boy of six and a half, whose natural mother had hardly visited since putting him in an institution at nine days old. She had three other illegitimate children, and reared none herself. She originally wanted her son adopted, but he had a heart murmur and was considered of low intelligence, so social workers planned for the mother to take him back. When it became clear he was physically sound and not retarded she was unwilling to place him for adoption. Although his foster parents wanted to adopt, the mother fantasised about a time when she would gather all her children together in a dream home. The foster relationship deteriorated, and the child became very disruptive.

Children who were adopted out of institutions after four and a half years did not experience anything like the same degree of acceleration in intellectual development which occurred for children adopted between the ages of two and four (who retained their lead through to 16 years). Both later-adopted and later-restored children had very poor concentration, more nervous habits and tempers, eating and sleeping disorders, and worse general behaviour compared to those who left institutions earlier.

The most important factor was whether the child sought or gave affection and became close to particular adults. Because of this, neither a below average IQ nor very difficult behaviour, or age at placement, seemed to prevent satisfaction with adoption, provided that mutual affection developed and the children became attached and successfully integrated into their new families, as most did once placed in permanent homes. What mattered to adoptive parents was the relationship they established and any gradual improvement they saw. Adoptive parents often regarded as natural or eccentric behaviour which most parents would have considered very difficult. The same situation was seen with the study of 21 late, multiple 'special-needs' children placed by the Children's Society,[19] where the success rate by parent and child evaluations was higher than might be expected from the objective tests of behaviour and well-being.

No adoptive child was removed by eight in Tizard's sample, while three natural mothers gave up with restored children. On the criteria of mutual attachment, there was an adoption failure rate of 16 per cent by this age. With restored children, nearly a half of parents believed the child was not attached to them, and more than half did not feel close to the child. One child was returned at four and a half after being abandoned at two months by a mother with three more illegitimate children, only to be ill-treated and removed again at six.

By 16, as many placements had broken down for the restored, at least temporarily, as had not, with children going into residential care or running away from home. In comparison, two adoptions broke down between eight and 16 and there was another case of mutual rejection. Otherwise, the family relationships of the adopted 16-year-olds were satisfactory to them and for their parents and differed little from those of ordinary non-adopted comparisons, who had never been in care. As at eight, restored 16-year-olds showed less affection to their parents than did any other group, and their parents had trouble showing affection to them. More restored adolescents felt that they were very unlike their parents (35 per cent compared to 20 per cent of the adopted). The restored group got on particularly badly with siblings, although both adoptive and restored children had more problems here.

However, poor adjustment at adolescence was most marked for those who were restored to their natural parent(s), while the problems found at eight had fallen most for the adopted group. More restored adolescents reported themselves as having been in recent trouble, fighting in school or in deep misery or depression, just as teachers rated them as far more anti-social, with high levels of absenteeism, compared with their control group and the adopted. Indeed, the majority of restored adolescents scored above the threshold for psychiatric screening, at 78 per cent, compared to 38 per cent of the adopted. Restored adolescents had more often been in trouble with the police than their control group, or adopted adolescents. Almost all had by now been referred to psychiatric services, while referrals for the adopted were not much different to those of their control group.

Was any other group of adolescents worse off than those who had been restored to their natural parents? Findings for those who were fostered or remained in residential care, instead of being restored or adopted, could not be statistically quantified because groups were small. However:

> None ...experienced continuity of care since we had seen them at age eight, none could be said to be progressing well, and several made it clear that they felt badly about aspects of themselves and their lives. Anti-social behaviour was common and in the absence of a family some adolescents revealed great anxiety about who would be there to support them when, as was soon to happen, they were no longer the responsibility of the local authority or voluntary agency.[20]

9

The Late Adoptee as Adult

I F there have been few studies focusing on the outcome of late adoptions, ones on late adoptees as adults are rarer still. After all, adoption after babyhood was uncommon and discouraged up into the 1970s.

A big exception is the Scottish study of John Triseliotis and James Russell,[1] involving 44 late adoptees as adults (average age 24), together with a sample of 40 people who had been reared in institutions run by statutory or voluntary organisations from before ten years of age until 16 (they had spent an average of 11 years in institutions). The adopted were 'hard to place' children born in the 1950s, who were settled with families between the ages of two and eight, and had been in care for an average of two and a half years.[2] A foster-care group, who had lived with a single foster family from at least the age of nine until 16, was also studied.

The natural parents of the children had been overwhelmed by social and personal problems. Their turbulent relationships were usually the immediate reason for the child's reception into care, particularly as these involved many separations and desertions. In many of the families there was heavy drinking and/or a history of criminality. Two-thirds of the children who went on to become adopted were in care when under a year old, compared to only one in eight of those who grew up in institutions. Continuity was frequently interrupted, with one child having experienced 11 moves before being placed. Both groups averaged nearly four moves between reception into care and final placement. The residential group experienced further moves within what was supposed to be their permanent 'home'. They may have been held back from adoption or fostering because of the presence of siblings or a tenuous link with their original family. Almost two-thirds of the adopted were described as having moderate to severe emotional and behavioural problems (compared to a fifth of the residential group). As with Barbara Tizard's sample, 'there were many doubts at the time as to whether these "high risk" children should be adopted at all'.[3] Professionals advised: 'only fostering, as child is very disturbed and demanding'; 'adoption postponed because of child's background, decided to wait and see how the child develops'; 'abnormally large head'; 'adoption postponed because of mother's background, mother was an unstable character'.[4]

They ended up adopted because of the perseverance of adopting couples, or because the agency saw the adopters as being 'marginal' like the children—in which case they would not be too bothered about poor heredity or adverse early experiences. There were more lower-class adopters in this study than is usual, which reflects the way in which agencies, especially voluntary ones, were more likely to pick higher-class adopters for babies from 'uncomplicated' backgrounds.

While 86 per cent of those who grew up adopted described their relationships as 'very good' or 'fairly good', compared to 60 per cent who grew up in homes, it seemed that 'real enthusiasm for growing up in residential care... was very rare'.[5] Only 15 per cent described relationships in homes as 'very good' compared with 45 per cent of adoptees. When asked about their total experience of growing up adopted or in residential care, 82 per cent of those adopted and 55 per cent of those who grew up in homes expressed very or fairly positive feelings.

While the residential group started out with significantly fewer behavioural and emotional problems compared to those going to adoptive families, only one-third of the adopted, compared to 70 per cent of those growing up in homes, had problems in childhood. Indeed, the emotional, behavioural and psychiatric problems of the residential group trebled. (This figure is almost identical to the rate of neurotic and anti-social disorders reported by other researchers for children in long-term residential care.)[6] During the adoptive placement and before leaving school, 14 per cent of the adopted and 35 per cent of those who grew up in homes were referred for psychiatric help.

Where there was dissatisfaction with adoption, this tended to centre on intense pressure from high status parents to achieve educationally—a point to which we shall return. However, while a greater proportion of adoptees referred to 'unreasonably high expectations on the part of their parents', this needs to be balanced against the way that more of the residential sample 'commented on the total indifference of some of the staff to their future'.[7] While the emphasis on achievement has its down side, it has been commonly found that improving the attainment of children of low academic calibre, who often come from homes with an unstimulating intellectual environment, leads to improvements in functioning elsewhere.

Overall, 70 per cent of those adopted and 50 per cent of those who grew up in homes continued their education beyond the compulsory school leaving age, compared with low rates for those who were fostered and a national average of 47 per cent in the late 1970s. This is similar to the 73 per cent found by Lois Raynor for baby adoptions.[8]

Adoptees achieved marked upward social mobility compared with their natural parents. Many in the residential sample achieved higher social ranking than their biological family. However, for the adoptees, there was no difference in social mobility between those who came originally from the most disturbed or disadvantaged backgrounds and others from less deprived circumstances. Both groups contrast with the children who grew up in long-term foster care, since these hardly achieved any upward generational mobility—a dismal result considering the circumstances of the original families. For those in work, 80 per cent of the adopted and over 40 per cent of those who grew up in homes were more or less satisfied with their present job. A total of 18 per cent of adopted people, compared to 50 per cent of the residential people, and 27 per cent of the foster-care sample, were facing serious or moderate financial or housing problems. During the previous year, adoptees barely made any claims on the social security system. Of those who had grown up in residential homes, a third of the married sample were on benefits, compared to two per cent in the general population, and 28 per cent of the single sample, compared with a national average of six per cent.

While nearly two-thirds of the adopted expressed outright satisfaction with their life as adults, only 20 per cent of those who had been reared in homes thought the same way. Overall, twice as many people who grew up in homes reported problems as adults compared to those who grew up adopted—whether in terms of dissatisfaction with marriages, police warnings, appearances before an adult court, and other indicators.

Difficulties present before an adoptive placement, or during placement, did not seem to continue into adult life to any significant degree. But earlier problems were more likely to persist for residential people. While 25 per cent of those who grew up in homes were referred for psychiatric help as adults, this compares to 11 per cent among adoptees. Over twice as many (38 per cent) of residential people were classified as having two or more forms of psychological or social pathology—including serious relationship problems with friendship or marriage, psychiatric referral in adult life, heavy drinking and a criminal record.

The factor which led to personal and social stability in the lives of residential adults was the extent to which they felt that they had experienced caring relationships with the staff—not a common experience. Not only do adopted people fare better in every way compared to children restored to natural parents or relatives: even when adoptees from the worst possible backgrounds are considered, their outcomes were significantly better than those for institutionally-reared people.

Psychiatric disorder was also generational for the residential people, so that disturbance in the child was correlated with problems in the families of origin, like alcoholism, severe relationship difficulties or mental instability. It seemed that early influences and genetic transmissions from the natural family found their later expression more often as a result of growing up in care than when adopted.

In contrast, any vulnerabilities which existed in the adopted group seemed to have been countered or managed by their new environment so that they usually failed to find expression. Adoptees with background histories that might include having alcoholic or retarded birth mothers, did not function much differently from the rest.

> The opportunity afforded to the adopted group to establish new attachments and relationships appeared not only to reverse early experiences of deprivation, but also to equip them with social and personal qualities enabling them to cope well with life. In contrast, the residential experience transmitted handicaps to the residential group.[9]

In adults, this vulnerability is likely to be compounded by a continued lack of family support and resources.

Other Finnish work has shown that, in healthy adoptive families, without mental illness or seriously contentious and otherwise dysfunctional behaviour, adoptees have little serious mental illness whether or not their biological mothers were schizophrenic. A disturbed rearing environment, as well as a necessary genetically transmitted predisposition, contributed to the emergence of schizophrenia. However, this and other studies suggest that genetic influences were not entirely mediated by the environment, since there was always a somewhat increased likelihood that children of psychotic parents would develop similar problems, independently of their childhood experience.[10] Michael Rutter's work[11] also showed a direct effect of parental deviance (or psychiatric disorder, criminality or drug dependence), but on outcomes for men only. For women, there was no effect of parental deviance that was independent of early disruption. Moreover, for both sexes, there was a major significant effect of early disrupted upbringing on later bad social functioning where, in the first two years of life, there were repeated short-term admissions into foster care, institutionalisation, or other separations due to family discord or disorder. As well as facilitating the appearance of parental deviance in the next generation, these were risk factors in themselves. Hence, parental abnormalities are transmitted to the children as much or more through the series of adverse experiences they set in motion, as by direct genetic routes.

While there tends to be a high genetic predisposition to social maladjustment and mental illness among adopted people, a stable home and the high level of careful parenting usually found in adoptive families provides a protective factor. Using the best parents for problematic children, adoption 'may mitigate, although perhaps not eliminate, the elevated risks of social and psychiatric problems in adolescence associated with children from high risk biological family backgrounds'.[12]

Why Adopted Children Do Well

Nothing has emerged since 1970 to challenge the 'unequivocally successful' rate of 74 per cent produced by Alfred Kadushin from all prominent studies on adoption then available that met a certain standard of rigour.[13] Adoptive children may often be 'harder to rear' when compared to their non-adopted siblings. However, adoptive parents are more resourceful than others, well prepared for parent-hood and have greater personal and social resources—being 'the only parents in our society who have to "prove" their ability to be good parents' before undertaking the task.[14] Adopting couples are more likely to have better familial and marital functioning, compared to other two-parent families, to be more integrated with their families of origin and their in-laws, and more likely to have shared friends.[15] As Victor Groze found for the families of special-needs adoptees, they tend to be more adaptable and cohesive than ordinary families.[16]

Not least, adopted children do well because the parents are so keen to rear a child. Alfred Kadushin identified the factors in the success of late adoptions as lying in the satisfaction parents got from their relationship with the child, their mutual identification and the occupation of parenthood itself as a lifelong interest. This gave satisfaction in helping a child grow and develop, through the successful navigation of the problems of child rearing, and the appreciation of the simple pleasures of life.

Adoptive parents also tend to have a pro-education ethos, which makes it usual to help children with school work and engage them in educational activities. We know how people who achieve education-ally tend to be better adjusted, as well as more successful individu-als. Reflecting this, those adult adoptees in Lois Raynor's sample with fathers in professional and managerial positions were most often satisfied with their adoption and the best adjusted. The small numbers with fathers in semi-skilled manual work were the least often satisfied or well adjusted. While nearly all adoptees who were themselves in social class I and II occupations were satisfied overall with their adoption, less than half of those in semi-skilled and unskilled occupations were. Even where these young adults had disliked school, many stuck it out and went on the higher education with the result of good jobs and good adjustment. On balance, they liked their parents to have high expectations and, when they obtained higher education and good jobs, they were well satisfied with themselves and the adoption experience. In families where little had been expected and little achieved, the adoptees were not very pleased with their jobs and the way their lives were going. These advantages could, however, become counter-productive pressures when 'parental expectations were not merely high... they could only be considered unreasonable'.[17]

Sooner or Later?

To say that human beings have a tremendous ability to overcome early disadvantages must not be taken as implying that neglect, abuse or physical deprivation are harmless. Moreover, it is commonly found that: 'the older the child at placement, the more likely is it that problems will develop'.[18] Rates of maladjustment, especially if these involve serious conduct problems, are likely to rise with age at adoption and in proportion to the adversities the child has endured in the pre-adoption years.[19]

Every year adds to problems. In one study comparing adopted children referred for psychiatric treatment with those who had never used such facilities,[20] it was noticeable that the average age of the clinical group at adoption was 33 months, while that of the non-clinical was 15 months. In turn, 29 per cent of the clinical sample had a history of abuse, compared to 18 per cent of the non-clinical sample. Similarly, depressive and manic symptoms in adult adopted males have been associated with events in the first two years—even after controlling for any significant relationships with genetic background and adult substance abuse and anti-social personality.[21] The disruption involved in late placements interacted with biological predispositions to make adult disturbance more likely. The message is that: 'Children cannot be put into cold storage while adults argue about what to do for them or pay attention to the needs of other adults'.[22]

One of the most ground-breaking and gratifying findings to emerge from adoption research concerns the high levels of attachment found for late adoptions. However, we can still discern the effects of age at placement, even with quite early adoptions. Questioned about their child's attachment to them in the early years, the replies of the adoptive parents in the Search Institute's study of adopted adolescents formed a gradient—from 91 per cent reporting that attachment was strong when the child was placed at under one month, down to 84 per cent when this was between 13 and 18 months. Hence: 'this study underscores the need for all efforts possible to be made to facilitate the earliest placements possible—for the good of the child'.[23]

10

Part of the Family?

EVEN when it is accepted that adopted children may enjoy many advantages, compared with similar children who were not adopted, the claim is made that none of these can compensate for the loss of a secure sense of belonging and relatedness, since identity formation may be particularly difficult for adopted children. Having been severed involuntarily from their original family and their roots, they cannot really become part of another family.

These criticisms of adoption seem to be based in an assumption that children in care, and even abused or neglected children at home, do not have similar problems. Even if they want for much else, the very thing they do *not* lack is their identity. It is particularly during adolescence that the adoptee purportedly 'really begins to understand what adoption means in terms of personal loss: they have lost a biological and cultural link, a portion of their personal narrative—something crucial is missing... how often, sadly, does the pain explode as aggression or teenage rebellion?'[1] In contrast:

> ...working through the tasks of adolescence, biological children have a sense of continuity, a link with past generations, a family identity which the adopted child simply does not have.[2]

However, a sense of detachment or estrangement from the adoptive family is not something which comes over from studies of adopted children. Adopted people overwhelmingly consider their adoptive parents as *their* parents, and the ones that matter. The natural family occupies an insignificant place in the pre-occupations and concerns of even later, 'high-risk', adoptees.[3]

Neither do most adoptees worry about their adoptive status. This is a fact which seems, at most, peripheral to matters of knowing and defining the self.[4] Because adopted people are secure with their families and themselves, they are not much perturbed or interested in their adopted status. For most adolescents in the Search Institute study, adoption had no emotional significance or heavy meaning in making them feel loved, special, proud, angry, confused, sad etc.: 'It is neither a burden nor a celebration. It just is'.[5] Indeed, about a third felt that this was harped on too much, and liked to emphasise that they were no different from anybody else. Only eight per cent felt that they did not belong to their families, and five per cent felt unwanted. Overwhelmingly, adoptees also express considerable satisfaction about their relationship with their family's biological children.[6]

Virtually all parents and adopted adolescents in the Search Institute's study saw no significant difference between adoptive and other families and rejected the view that adoptive families were different: 'nearly all children and parents in this study downplay the differences'.[7] Indeed, adopted youngsters tended to rate their relationships with their parents more positively than a national sample of adolescents, judged by their responses to statements about communication and parental involvement (see Table 10:1).

Table 10:1
Family Dynamics: Adopted Adolescents and National Sample Compared

Domain	Indicators	Adopted Adolescents (%)	National Sample Adolescents (%)
Warmth	There is a lot of love in my family[1]	78	70
	My parents often tell me they love me[1]	83	71
Communication	I have lots of good conversations with my parents[1]	65	48
Family Harmony	My family life is happy	77	68
Discipline	If I break one of my parents' rules, I usually get punished[1]	61	54
Parental Involvement in Schooling	My parents talk with me about school curriculum[2]	63	53
	My parents attend meetings or events at my school[2]	52	36
Support	If you had an important concern about drugs, alcohol, sex, or some other serious issue, would you talk to your parents about it?[3]	52	47

[1]Sum of agree and strongly agree.
[2]Sum of often and very often.
[3]Sum of yes and probably.
Source: Search Institute, Minneapolis, *Growing Up Adopted*, p. 46.

Who is 'Nobody's Child'?

Even amongst late, high-risk adoptees, the vast majority: 'had positive self-concepts and did not feel different. Negative self-concepts were characteristic of very few' in adulthood.[8] The percentage of adolescents adopted as babies reporting high self-esteem for the Search Institute was greater, at 55 per cent, than in the national sample, at 45 per cent. These were also as likely to report positive identity as their non-adopted siblings, whether in terms of sense of purpose, clarity about who one is, or self-affirmation (see Table 10:2).

Table 10:2
Measures of Identity, By Age and Gender

Measures of Identity	Adopted Adolescents (%)			Non-Adopted Siblings (%)
	Boys	Girls	All	
Sense of Purpose				
I have a good idea about where I'm going in life[1]	69	74	72	66
Clarity				
I have a good sense of who I am[1]	83	76	79	77
I feel confused about who I am[1]	8	14	11	14
Self				
I'm glad I was born	86	86	86	87
Affirmation				
I think I am lucky to be me[1]	78	74	76	79

[1]Per cent often or always true.
Source: Search Institute, Minneapolis, *Growing Up Adopted*, p. 17.

If there is confusion anywhere, this seems to be more attributable to rejection by the original family, where children could never be a 'worthwhile person' in the eyes of their birth parents, rather than any feeling of being unaccepted by adoptive parents.[9] It needs to be borne in mind that maltreated children not only tend to have difficulties with identity and self esteem, but with depression, acute anxiety, poor impulse control, marginal peer relationships, aggressiveness, attachment, abuse fantasies, provocation, punishment-seeking, impairment of achievement and cognitive functioning—which can last well beyond childhood.[10]

An acceptable self-image and identity, as well as a feeling of kinship, is connected to feelings of similarity between adoptive parents and children. It might be imagined that similarity is something which is generally difficult to engineer in adoptive families. However, families can share interests and values as well as physical likeness, abilities or temperament. These similarities may be the result of living together: 'indeed, they may be matters of belief rather than actuality but nonetheless effective for all that'.[11]

Neither denial nor emphasis on the child's 'difference', but acceptance, promotes the healthiest outcomes, where 'my mother/father knows I am different but makes no big deal about it', or 'my mother/father likes the things that are different about me'.[12] Interestingly, the biggest threat to well-being reported by parents and adolescents by the Search Institute was the stigma attached to adopted people and adoptive families.[13]

Don't They Have More Problems?

Where increased problems have been recorded for adoptees during childhood and adolescence, these tend to be conduct disorders rather than low self-esteem, suicidal inclinations or neurotic symptoms. We do not know the proportion of people in the general population who are dissatisfied with their upbringing. In one study, when adoptees expressed definite disappointment, this focused on the 'strictness of their parents, their high expectations... the absence of sufficient love and caring, and frequent reference to their adoption as something to regret'.[14] This was most likely to happen when they grew up in high-status and very ambitious families. Similarly, Lois Raynor pinpoints that 'little group of dissatisfied adopters' who were unhappy with children who could not carry on their profession. Haunted by a 'fantasy birth child'[15] these:

> ...felt urgently the need to mould the [adopted] child to their own ways, but believed they had failed in this... They had tried to prevent the child from developing in his own way, and had worked harder and harder to squeeze him into the imagined likeness of the ideal child who should have been born to them.[16]

These efforts 'were markedly unsuccessful and resulted in much unhappiness'.[17]

This is a thread running through the literature on adoption discontent. One American long term study of 43 children until 16, mostly placed as infants, found that, while most of the adoptees had adjusted well, and adoptive status was unrelated to the development of emotional problems, there were more school difficulties. The factor which seemed to be instrumental was high parental expectations.[18] The feeling that adoptive parents must 'prove' themselves, or do demonstrably better than biological parents, may mean a particularly heavy emphasis on the child being a 'credit' to them, with some adoptees claiming that their parents wanted 'children to be perfect'.[19]

Notions about the overpowering influence of environment over endowment may also have encouraged some parents to believe that the adopted child is even more of a 'blank slate' than a biological child might be.[20]

Currently, with 'many special-needs children being adopted who have severe emotional and behavioural problems as well as an array of significant learning difficulties', these expectations are going to be even less realistic than in the days when the ethos of adoption societies was to place the 'perfect' child with the 'perfect' couple.[21] However, adoption of older and special-needs children has also gone hand in hand with the erosion of the notion that adoptive children must pass as the adoptive parents' biological children. In turn, adoptive parents cope well with retardation that is obvious and explicable.

Lost Souls?

It has been claimed that adopted people are disadvantaged because they lack the knowledge of the past which makes the present intelligible, and gives the continuity so important to the formation of the self. However, this argument against adoption overlooks the fact that 'late' restorations to the natural family may be more problematic for the child than placement with a new family, due to the likely ambivalence of parents about having the child return to them, as well as changes to the family itself while the child has been in care.[22]

In Barbara Tizard's sample,[23] whether late-adopted or restored children took to parents or not depended on how much their adoptive or natural parents really wanted them, and were prepared and able to spend time with them. While the extent of parent/child activity in adoptive families was much greater than in most middle-class homes, the natural parents of restored children played with them less and encouraged them less than working-class parents. They expected restored children to be as independent as working-class children of the same age, while adoptive parents accepted and dealt with the child at his or her level of development which, for older adoptees, was often retarded.[24] In no case did a step-parent feel close to an ex-institutional child.

Moreover, what coherent picture of their past and future do children possess who can make no stable relationships with committed adults and who grow to adulthood affiliated to no-one, and without a base to which they can return? What confusion ensues when a child has been 'brought up to believe that both his parents were alive and coming for him one day' and is then 'told that his father was in prison and his mother was dead'.[25] In John Triseliotis and James Russell's work, it was the residential people who were:

> ...very preoccupied with their circumstances, their families and their future. This preoccupation seemed to be an emotionally draining experience which affected their social and academic functioning.[26]

Children in institutions and foster homes ask 'Why am I in care?' and 'What will happen to me?'. It is they who are most likely to have trouble coming to terms with their past, and to be looking towards a troubling future. The adopted have a family caring for them, with supportive relationships in which to invest. In comparison, residential people tended to be haunted by feelings of rejection: 'I felt unwanted and rejected by my parents... they didn't care about me, that's why they put me in a home'. While they were negative about parents for having deserted them or put them away, those who remembered life at home had few regrets about leaving. In another study of 52 children adopted by their foster parents,[27] most had unhappy memories of fighting or ill-treatment at the hands of natural parents. Only three spoke positively about life before care.

Children growing up in care may have as little or even less information about their original families than the adopted. Four out of five of those who grew up in homes in one study maintained that their circumstances were hardly, if ever, discussed with them: 'often being unaware whether their parents were alive or dead, or whether they had siblings or not'.[28] One person described how: 'you couldn't understand how he could be a brother and you hadn't seen him in your life before'. There was resentment at being separated from siblings: 'I hated being moved from E. Home and from my brother because he was all I knew... my brothers were fostered but I was left. I couldn't understand it because I didn't know why I was there'.[29]

Many residential people are reported to be 'particularly bitter and critical' about institutions: 'comments such as "erase", "abolish" or "close" them were made... only a minority said that institutions were beneficial'.[30] They felt that the experience had 'spoiled' and 'wasted' their childhood and was a blight on their adult lives. It was they who saw themselves as different from others; as having had no parents and having lived excluded from normal society. Such an overwhelming sense of alienation, rejection and inadequacy affected few adopted people. For them: 'it seemed to have no meaning because, as many put it, they were wanted by their adoptive parents'. Some remembered living in institutions, but they much preferred the 'opportunity to grow up with people who wanted them'.[31] Even if adoption should 'aggravate some identity issues... few youths would trade those... for a lifetime of being completely on their own after age 18'.[32]

It is curious that adoption should be perceived as such a threat to identity, when it is institutions which have been so clearly identified with this role in modern social theory—even defined in terms of social death.[33] The identity of children growing up in institutions is negatively affected by ignorance about their personal history, the absence of significant, close relationships, and the feeling that they are perceived as 'worthless'. Measures which are counterproductive to children's development can seem necessary to the welfare or smooth functioning of institutions, which requires administration and housekeeping, not personal care and relationships. Individualisation is disruptive to institutions, whose existence and efficiency depend upon the routine ordering of almost every aspect of life, and the interchangeability of staff.

Whether satisfied or not with their residential experience, youngsters feel themselves stigmatised: 'Often in the back of people's minds were notions that they had done something "so bad and terrible to get in a home" ',[34] with staff telling children that the 'social work department don't give us enough to keep the likes of you here', or that 'they were not in the home for the good of their health'.[35] The stigma attached to care was the major theme running through responses to all aspects of a recent self-reported survey of children in care by the National Consumer Council.[36] The young people felt it particularly acutely in their education, where the strain of dealing with this, on top of so many moves, disrupted their schooling.

In contrast, the adopted child is identified:

> ...with a well-organised family of father and mother who act in a responsible, respectable manner. He now receives messages which proclaim his acceptability, and support, reinforce, and strengthen whatever components, however limited, of self-acceptance he has been able to develop as a result of whatever small amount of affection he received in his former home. The effect of positive parent-child relationships within the home are now buttressed by social relationships outside the home.[37]

As found with fostered children who were subsequently adopted, the adoption itself achieves self-verification. They gain self-worth, as much as acceptance, through the transfer of legal ties from a family that has failed to one that has positive status.[38] Children in the public care system suffer discontinuities, the absence of family membership and the degradation of being accountable to welfare agencies. Adoption neutralises these.[39]

Searching Out the Self?

At 18 the adopted child has a potential 'choice' as to whether the adoptive family is to remain the lifelong family, or whether he resumes a relationship with members of the birth family. Tremendous publicity has been given to cases of re-unification with natural parents. It is difficult to know what proportion of adoptees seek further information about birth relatives, or are even reunited with them, and to what extent they are representative of adopted adults as a whole. It is estimated that about 15 per cent of adoptees might seek information about their origins at some point in their adult lives.[40]

Despite the impression given by the media, many adoptees are not particularly interested in their original family and, if they are, this need not mean that they have been unhappy with their adoptive family. Moreover, a need to know is not synonymous with a need for contact, and it may reflect curiosity, rather than identity problems or rejection of the adoptive parents. People are often satisfied with just having information about their biological and genealogical backgrounds.[41]

Overall, 27 per cent of the older adoptees in one study[42] had maintained or established some contact with a member of the original family, but this often did not go beyond satisfying natural curiosity. In another sample,[43] of those adopted as babies, only a quarter wished to contact birth parents, although many would have welcomed more information about their background. Those who showed an interest in contact were more likely to be dissatisfied with their adoption than those who did not, although the adoptee's desire to meet birth parents may reflect the urge to tell them that they are happy and well.[44]

When it comes to contact during childhood between the adopted child and the birth parent(s):

> Current trends, which promote the value of maintaining contact and also ideas about the benefits of greater openness in adoption, are in danger of giving support to the concept that all contact is good and that the greater the move toward direct contact (meetings) between child and birth parent, the better.[45]

A good arrangement might be one where the birth and adoptive parents are in touch, but there is limited or no contact between birth parents and child. As with adult adoptees, the desire as much as the need for contact between adopted child and natural parent(s) may have been exaggerated.[46] What seems to have become almost unmentionable is that there are 'children whose sense of attachment to their family of origin appears... to be non-existent'.[47]

There may be 'little to build on through continued contact', and children may find it 'very difficult to settle or feel protected if they are still in contact with people who have abused them in the past'.[48] Children may be exposed to 'painful and destructive contact out of a misplaced belief that preserving contact is always beneficial'.[49]

Instead of being able to recover and move forward, they are pulled back by traumatic events being kept alive.

The move towards openness may owe more to the wishes of (some) birth parents than the interests of the adopted child.[50] On the other hand, birth parents who want to completely relinquish their children may not only be pushed into rearing children they do not want, but into retaining contact they do not want.

None of this is to deny that adoption does have its ambiguities, even when totally accepted by society, and that these centre around the way that the child does not share the adoptive parents' ancestry. However, it is interesting that similar claims about threats to identity, as well as the other adverse consequences attributed to adoption, are hardly ever made about children produced through reproductive technologies—whether egg or sperm donation, or surrogacy. When these fears are raised about adoption, we are probably witnessing a feminist position on women's rights masquerading as concern for children's identity.

11

Colour Blind?

THERE are few areas of the adoption debate which are more controversial than trans-racial adoption, or the adoption by parents of one racial group (usually white) of children from another group or groups.

The Question of Black Identity

Childcare professionals have become increasingly dogmatic on the issue, preferring to abandon the possibility of adoption altogether for a child for whom adoptive parents of exactly the same racial profile cannot be found. The British Agencies for Adoption and Fostering (BAAF) insists that 'children need parents of the same racial background'.[1] This is because the supposed identity crisis of adopted children is:

> ...compounded when the adoption is trans-racial because the child has to make sense of their place in a world where, every day, the differences are manifest, where frequently they will have to struggle with the fact of racism, yet may feel isolated in a family which does not share that experience.[2]

With the black identity question at the heart of the case against trans-racial adoption, the argument is that:

> Black children growing up in white families grow up with a very confused sense of themselves. They feel white but they are regarded by the outside world as black. They experience racism as a black person and, however well-meaning a foster parent, there is no way that a white person can have that experience of racism or provide positive role models.[3]

The black identity or 'black consciousness' which the white adopter is incapable of nurturing is linked to 'coping mechanisms'. These arise out of the 'black experience', or the indignities and sufferings inflicted on black people, and are generationally transmitted. White adoptive parents cannot satisfy the 'psycho-survival needs' of the black child, because they cannot pass on tendencies towards doubt and the suspension of trust which black people employ when faced with racism. According to a guide for *Explaining Adoption* to your child: 'The black child in a white family is not only a minority in

105

society but in their own family'. The white adoptive parent is ignorant and helpless when it comes to enabling their adopted black child to 'cope with what the rest of society is presenting them with'. They must get 'the support of black people who share the experience and so understand better than you do what your child has to face'.[4]

All in all, trans-racial adoption is blamed for leaving black children unable to cope in a black world and unacceptable to a white society, or marginalised pariahs to both.[5] Indeed, since individual and 'institutional racism' permeate all aspects of society, this will be internalised by white adopters.

When it comes to a factual basis for claims that black children with white parents do badly or lose out, we find Ravinder Barn quoting the letter of one unhappy Afro-Caribbean girl to her social worker. Placed with white foster parents, she complains how:

> This sort of life was alright for me when I was younger because I deserved it. I think that one of the happiest times of my life was when I was at the children's home. I would love to go back there, because... there were more of my kind there.

This, it seems, is the proof of the:

> ...plight of trans-racially placed black children. There is no comprehensive study to date which has explored their pain and anguish in an adequate manner. It would appear inevitable that the majority of these young children, fostered or adopted by white couples before the 'same race placement' policy came into being, will suffer the consequences in later years.[6]

Actually, there are enough investigations involving trans-racial adoptions to enable us to see whether or not it is 'inevitable' that trans-racial adoptees will be racked by 'pain and anguish'. All show that they seem to enjoy much the same degree of success and satisfaction as same-race adoptions. Neither does there appear to be evidence of higher breakdown rates for trans-racial placements as the proportion of special-needs and older children have grown.[7] Whatever their race, the same factors help adopted children adjust well—lack of delay in placement, love and security in the family, good relationships with adoptive parents, siblings and other relatives, as well as an open, relaxed approach to appearance and background.

Trans-racial adoption in the USA was investigated in the early 1970s using groups of 44 trans-racial adoptions involving a black child and 44 white couples with a child of their own race.[8] According to both the parents' and investigators' reports, there was no difference between the two in the high levels of satisfaction.

Soon after, another study reported on 125 trans-racially adopted children who had lived with their adoptive families for an average of seven years. At nine years of age the picture was of predominantly well-adjusted children, living with parents who were very satisfied with their adoption experience. The success rate of 77 per cent was much the same as that of other studies that had looked at white baby or older child adoptions.[9] Similar adjustment rates of three-quarters or more have been obtained on both sides of the Atlantic from follow-ups of trans-racial placements.[10] There is a striking similarity of outcomes for different racial groups and at different ages—illustrated by a follow-up of Colombian, Korean and Afro-American trans-racial adoptees aged between seven and 25.[11] The Hispanic and Korean adoptees were, if anything, doing slightly better than in-racially adopted whites in terms of adjustment. The Afro-American children had slightly poorer adjustment, attributable to their older ages at placement and more troubled histories.

It was noticed in *Adoption and Race*,[12] a report on the families of largely trans-racially adopted children with an average age of 14, that the study children were doing better academically than their age mates. Barbara Tizard had previously found that mixed-race children adopted by white families were the most intellectually gifted of the adopted children, with reading attainments generally above average, while their problem scores did not differ from those of white children.[13] This is underscored by results from other studies conducted in the USA at about the same time, which reported significantly higher IQs for adopted black children compared with the average for black children and for those reared in their birth-homes.[14]

In Barbara Tizard's research, some of the most unhappy children in the least successful placements (by any criteria) were mixed-race or black children restored to a reluctant natural parent at the insistence of social workers. Another study reported much the same a few years later when it compared 27 mixed-race adopted children with others in care or being reared by lone mothers. Even in relation to white adopted children, and white children at the same schools, the adjustment of the trans-racially adopted children was excellent.[15]

But Are They Black?

As black researcher J. Ladner found in the late 1970s, white adopters of black children generally tend positively to accept the difference between themselves and their black children.[16] There is, of course, no reason why white adopters should not be able to talk to black children (or Chinese children, or Korean children, or Romanian children etc.) about the history and culture of their ethnic group, or encourage them to have same-race friends.

In an attempt to comes to grips with how adopted black children see themselves, Rita Simon and H. Altstein assessed racial awareness in families, each of whom had adopted at least one non-white child as a baby or toddler (which involved 388 children between three and eight years).[17] They found that trans-racially adopted children actually had a much more accurate and positive perception of their race than other black children. At the same time, they were more indifferent to race as a basis for evaluation than any other group reported in any previous study on children in the USA, Hawaii, New Zealand, and other parts of the world.

> They found black children who did not think that white children were smarter, cleaner, or more attractive than themselves. They found white children who did not think that black children were dumber, meaner, less attractive, and so on. They found that most of the fathers and mothers believed that race did not figure greatly in how people perceived and evaluated each other. They found that, on the whole, the parents were extremely optimistic about what relations between different racial groups in the United States would be like... They did not seem to be hiding their heads in the sand... they believed that their problems would not be insurmountable and that their children would grow up to be emotionally healthy, well-adjusted individuals, able to relate to the culture and society of their adopted parents and to the society of their ethnic origins.[18]

One hundred and thirty three of these children were followed up at 11.[19] Around 20 per cent of the adopting parents described problems relating to the children. One (which occurs with same-race adoptions) was the 'rather painful discovery that their adopted children had physical, mental, or emotional disabilities that were either genetic, or the result of indifferent or abusive treatment... received in foster homes'.[20] Another problem was that the children born into the family sometimes felt left out because the family had changed its lifestyle so much (in terms of churches, schools, holidays and so on) to meet the needs of the inter-racially adopted child. However, most of the parents reported that the adoption had brought happiness, commitment and fulfilment into their lives, being the 'wisest and most satisfying decision they had ever made'.[21] In turn, 74 per cent of the adopted children were doing well in school and appeared to have no difficulties. As a group, the children themselves were not only more comfortable about their own racial identification, but also more racially 'colour blind' or indifferent to race as a way of evaluating people.

Similarly, in a longitudinal study,[22] children placed trans-racially had a good sense of racial identity at age eight, but this had not increased from earlier on to the extent that it did for those with black families.[23] Barbara Tizard's findings also indicated that trans-racial adoption, far from inhibiting black children from acquiring an accurate and positive image of themselves, was more likely to encourage that process, without race becoming a prominent issue. It was the children restored to their biological parents who showed more confusion and negative feelings about themselves.[24] While the black adopted children were not taught 'to be proud of their colour', what they did have was 'the self-confidence that came from knowing they were attractive, talented and much loved'.[25]

Any child may feel unattractive and have low self-esteem if they are neglected or unloved. What every adopted child intuitively understands is that:

> Adoption is not easy. No matter how much a child's family looks like him, it does not alter the fact that someone gave him up. Having the same skin color as the people in the household does not erase that. Only love does.[26]

The concerns of trans-racially adopted black children are the usual concerns of children—success at school and with friends, achievement in sports, the dilemmas of adolescence and worries about future employment. Race may not be a crucial determinant of the child's world.[27]

Identifying with both aspects of their heritage is also more important to children than being made to decide whether they are black or white. We might ask why it is assumed to be 'healthy' to have a single reference-group orientation and not a bi-cultural orientation? After all, mixed-parentage children—and many cultural minorities—have, over time, developed 'a dual-culture group-orientation' with which they are quite comfortable.[28] This works to the benefit of their own group and the cohesion of the wider society.

A third of the Search Institute's sample was made up of trans-racial adoptees. Although trans-racial male adoptees were less likely to report high self-esteem (55 per cent) compared to same-race adopted boys (63 per cent), this was still higher than in the national sample of adolescents (51 per cent). The same proportion of trans-racial, as same-race, adoptees, had a strong sense of self (78 per cent), and an identical eight per cent felt as if they did not belong to their family. The vast majority of trans-racial adoptees were comfortable about their adoption (see Table 11:1). The study provides no support for claims that: 'sadly, many young and older trans-racially adopted people... have been given *no* meaningful sense of who they are, where they come from, or where they are going'.[29]

There was a tendency in the Search Institute work for trans-racially adopted youth to be more likely than those in same-race families to be highly attached to both parents.[30] The same applied to the quality

Table 11:1

Identity for Trans-racial and Same-Race Adopted Adolescents

Measure of Identity	All Trans-racial (%)			Asian Trans-racial (%)			Same-Race (%)		
	Boys	Girls	Total	Boys	Girls	Total	Boys	Girls	Total
Sense of Purpose									
I have a good idea about where I'm going in life (% often or very often)	66	72	70	71	75	74	69	76	73
Clarity									
I have a good sense of who I am (% often or very often)	79	78	78	75	77	76	84	74	78
Social Isolation									
I feel unwanted (% agree)	6	5	5	5	5	5	3	9	7
I feel like I don't belong in my family (% true)	6	8	8	3	7	6	7	11	8
Self-Affirmation									
I'm glad I was born (% often or very often)	80	86	84	83	87	86	88	85	87
I think I am lucky to be me (% true)	71	77	75	68	77	75	80	72	76
Self-Esteem									
Percent, high self-esteem[1]	55	51	52	53	53	53	63	43	58

[1]High self-esteem is defined as a mean of 4.0 or higher on a 5-item index of self-esteem with a range of 1-5.

Source: *Growing Up Adopted*, Minneapolis: Search Institute, p. 99.

of the parent/child relationship, family warmth, and parent/child communication. (Families of trans-racial adoptees were higher on acceptance, and therefore less likely to deny or insist on the child's difference, than was true for same-race families.) Only three per cent reported that they were 'often' or 'very often' ashamed or embarrassed about their racial background. With the African Americans, 70 per cent reported that they were never embarrassed about their race, and 74 per cent reported racial pride.

An important variable associated with positive adjustment in trans-racially adopted children is whether or not the adopters have the support of relatives and friends—a factor applying to all parenting. In the longitudinal study of Rita Simon and H. Altstein only 12 per cent of adopters reported a continuing rift with their own parents over the adoption; slightly more reported that they were closer and, for the large majority, inter-racial adoption had made no change to their family ties. It has also been observed that 'preferential adopters' (who may already have biological children) are more prepared to adopt black children than people who are involuntarily childless, who presumably want a child more like their 'own' might have been. However, as adoptive parents, the two groups do not differ in the time they spend discussing the children's cultural and racial background with them, and the children feel the same about their racial origins.[31]

Child Welfare or Race War?

As June Thoburn emphasises, in a review of research for the Department of Health, there are no 'studies which support the fears of black social workers about the dangers of trans-racial placements'.[32] She was only able to come up with a sample of adoptive families seeking help because of behavioural difficulties, in which 23 per cent (where the race was known) concerned trans-racial placements.[33] Whatever the problem may have been here, why assume that it has something to do with race?

Bans or barriers to inter-racial adoption exist not only regardless of the disproportionately high numbers of black children in care who need a permanent home, but despite the findings of research, and the traditional principles of childcare. Directed by a political ideology: 'It is a mark of the debate that although concepts such as the "black identity" and "cultural genocide" are rarely defined in any systematic or coherent manner this has not prevented them from being uncritically accepted into the language of adoption and childcare'.[34] They are backed up by references to obscure psychological mechanisms possessed by black people, and to 'explanatory' concepts like 'institutional racism'. Blackness seems to amount to 'a collective state of political being... which overrides all marks of individual identity'. All individual differences of need, character, aspiration or talent 'are submerged beneath the historical consequences of skin colour'.[35]

Unfortunately, nothing is permitted to falsify claims about the perniciousness of trans-racial adoption. It is apparently demonstrated even when families 'treat their adopted relatives as what indeed they are—members of the family', on the grounds that full acceptance amounts to 'further denial of the difference both of adoption and of ethnic background'. Acceptance is cast as 'a kind of "benign" racism', which is 'deeply rooted in a white supremacist mythology based on centuries of (mis)education about the supposed inferiority of people from different cultures, races, or origins'.[36]

There are two responses to the frequent finding that black trans-racially adopted children are not much preoccupied with their own, or anybody else's, race. One is to optimistically observe that '[i]f the goal is a society that embraces diversity, trans-racially adopted children may be a source of positive modelling for thriving within a multi-cultural nation'.[37] As 'needed bridges between worlds' they 'promote a society in which the individual can be a real part of more than one culture'.[38] The other is to treat this 'multicultural competency' as a way in which racism has negated the will to struggle against an oppressive society, by extirpating black identity. In *Adoption and Race*[39] Gill and Jackson reported that there was no evidence that their black sample felt isolated or estranged within adopted families, and had none of the expected problems of identity and self-respect. Nevertheless, they worried that the children 'saw themselves as white in all but skin colour and had little knowledge or experience of their counterparts growing up in the black community', because, it seemed, 'the large majority of parents had made only limited... attempts to give their children a sense of racial pride and awareness of their racial origin'.[40]

If language like 'racial pride' were used in respect of white children, how would this be received? White children are expected to be 'colour-blind', while black children are expected to be obsessed with race. The consequences of the view in which the creation and survival of black identity is defined in terms of continuing racial antagonism are socially and personally destructive. It:

> ...entails that instead of race being treated as one factor in deciding on the interests of the child, the child becomes a factor in deciding on the interests of the race.[41]

Hidden Families?

Many of the children who, it is often insisted, must not be adopted or even fostered by white families are mixed-race children, often born out of wedlock to white women by black men. There are reasons to believe that 'black' children are over-classified—so that, for example, a child of swarthy appearance, whose father is unknown, may be counted as black, along with children with any black ancestry. However, were these children restored to their original families, they would be largely reared by white women, or in racially 'inappropriate' placements.

However, the disproportionate numbers of black and mixed-race children in the care system have been laid at the door of the ethnocentrism, or racism, of white social workers, who are incapable of appreciating the strengths of black families. When white people think that a black child has no one to care for him, it is apparently because they are too prejudiced to see how the 'extended' or 'multiple-mothering' black family enjoys a thriving existence, where '[f]or aunts, uncles, older siblings to share the responsibility of the child's upbringing is a perfectly normal, reasonable, caring thing to do'.[42] Indeed, the 'Eurocentric model of the nuclear family supports and reinforces this denial of the child's right to be loved, valued and validated for themself' (sic). [43]

In one study of children in care,[44] the proportion of black children with lone parents (83 per cent) was significantly higher than among whites (64 per cent). Black children also had double the proportion of mothers in white-collar and skilled occupations.[45] The black child's entry into care was far more likely to be voluntary, with white children more likely to be removed for parental neglect/inadequacy, failure to thrive, child abuse, non-school attendance and so forth. However, the police were more likely to refer black children for behaviour, as were health services to refer black mothers because of mental illness.[46] For both races, '[s]ocial workers played a very apathetic role in planning for the children's future after the initial admission into care' so that, children left at 18 or were withdrawn from voluntary care by parents, although those whose status had become compulsory had 'virtually no chance of leaving care'.[47]

The voluntary nature of many black care admissions may seem difficult to explain in terms of social worker prejudice against black families. But this is achieved by claims that, as black victims of racism 'are the most disadvantaged group in society', this victimisation has robbed them of the power of choice: 'the "voluntary" concept bears little relevance to the situation', as their deprivation 'forces them to seek the help of welfare agencies'.[48] That proportionately more black care children than white care children are from better-off backgrounds also becomes proof that 'issues of race, via institutional, individual and cultural racism' culminate 'in discriminatory practices to the detriment of black people'.[49] The evidence is an anecdote about a black mother threatening to go and steal and leave her 'kids in care' if social workers did not give her money! (This is a 'failure of preventative work, that is the provision of financial assistance'.)[50]

There is clearly no way that welfare agencies could behave that would remove accusations of bias and failure to 'recognise the onslaught of racism upon the lives of black clients'. They are held to be jeopardizing the chances to rehabilitate black children by not putting them 'home on trial' as much as white children—illustrated by cases of white children being returned to parents for horrifying abuse. Could we be sure that, were black children sent home in similar circumstances, there would not be accusations of callous disregard?[51]

A *lack* of spousal and extended-family support clearly contributes to the high numbers of black and mixed-race children received into care.[52] The levels of one-parent households amongst Afro-Caribbeans tend to run at more than double the level among whites. Poor levels of family integration are likely to contribute to the lack of prospective black adopters and foster parents. In the circumstances, insistence on same-race matches will leave many children without a permanent home, particularly when combined with the over-classification of children as black. Of course, some local authorities are more successful than others in finding black adoptive homes, just as some use adoption more than others. However, the simple answer may not be just to 'try harder' to find black homes, if this means lowering standards.[53] Already, there are high proportions of black single adopters.[54] Considering the practicalities of raising any child alone, there is cause for concern if one young woman may be caring for a number of foster and adoptive children, including older boys. When there are 'insufficient placements for children within their own cultural and racial groups',[55] trans-racial adoption is clearly a viable option for black children. Institutional or foster care for non-white children, or restoration to unwelcoming homes, or placement in any black home willing to take them, irrespective of whether this meets their needs, 'must be considered a form of race prejudice'.[56]

Section C
The Alternative: 'Care'

The outcomes for children who are in long-term care placements are poor, but the problem is evaded by insisting that care is only for short-term placements. Theoretically children in care are going to be returned to their families soon, but in reality many just stay in care indefinitely. As a result of this method of evading the issue, many local authorities have unstructured and unplanned care systems, sometimes operating chaotically, using untrained staff and, increasingly, small and unregistered homes. The system has shown itself to be open to widespread abuse by active paedophiles. Social services departments have proved to be either unable or unwilling to protect underage children who are the victims of illegal sexual acts. One in seven of all girls leaving care is either pregnant or a mother. Boys and girls have been engaged in prostitution whilst 'in care'. The increasing awareness of problems with children's homes has led to an increase in fostering, but this is also beset by problems of untrained carers and lack of proper monitoring. Children who remain in the system 'long-term' experience multiple changes of carers, resulting in the inability to form relationships.

Children who have spent time in care are the most disadvantaged of the child population. They are more prone to psychiatric disorders, they suffer in terms of education and health, and they often 'graduate' from care lacking the most basic life-skills. Deprived of the kin-support systems which re-affirm and sustain most young adults, they are more likely to become homeless, unemployed or in prison. The problems are intergenerational: graduates of 'care' often see their own children absorbed into the same system.

12

From Pillar to Post

THE outstanding characteristic of adoption to have emerged from the review of research into outcomes is clearly the success rate—whether in terms of stability, child development, education or satisfaction. Adopted children have far fewer problems than non-adopted children from similar birth circumstances—whether we are talking about early or late adoptions, whether we ask adoptees or adopters, and whenever in the child-rearing cycle we ask the questions. Adoption is 'perhaps the most therapeutic of all therapies',[1] the most successful form of preventive intervention or rehabilitation for children from disturbed backgrounds. Insofar as anything works, only a permanent substitute family seems up to the task of bringing troubled children to adulthood. However, the most probable response to the needs of children who, for whatever reason, cannot live with their biological parents, will be to rear them in the public care system. Because of this, the role, the operation and—most importantly—the outcomes of care need to be carefully scrutinised.

The Legal Situation

In law, local authorities have a duty under the Children Act 1989 to safeguard and promote the welfare of any child they are looking after. Their powers and responsibilities, as elaborated in *The Children Act Guidance*,[2] are assumed to be consistent with those of the 'good parent'. The obligations cover material well-being, provision for appropriate education and training, health care, employment, leisure and continuing interest and support after discharge from care, and—ambitiously—helping the child to develop personal skills and preferences, a sense of personal identity and worth, a sense of security and even an understanding of family life.

Whether a public care system does, or ever could, play the 'good parent' is debatable. The immediate achievement of care and what is 'so evidently its primary purpose in many cases' is control over children, parents or both.[3] It provides a protection and rescue service for children in danger, and some kind of public protection from dangerous children, as well as providing a range of services for families in difficulty.

Theory and Practice

It has been the perennial hope of child welfare services since the 1940s that the 'era of the child in really long-term care is drawing satisfactorily to a close, that plans for rehabilitation usually work and that hopes for preservation of family ties are being realised'.[4] In spite of the fact that this is obviously not the case, and that some children spend many years—perhaps the whole of their dependent lives—in the care of the local authority, there has been an unwillingness to face up to this.[5] In theory, care holds the family together during brief periods of crisis. In reality, many of these children may not have a family in any meaningful sense. Care children are in perpetual transit, or warehoused in waiting for that elusive family reunion. The overall effect has been described as one of 'constructed insecurity',[6] in which:

> ... the majority of children in long-term care will be either moving between foster homes which disrupt and residential placements, or be in foster placements which were initially intended to be short-term and have become long-term. They are likely to have lost touch with members of their birth families, and yet the placement will be unlikely to offer them a sense of permanence since social work practice will be geared to a fostering status and regulations which imply *impermanence*.[7]

Even if fostering may lead to adoption, the original or overt intention is likely to be that fostering should not be permanent. There is a common failure to distinguish between foster carers working with social workers and birth parents to reunite the family, and those who are really substitute parents because restoration is unrealisable or unrealistic. No one expressly espouses instability and changes of placement. However, the alarm is supposed to be raised if foster parents are developing an attachment to their foster child, and they must be alerted to the difficulty of working for the child's restoration if he remains with them. Fostering is not something which provides a child with relationships within which to develop, but is '...meant to be a support to birth-parents, enabling them to overcome a situation, rather than provide an alternative family ...and preparing a child to return',[8] irrespective of whether or not this is likely to occur. The term 'foster carer' has been coined to avoid any suggestion that the birth parents are unable to parent their children adequately, or that the foster parents are competing for the children's affections.

If care is 'by its very nature missionless', it should not be surprising that a prominent and recurrent theme of reports is the lack of a coherent policy framework for care services. Aside from sweeping statements like 'serving the best interests of children and families', there is 'administrative avoidance of an articulated vision or clear agenda for action, characterised by limited organisational communication, fragmenting units and institutional confusion'.[9]

The social services department which is efficiently run, with a clearly articulated childcare policy, is a rarity.[10] Investigators have mentioned 'common difficulties in identifying what policy actually was, and how it linked with practice', there being 'no consensus in the literature, and none in department policies either'. There might be 'disjointed or disparate pieces of policy [that]... emanated from a variety of sources and originated at different periods of departmental history'.[11] Staff at various levels may be ignorant about the existence, let alone the content, of policies as distinct from procedures.[12] Moreover, 'apart from the very broadest statements to support family life, childcare policies did not necessarily command a consensus within the departments, or even within the small teams of social workers at the operational level'.[13]

If many social services departments have no view of the purpose or rationale of care, it is not surprising that expectations about the role or functions of institutions are absent. Only a minority of local authorities are able to make any kind of broad strategy statement relating to children's homes. Even then, it is impossible to say how the outlines on paper have any 'impact on practice (though "crises" inspections ...suggest the gap is wide)'.[14] Few authorities have developed satisfactory ways of monitoring their community homes.[15] With 'little sense of direction', the delivery of residential children's services 'related more to crises than careful and well-informed planning'.[16]

The Therapeutic Institution?

The care system has undergone periodic contractions and expansions, depending on whether it is seen as a place of last resort, or as offering some form of therapeutic benefit.

Foster care was increasingly seen as a viable alternative to large, harsh institutions in the wake of the Curtis Report (1946), which formed the basis of the Children Act 1948. Foster care then went into disrepute in the 1960s because of difficulties over recruiting and keeping foster parents, role confusion and high breakdown rates.[17]

At the same time, residential care underwent a renaissance with major changes to the juvenile justice system under the Children and Young Persons Act 1969. Giving social workers considerable discretionary powers at each stage of decision making, it was based on the assumption that the young offender was simply one species of deprived child, so that it was pure chance whether or not he went into care because of abuse or neglect, or had committed a crime.[18] The aim was to make the 'best possible use of all available resources to deal with the actual problems of children and families... without being inhibited by distinctions which are not relevant to the diagnosis of needs'.[19] The approved schools passed to the social services as mixed community homes for non-offenders and offenders.

The reformed juvenile jurisdiction was the flagship of the new comprehensive 'generic' social work departments, established in the wake of the Seebohm Report in 1968.[20] Along with professional status, social workers laid claim to specialist insights and expertise. They promised to prevent the deprived and delinquent children of today from becoming the deprived, inadequate, unstable or criminal citizens of the future.[21]

The explosion in care orders in the early 1970s was matched by the almost exclusive concern of the DHSS and its Childcare Development Group with the therapeutic community,[22] or for 'care and treatment in a planned environment'.[23] Yet, while the Curtis Report in 1946 had attributed the unsatisfactory standards of care in children's homes partly to poorly trained staff, there was no sign that the situation had improved in the intervening years.[24] Neither had there been any great breakthroughs in knowledge or techniques that might transform the social and emotional development of children for the better. It was therefore somewhat implausible that a child could be re-socialised or made 'better' by a spell of residential treatment, particularly if problems existed within the environment which he usually inhabited.

The existing evidence on outcomes was unpromising. When young people were looked at two to three years after leaving the care of Glasgow Corporation, their employment records, educational achievements, intellectual ability, and conviction rates were worse than those of working-class boys who had not been in care.[25] As the news came in from the 'therapeutic communities' in the 1970s, it was of unremitting failure. The more healing and 'intensive' the intervention purported to be, the worse the results.[26] There was no difference between the subsequent offending rates of those who entered as non-offenders or minor offenders and those who entered as seasoned offenders.[27]

As the disastrous foray into delinquent rehabilitation reinforced the longer-term disillusionment with institutions, the closing of as many as possible became a major objective in the 1980s. However, a review for the Department of Health in 1991 (following the Pindown scandal in Staffordshire) spoke of the way in which: 'the collapse in the number of residents... an associated loss of purpose... deficiencies in policy and management, a largely unqualified and inexperienced staff, and problems of control in homes', had exacerbated profound, long-term problems of staffing, expertise and morale that had never been addressed.[28] By the mid 1990s, 'residential childcare has shrunk as a national service to a level below that at which a reasonable choice of placement is possible for a child'. With children being shoe-horned into 'vacancies in unsuitable establishments', exposing them to 'unforeseen harm', all the 'assessments, plans and reviews are a mockery if a reasonable range of services are not available to fulfil their purposes'.[29]

Residential workers need 'exceptional skills' to deal with youngsters who may have been grievously abused, rejected by their families, be unloving as well as unloved, and badly behaved. Yet, only a third of officers in charge at community homes held a Certificate of Qualification in Social Work in 1991, and 20 per cent had no qualifications. A 'deplorable' 70 per cent of all staff were completely unqualified,[30] and 45 per cent had been in their posts for under two years—no better than ten years before.[31] (Anyone who gets trained tends to leave for field social work where the pay and promotion prospects are much better.) In 1997, staffing was still a 'chronic problem' and while 'progress is made here and there by dint of determined and persistent effort, the overall impression is of progress too slow to redeem the sector as a whole.'[32]

Residential care always presents problems of management and supervision since 'the physical isolation of an establishment... may set it out of mind as well as out of sight'.[33] But the uncertainties over policies and management weakness in children's services have been a particular 'recipe for confused leadership', with the 'risk that homes would operate individualistically' and be managed idiosyncratically. If such has been the position of homes under local authority control, what is the situation with the small unregistered children's homes springing up in the 1990s? After adverse accounts to the Department of Health from many quarters, an area report in 1993 giving substantial cause for concern, and an ineffectual circular urging local authorities to fulfil their responsibilities under the available legislation, there came a shocking national report in 1995.[34]

Only eight of the 42 English and Welsh authorities admitting to using such homes showed any signs of having procedures governing their use. Fourteen who said they were non-users were current users, making placements without reference to senior staff, or counter to departmental policy. While some homes offered care of a high quality: 'an unacceptably high proportion... do not achieve a satisfactory standard... do not produce good results and... do not provide value for money'.[35] Consequently: 'children are being placed... in accommodation which, at the very least, is unsuitable and, in some cases, is placing them at risk'.[36] Used for those for whom other residential care or fostering had failed: 'Some authorities even went as far as to suggest that they were using such placements in "desperation" for those children who had reached the "end of the line"'.[37]

While charging fees of £1,000-£1,500 per week for what were often, at best, no more than foster placements, the homes were often staffed by students working part-time or on short-term contracts, or by the homeless in exchange for accommodation.[38] The high staff turnover 'can do little to reassure the young people... most of whom have been placed with the intent of securing greater stability'.[39] Unskilled people did therapeutic work and counselling without professional oversight and education was sometimes 'very poor' or non-existent. Homes might be part of larger, profit-oriented enterprises, with some operators paying fees to agencies to find them children. There are:

> ...very unsuitable, unsatisfactory people moving into this area of provision. There were some who had a history of financial misdealing and who were subsequently convicted of fraud. In one case a proprietor fled with money collected from a local authority for the care of three young people. There were others against who allegations of both physical and sexual abuse had been made prior to them setting up small homes, and some of these have subsequently been convicted and sentenced... local authority checks had not been sufficiently robust to prevent them from placing children in the care of these people.[40]

Placements in these homes are still growing, and they do not, as yet, have to undergo inspection or staff checks.[41]

A Playground for Paedophiles?

No doubt some children's homes 'engage people of skill, imagination and persistence' to work with those with whom 'no one else wants to be bothered'.[42] However, a system so deficient is conducive to abuse. 'People who wish to exploit children seek occupations or voluntary work where they have access to children. They will find the weak points in our defences... residential work as an employee or volunteer provides the abuser with a captive group of vulnerable children.' The massive dimensions of abuse over the last few decades are still being revealed, leading to a major review of the 'widespread sexual, physical and emotional abuse of children... over the preceding 20 years',[43] and numerous moves by the Department of Health in the 1990s to get local authorities to bring about changes in management and personnel practice.

It is no longer possible to treat as aberrations cases like that of Frank Beck (a foster carer), who abused dozens of children in Leicestershire between 1973 and 1986, or the Pindown experience, where Tony Latham used a distorted version of Pavlovian conditioning to control children with long periods in isolation. Since 1990 Leicestershire, Staffordshire, Cheshire, Merseyside and North Wales have faced huge police investigations. Peter Howarth, John Allen and Steven Norris, among others, are serving long prison sentences for a sample of their crimes against children in Wales, where a Tribunal of Enquiry is investigating events in Clwyd and Gwynedd.[44] At Bryn Estyn in Clwyd, where staff abused boys 'on an almost unimaginable scale',[45] the children also suffered serious physical and sexual assaults at the hands of each other, as staff encouraged peer control to make their job easier.[46] Some of those abused in care themselves become abusers: three from Gwynedd are currently serving life sentences for murder. (The assessment centre in Gwynedd, where so many other abuses took place, closed after its regime collapsed and police were called in to quell disturbances.) Hard on the heels of the scandal in Clwyd—at least 100 children sexually abused over 20 years, of whom 10 have killed themselves—came that in Cheshire. By 1997, eleven care workers had been jailed for a multitude of sexual and physical assaults, with more trials pending.[47] In Hackney, Mark Trotter died of AIDS, with many children alleging he had abused them, and when he was due to be charged with abusing children while working in Merseyside.[48] Islington has already been censured in a government report for its neglect over abuse allegations in its children's homes.

While no work has been done on the incidence of abuse against disabled children in the UK, the situation is unlikely to be much different from the US, Canada and Australia, where they have been found to be up to twice as likely to be physically abused as well as emotionally neglected, compared to children without disabilities. It is also estimated that some impairments found in care children are likely to be the result of abuse.[49]

Research in the UK testifies to the extraordinary amount of physical punishment meted out in children's homes.[50] A witness speaks of how, in a children's assessment centre:

> ...she found a senior member of staff slapping girls across the face. He went on sick leave, to be replaced by a man who started 'laying into' an 11-year-old boy. 'He was beating the living daylights out of him, trying to force him to kneel down and lick his shoes'.[51]

In one investigation, over half of the institutionally reared people said that beatings were the main form of control.[52] (They were quite able to distinguish between 'unfair' and 'fair' punishment and that what, at the time, might have seemed unfair was deserved in retrospect.) A small number experienced benevolent and reasonable regimes. More often, rules were 'rigid, inflexible and sometimes unreasonable which almost made it inevitable that they would be broken'.[53] Almost two-thirds felt that punishment was often or almost always 'unfair', and quite frequently downright harsh and cruel: 'if they started hitting there's no chance of them stopping. They would go on and on. I got battered on the backside when I was six for standing on a heap of soil'.[54] There were severe beatings for bed-wetting, for not eating fat, or 'when it pleased them [the staff]'.[55] Children 'were terrified... sometimes they would promise a cake, if you were good, but if you asked for it later you got leathered'.[56]

Children's homes seem to veer between harshness and abnegation. A circular from the Department of Health and Social Security stated in 1981 that corporal punishment was incompatible with the principles on which control and discipline in community homes were based. This appears to have been widely ignored.[57] However, staff may have little help, advice or training on what is supposed to replace physical discipline. Taking the line of least resistance, they may abandon all control, as at Grove Park in Southwark, south-east London, with its transvestism, sexual assaults and drug-taking.[58]

In Care and Unprotected

At least one in seven young women leaving care is either pregnant or already a mother. Sexual intercourse with a girl under 16 is, of course, against the law. Much underage sex is also exploitative. Girls have clearly not been protected from the predatory attentions of either males in the system or outsiders, who may lure or force them into prostitution and live off their earnings.[59] There are allegations too that youths are allowed to work as rent-boys, and to visit the gay scene.[60]

JANE, 13, was sexually abused by a relative from the age of eight. It was three years before her mother found out what was happening. Both her parents were heroin addicts.

Taken into care at 11 years-old, she was introduced to prostitution a year later by 14-year-old girls in the residential home... She claims care workers know what she is doing—but are powerless to stop her.

LEE has just turned 16. He started working as a rent boy three months after being taken into local authority care at the age of 11. He has lost count of the number of men he has had sex with... He ran away to London... and was put into secure accommodation when he returned. But that was only for three months—and, in his view, little else was done to dissuade him from prostitution. He is now HIV positive.

JILL was abused by a relative from 12 months. She was taken into care when she was five, because her mother was not able to protect her. She has learning difficulties and behavioural problems. She learned to be a prostitute from older girls in care from the age of 11.[61]

A survey by a national drug and alcohol agency found that 44 per cent of its clients had been in care at some time in their childhood. Over a third claimed that they had started using drugs while in institutional or foster care.[62]

Large numbers of children are able to abscond and 'go missing' while in care. The Central London Teenage Project—a 'safe house' for young runaways—reported that a quarter of those admitted (in its first two years of operation) had run away from care. Over half were persistent absconders and had already run away at least five times. Among the reasons they gave was that the placement was too far from home; they had been in a temporary placement for assessment too long; no one had taken an interest in them; they disliked the rules and regulations; and they felt stigmatised by being in a home. A further reason was that they were alarmed by the prospect of imminent 'independence'.[63]

Such youngsters make ideal victims. An investigation prompted by the case of mass murderers Rosemary and Frederick West, whose home was a haven for runaways from a local children's home, also discovered that the local social services department had lost files on nearly one in seven of the children in its care.[64] (These children may have already been running from abusers: 'one of the worst features of earlier scandals is that children who ran away from abuse were continually returned to the abuser's care'.[65]) Reacting to the news that, over the years, thousands of young people may have been 'lost' to the care system, the social care workers' magazine *Community Care* declared:

Make no mistake, the appalling neglect, and sometimes abuse, of young people at every stage in the care system (including when they leave it) is the single most damning indictment of the way social services departments are managed and the way some professionals within them operate.[66]

Responsibility for supervising youngsters in care may be shrugged off by appeals to rules that forbid doors to be locked, or prescriptions about 'non-judgmental' attitudes and the need for 'therapeutic freedom'. Half of the abuse reported in institutions is probably peer abuse, given the 'unconsidered mix of fearsome and vulnerable residents'. But staff 'may dismiss abusive sexual behaviour as "normal" and deprive children of the protection they rightly expect by consciously or unconsciously colluding with what is going on'.[67] The Children Act 1989 is widely read to mean that carers are constrained to abide by the child's wishes, when what Section 22(5) actually says is that when an authority is making any decision about the future of a child, it shall give 'due consideration having regard to his age and understanding, to such wishes and feelings... as they have been able to ascertain'.[68] Recently, the Health Secretary[69] had to remind local authorities that the guidelines[70] made it clear that staff can and must use their authority, or the parental responsibility which is invested in them, to stop youngsters leaving homes if they might be putting themselves, others, or property, at risk.[71]

In his 1997 review Sir William Utting concluded that the residential childcare sector 'as a whole now lacks the capacity to initiate widespread improvements in standards'. Whether in the public or private sector, there was 'no grouping of services of sufficient strength—and not enough confidence or stability in the sector as a whole—to provide the basis and the motive power for the development required.[72]

Is Fostering a Better Option?

The drawbacks of institutions have always made foster care appear attractive, but this has its own problems. Around two-thirds of social services departments claim to have trouble recruiting foster carers,[73] particularly ones who can deal with the physically or sexually abused, disabled, or difficult child. The number is dwindling and turnover is high: one investigation found that 60 per cent had been fostering less than a year. The result is inadequate placement choices for 75 per cent of children. Only one-third of children have a proper assessment of their needs and a care plan.[74] Only 20 per cent of authorities can offer a placement choice for children under 10, and only three per cent have a choice for an older child.[75] Consequently, the child goes to the only available placement, not one that can meet his needs.[76] Despite some increase in specialist foster schemes, the service provided is mainly short-term temporary care, and it is estimated that a half of carers have no training at all.[77] No social services department has an effective monitoring system to ensure that statutory requirements are being met. Record keeping is poor and it is difficult to know how decisions are being made.

An irony is that small children's homes are effectively being created. Indeed, some proprietors offering accommodation in small homes are moving into the area of independent fostering as desperate local authorities bid up payments. A family finding business, operating as a voluntary agency offering foster placements, may be allied to a 'for-profit' enterprise running small homes.[78] But these homes do not provide carers with the same resources to cope as institutions, so that the more 'difficult' children move on to another placement.[79] They may also be caring for children from several different authorities. This scattering of placements, and dissemination of control and supervision, as well as chronic shortages, militates against the maintenance of standards and the check of abuses. There is a '"negative incentive" ...not to ask too many searching questions about the placement lest it be proved to be unsuitable'.[80]

Moving On

Movement through a multitude of placements is a foremost feature of children's care experience.[81] The Dartington Research Unit found that, out of the 170 children who remained in long-term care (two years or more), 60 per cent had experienced three or more placements of various kinds, and 14 per cent had experienced at least five.[82] Very recently, an assessment of previous moves by 145 children entering Barnardos projects in Scotland showed an average of 3.7, with a small number of youngsters having between 15 and 40 moves. The child with 40 moves was of primary age, and 26 of the 64 primary-age children had experienced between two and five moves.[83] Moreover, forty children had experienced three or more changes of school on top of those usually experienced by children of their age. One child had experienced 11 changes.

Foster care has generally deteriorated in recent years as family preservation and low care admission rates have been equated with good childcare. As a result, a 'last resort' stance means emergency admissions into hastily arranged placements as social workers, struggling to keep children out of care, intervene too late. Contact with or repeated restoration to abusive, neglectful and highly unstable families means going in and out of accommodation.[84] Then, as many move 'from one unsuitable (because badly matched) foster home to another' there are 'children of 10-years-old who have had 10 foster homes since the age of five. My record is a 14 year old with more than 20 moves. Many such children can attach to no one. They run off and "get lost"'.[85]

Even after being in care for only six months, a quarter of the children in one[86] study had made three or more moves. Sixteen per cent of those who had entered by the compulsory route had moved five to seven times. The results were similar to those from another study[87] which found that two-thirds of the placements that broke down within six months did so in crisis conditions when, once again, the child often moved on to another inappropriate placement likely to break down.

13

Children with the Odds Against Them

THERE is little doubt that care children are the most disadvantaged of the child population. A significant proportion of children diagnosed as having a psychiatric problem has been in care,[1] and the pattern has scarcely changed over time.

One comprehensive investigation followed up 624 young people five years after they had entered care in New York State in 1966. Between a quarter to a third of those remaining in foster and institutionalised care at the end of the study showed various signs of psychiatric impairment.[2] Care is supposed to help them. As Michael Rutter and colleagues tartly observe in their study of institutionally reared adults in the UK, as children they:

> ...had been admitted to the Group Foster Homes because of a concern that they were at risk from being reared in severely disrupted families or from a breakdown in parenting. It is chastening, therefore, to note that of those admitted before age two who remained in the institution until age 16 or older, 44 per cent of males and 45 per cent of females showed poor social functioning at follow-up, giving little indication that their institutional admission had proved protective. Of course, it is possible that their outcomes might have been worse had the children remained with their biological parents.[3]

Studies of children in foster, rather than institutional, care, do not present a more cheerful picture, with their high rates of disturbance as well as breakdown. One looked at foster children aged between five and 17 who had been in placement for at least a year. Nearly 40 per cent showed evidence of disturbance on objective measures, compared with seven per cent of children generally from the Isle of Wight, and 25 per cent of boys, and 13 per cent of girls, living in Inner London.[4] Another, again dealing with children who were in longer-term, and thus far more stable placements than is often the case, was restricted to those in placement for five years, mostly starting before five. Disturbance rates were 30 per cent (compared with only 11 per cent for the children adopted by their foster parents).[5]

Positive school experiences are the main help for care youngsters, given the dearth of other sources of self-esteem, satisfaction and accomplishment. However, the education of children in care is often impaired, or undermined, by peer group pressure, low expectations of school attendance, stigmatisation at school (with the consequent bullying),[6] as well as by the many moves. Audit work has shown that over a third of children in residential care are not receiving education at all, producing a 'scandalous situation in which the life prospects of these young people may be irretrievably damaged'.[7]

Similarly, the health of care children is neglected. For parents, a child's health is a 'primary and primal' concern. But, in care, there is 'no one person who sees it as their job to carry out the daily monitoring which most parents do without thinking'. With responsibility for health care borne by professional and often temporary carers, knowledge of the child's normal state of health, his health history and all those 'minor daily signals whereby a parent is sensitive to a change in a child's health' is missing.[8]

The long-term development of children in the public care suffers in two major ways.[9] There are the effects of separation, loss and/or ill treatment with respect to birth families, and then the secondary effects which come from being in care itself. The more years spent in care, the more the risk of 'system abuse', from inappropriate placements, high rates of breakdown, abuse in care and while on the run. Back in 1967, one study concluded[10] that care provides a psychologically, culturally and educationally restricted, even impoverished, environment. In 1976 another researcher[11] could find no new evidence which contradicted these conclusions. Nor is there any now. Care is: 'insecure and unstable, subjecting children to repeated changes of placement and caretakers, or to institutional environments where emotional links are hard to forge'. It can leave a child 'isolated, without any close ties to others, and grossly unprepared for adult life'.[12]

After Care?

Care-leavers account for less that one per cent of their age group, but they are massively over-represented amongst the disadvantaged. More than 75 per cent leave school with no qualifications—a rate which is 12 times higher than that for children in general.[13] Only between 12 and 19 per cent go on to further education, compared to 68 per cent of the general school population. Between 50 to 80 per cent are unemployed: fourfold the rate for youngsters between 16-24.[14] In turn, 23 to 26 per cent of adult prisoners (depending on the sample) and 38 per cent of young prisoners have spent time in local authority care before 16, as have 30 per cent of young, single homeless.[15] Overall, care children are 60 times more likely to join the ranks of the homeless and 50 times more likely to be imprisoned.

The statistics are similar in the US where 40 per cent of the children leaving the system end up on welfare, and between 23 per cent and 39 per cent of homeless youth are former foster children, who also make up nearly 14 per cent of America's prison population.[16]

Investigations of ex-care populations all conclude that many are not only retarded in their emotional and social development as children, but also in adulthood.[17] Michael Rutter and colleagues[18] studied nearly 100 men who had been reared in children's homes (run on group cottage lines) because their parents could not cope. Nearly 40 per cent were seen to have a personality disorder, with abnormal interpersonal relations associated with definitely impaired social functioning, compared to just over 10 per cent of controls who had never been in care. Nearly 50 per cent possessed a criminal record at, or after, 18, compared to just under 15 per cent of the controls, even given that the control group from inner London contained more socio-pathology than a general population sample. The ex-care women were more likely to marry deviant men (52 per cent versus 19 per cent for other women, when comparing the first spouses of those who had ever married/cohabited). Institutionally-reared women are eight times more likely to be teenage parents (or 40 per cent to five per cent for women in general).

Any time spent in care in childhood seems to be socially and psychologically damaging. In the longitudinal National Child Development Study[19] experience of care was a risk factor for high maladjustment at 16, involving a quarter of subjects of both sexes, compared to just over five per cent for those reared continuously by both natural parents. Of the entire cohort, seven per cent were at risk of psychological problems at 33, compared to 20 per cent of the care group. Care under the age of 11 was associated with particularly high levels of mental ill health in men. The results are not explicable in terms of any of the pre-existing problems of children who enter care.

Goodbye and Good Luck

Each year about 8,000 young people leave public care for independence, or 'age out' in American parlance. About a third leave at 16 and most of the rest before their 18th birthday.

As their family of origin was not ready or prepared to take the youngster back at 14, or 12, or 10, it is unlikely to be more willing to do so now that he is 16 or 18. Many parents will be dead, insane, alcoholic, chronically sick or otherwise incapacitated and hardly in a position to look after themselves, let alone offer support and help to an older teenager. Moreover, as the families of care children are often transformed in a very short space of time, it is often going to be difficult to identify a 'family' after so many years. What is often apparent is that the return home is blocked by a new step-parent or boyfriend. (The hostility of new 'partners' to the children of previous unions is also, of course, a foremost reason for young homelessness anyway.) Adults who have been in care at any stage in their childhoods have low expectations of help from parents or other relatives.[20]

What is on offer as preparation for living alone in the outside world is 'mostly a haphazard and spasmodic effort rather than a well thought-out and planned activity with close co-ordination between residential and field services' and one 'rarely sustained and continued with follow-up services'.[21] A prominent study found that only one of the homes involved ran a hostel to which youngsters could move before leaving care and learn to look after themselves. (Another avoided the need by pushing the boys towards the armed forces.) More than half of the young people said they received no help whatsoever in managing money or with employment.

The Children Act 1989 provides the statutory context for what promised to be the better preparation and aftercare of those who have been 'looked after'. Local authorities have a duty to 'advise and befriend' young people after they leave care, and have powers to provide assistance in cash or kind, as well as help with education, employment or training up to the age of 21. However, even where the services exist, they are still minimal:

> At 16 I was put into a flat found by Social Services, I had to do everything for myself: cook, clean, pay bills, things I had never done before. The worst thing though was coping with the loneliness. I didn't see my social worker for seven months and I didn't know anyone in the area.[22]

The central and irreducible characteristic of family ties is that people are involved in responsibilities which are imperative and enduring. This cannot be replicated by social service functionaries, whose interest and efforts, however conscientious, are delineated by the hours, terms and length of their job contracts. How well a young adult fares depends on having people who care not just for him, but about him, at age 24 as well as at 14 or four years of age. While families usually keep some track of their members' whereabouts and fortunes, local authorities, voluntary and private units do not even record where young people live after leaving. It is questionable how even the suggested mandatory monitoring of all care leavers could provide a similar function on an impersonal and bureaucratic basis.[23]

The ordinary population of more 'advantaged children' will be leaving home, on average, between 20 and 22 rather than 16 to 18.[24] Even then, there will be obligated kin in the background, or a home where they have to take you in, or help you out. As the National Child Development Study's investigation of 33-year-olds underlines, for most people the family is the first port of call for all types of help.[25] The drawbacks of care do not only relate to the absence of committed parents to take personal responsibility for the child's welfare in the dependent years. There is also the lack of a stable and supportive kin network which provides the continuing involvement, protection, affirmation, interest, influence and control which is strongly associated with successful adaptation in adult life.[26] This problem receives virtually no recognition, it being usually assumed that what care leavers need is another course, or more lessons in cooking or budgeting, or help with filling in benefit forms.

When the subjects of one study were asked whether they felt they could go back to the home for help and support: 'most of them either did not want to have anything more to do with the home or the impression they were left with on leaving was that they would not be welcome'.[27] Others discovered that the house-parents they knew had moved on (a common occurrence with staff turnover running at around a third a year) or were told: 'You don't live here any more'.[28]

None of this means that all of those leaving care must inevitably fail, or that every statutory or voluntary service is inadequate in caring for these children or preparing them for adult life—only that, proportionately, care leavers do much, much, worse in most important respects than children from families in general.

Pass It On

The malign effects are inter-generational. Among women leaving care, pregnancy plays an important part in the processes associated with relationships to unsupportive, deviant men. Starting one's own family partly reflects a tendency to seek escape from an unhappy background and a 'pervasive lack of planning'. But institutional upbringing is strongly associated with parenting, as well as marital, breakdowns. This leads to the offspring going into foster or institutional care for another generation, or at a rate 66 times greater than the children of those who have never needed substitute care.[29] This is underlined in Jean Packman's work on care referrals, where a half of the mothers had been separated from their own parents, whether through death, divorce or other reasons, and one in five had lived away from home, whether 'in care' or in a similar private arrangement.[30] Almost a quarter of the mothers felt that their childhoods had been sad or dreadful: 'and every "dreadful" description belonged to a parent of an admitted child'.[31] The worst start in life that a child could have is to be born of a young mother who has come out of the care system: 'Nowhere is the cycle of deprivation more obvious than in the admission to care of children whose parents were themselves "in care"'.[32]

The review of residential childcare for the Department of Health in 1991 observed that not only is the 'public parent... not necessarily a successful parent', but that it is misleading to ever couch expectations about public care in terms of the parental role or parental responsibilities.[33] Public care can never 'replace or replicate the selfless character of parental love'. Even 'a warmth and personal concern... goes beyond the traditional expectations of institutions'.[34]

Clearly, the low rating of adoption as a placement option by social policy theorists and social service practitioners not only occurs despite its highly successful track record, but in the face of the failures, and oft-times the horrors, of so much that still passes for official or professional childcare.

Section D
Policy Responses

All current proposals for reform of childcare arrangements are loaded against adoption. The 'party line' is that more resources should be channelled into keeping dysfunctional families together, and that poverty must be eliminated. This approach assumes, firstly, that virtually limitless resources and sweeping redistributive policies are feasible, and secondly that poor parenting could be eliminated by cash transfers. Both assumptions are flawed. In spite of the poor record of local authority care, there are new plans to revive and expand it, removing the stigma attached, so that it would come to be regarded as normal for parents to put their children into care for spells whenever they feel pressed. This would fulfil the aims of the Children Act 1989 which sought to make the upbringing of children a co-operative venture between parents and the local authority. The scope for creative social work within such a framework is considerable, and in some cases families might receive payment for bringing up their own children. There are also plans for 'limited adoption', 'permanent fostering' and guardianship half-way houses between fostering and adoption. The research indicates that outcomes for children are not encouraging from these arrangements, and, if they are equated with adoption, it will have the effect of diminishing adoption by association. Children themselves prefer to be adopted: it confers a publicly recognised status, like marriage. It may be 'only a piece of paper' but it affects people's sense of well-being.

The current overriding concern for family preservation should be replaced with a concern for permanency in the child's placement, to save children from the known ill-effects of being shunted about for years. Local authorities should be accountable to the courts; the grounds under which they may intervene in family life should be narrowly defined and any child removed from home should have a permanency plan. If the child cannot be returned to the natural parent at the end of—say—12 months, then the procedures to free the child for adoption should be instigated. Any child left voluntarily in care for six months should be treated as abandoned and similarly made available for adoption. Sanctions are needed against bureaucratic inertia. Local authorities should be required to publish details of the number of children in their care and how long they have been there. Local authority social services departments are cumbersome and bureaucratic, as well as being often hostile to adoption on ideological grounds. Adoption services should be removed from them and vested in voluntary specialist agencies.

14

New Ways To Go Backwards

IF state intervention is to be judged on how it harms or benefits children,[1] then subjecting them to lengthy public care, especially involving multiple placements, clearly causes both short- and long-run serious harm. The plight of children in care is a national scandal, and the record of the system one of massive shortcomings, incompetence, and no little corruption. It was usually so. While there is much preoccupation with the 'rights' of all manner of minorities, we still tolerate two castes of children, where one is socially excluded and stigmatised, with life chances very much poorer than the other.

However, while the debate is widening to involve the vision of what 'a "good" childcare service would look like', and how all the manifest inadequacies of the present system might be 'turned around to produce a new childcare service for the next century',[2] proposals for revitalising child welfare services largely represent developments within the familiar framework. They are intended to more or less preclude adoption and all attempts to get children out of public care. Indeed, after its contraction of the care system under the 'last resort' policy of the 1980s, suggestions now abound for reviving, reformulating and expanding it as an everyday family support service. There are also calls to pursue alternatives to adoption like 'permanent fostering', 'limited adoption' and guardianship, which avoid the explicit replacement of the original parent(s).

Preserve the Families in the First Place

Even when the success of adoption is acknowledged, it may be attributed to the failure of the state to support the natural families of the children properly. This is not unreasonable, considering that there might be parents who could keep their children if they had the right assistance, and given that there has been little systematic development, assessment and evaluation of ways to help and who is likely to benefit. However, it is a different matter to argue that, until we have all the means to improve or transform inadequate parents, and there are effective preventive and restorative programmes—which

137

might be never—'[t]he temptation to use adoption as an outlet for the children of the most disadvantaged must be resisted'.[3] Indeed, it is further argued that: 'adoption cannot be practised as a "childcare service" without at the same time consideration being given to the forces which generate childcare need'.[4]

These 'forces' may relate to social and economic inequalities, and discrimination. It is true that families generally have become more economically disadvantaged compared to other groups over recent decades. It is true that this has implications for the quality of parenting and family structure (although the blatant connection between family disintegration and child abuse is invariably ignored in social work texts). However, while children from low-income homes are more likely to be victims of aggravated abuse, most children from low-income homes are not victimised. Moreover, alcoholism and drug-abuse lead to both poverty and child maltreatment, and there is a distinction to make between poverty as a 'marker' for risk factors, such as stress, poor health, or lack of social support, and poverty as a cause of risks. 'If parents who are depressed are poor because depression makes it hard to earn a living, transferring money to them will not reduce their depression'[5] or, indeed, alter their paedophiliac propensities, retardation, and so on.

There are reasons to be cautious about notions that child abuse necessarily lies at one end of a continuum—so that 'anyone' can abuse or neglect their child when life's stresses and frustrations outweigh the supports.[6] It is possible that, even were there redistribution to accord with the dreams of any socialist, some people would still reject or abuse their children, or fail to display even elementary caring behaviours. In any case, should we wait to find out? Is it right for children to suffer until we can rectify all the injustices to their parents?

The retort might be that we could at least devote the resources we put into public care into keeping the original birth family to-gether—not least by providing services in the home. Family preservation, which means working with families before a child is removed, is thus presented as the alternative to family re-unification. Such considerations led to the requirement in 1996 for local authorities to prepare Children's Service Plans. These are intended to ensure that arrangements are put in place across all children's services, in order to recognise those potentially at risk and act on warning signals in a coherent, co-ordinated way.[7] Family preservation exponents want that action to involve 'long-term or intensive work', as well as 'flexibility and quick response to need', using:

... a range of resources... such as day-care provision, supported accommodation, home-help services, peripatetic foster parents, even payment of the parent(s) to stay at home and look after their children where this could prevent their reception into care.[8]

Enthusiasm for family preservation continues to grow in the UK, while US specialists conclude that: 'The days of conceptualising family preservation as a placement and cost-reduction strategy are numbered'.[9] The selling of family preservation in the US has now cooled off, but a decade ago it was all the rage. As in the UK today, family preservation seemed to offer the best way to resolve the problems plaguing the child welfare system: it could support families, obviate the need for permanent alternatives, yet reduce the resort to harmful public care. The 1980s boom in the US care population lent urgency to the development of measures to prevent children from being placed away from home. For social activists, child advocates and service providers, it was money for an overburdened system. Preservation programmes 'could, if properly marketed, become the new funding stream that could plug the gap between service needs and resources'.[10]

None of this was proof that family preservation programmes worked. Extensive evaluations of programmes in the US have found no evidence that they are effective in reducing out-of-home placements—the most important indicator of success.[11] However, it has been argued that 'reducing placements should not be the measure of success. The main outcome variable should be *child safety*',[12] and whether children are better protected, and their health and development improved.

This was one of the outcomes explored in a vigorous four-year evaluation of the Family First placement prevention programme in Illinois, which included experiments in six areas comparing the results of family preservation services with regular child welfare services.[13] Homebuilder therapists were available 24 hours a day, seven days a week, serving two families at a time. They taught skills, and set clear, specific goals, using a range of techniques like modelling, values clarification, cognitive-behavioural strategies, and problem management. In turn, 89 per cent of Family First cases received services like food, clothing, housing and transport, and three-quarters were given cash assistance. Intense 90-day programmes were intended, but caseworkers extended their work as they thought necessary.

Participating in a Family First programme did not lower the risk of the child going into care or being maltreated, with some children continuing to be abused even during periods of intensive interven-tion.[14] There was no lasting effect on the length of time that families remained in the child welfare system, nor on the likelihood that families would return to this system. It did, however, have a 'net-widening effect' in that more people became dependent upon services in the public childcare system. Understandably, there were no savings in care costs. These results were reflected in a state-wide analysis of the performance of California's 'reformed' child welfare system over the last decade.[15]

Workers struggling to save families who seemed to have little interest in being preserved 'viewed lack of acknowledgment of problems by the primary caretaker to be the number one reason for case failure'. Apart from 'resource deficits' clients often did not view other problems 'as important and did not want to work on them'.[16] Richard Gelles, a pre-eminent child-abuse researcher, who was an optimistic advocate of family preservation programmes, now con-demns as naïve the 'notion that anyone can be a fit and loving parent if only appropriate and sufficient support is provided'. He has seen too many:

> ... studies of children who were returned home only to be abused again or even killed. These studies show dramatically that some abusive parents cannot be rehabilitated. In these cases the appropriate care of the child is to terminate the parents' rights as quickly as possible and place the child with a permanent caring adoptive family.[17]

It is easy to maintain that not enough, or the wrong kind, of family preservation efforts are being made. This is a reason why general family preservation directives are dangerous, because they set no limits, and provide no guidance about when and where to stop. Those at the top of social services may appreciate the need to balance child safety and family preservation, and believe they know when and how a balance can be achieved. The field worker, 'sold on the effectiveness of family preservation, working under the mandate of reunification, and not provided with a credible or useful set of rules'[18] on which to base decisions, will often press ahead even when there are risks. After a two-year study of fatal child abuse and neglect the US Advisory Board on Child Abuse and Neglect[19] recommended that all family programmes adopt child safety as a major priority, and that all legislation should explicitly identify child safety as a goal.

What's Wrong with Care?

From amidst the ruins of the Family First placement prevention programme the researchers argued that, if children cannot be kept out of care, then we could at least be more positive about this. It is claimed that placement is only traumatic for a child because of the way the 'system handles it', when it would 'be useful to blur the distinctions between in-home and out-of-home care, to make movement between them somewhat easier'.[20]

> Under this conception, in-home and out-of-home services would constitute a continuum and the movement between placement and home would be made easier. Placement should be viewed as a step in the process of helping that need not always indicate failure. Placements can often be thought of as respite from caretaking responsibilities and more use should be made of voluntary placements.[21]

In the UK this 'conception' is well advanced among welfare specialists, and the positive use of accommodation by parents is characterised as a necessary expression of the partnership with the state attributed to the Children Act 1989. As conflict between parents and social workers is blamed on the way in which social services have regarded prevention and substitute care as opposites, it is claimed that antagonism over children's protection and welfare will evaporate once these are treated as complements. Most importantly, were care perceived as an extension of the family, it could not be contrasted with family life (and there would be nothing to adopt children out of). The illusion is then complete that virtually no child in the care system actually lacks a family, or could need a substitute home. It is accepted that: 'Drift in care within unstable and changing care situations and relationships mostly results in damaged children who later become damaged adults'.[22] However, with admissions to institutional and foster care seen in terms of 'respites', or breaks, for parents, this represents 'permanency of care within the child's immediate or wider family', and actually reduces 'significantly the need for any child to be placed permanently out with his or her own network'.[23]

The Fantasy World of 'Respite Care'

With the recasting of public care as a general 'respite' service for families goes a vast increase in its potential clientele. 'Non-stigmatised respite care (or as the White Paper leading to the [Children] Act called it, "shared care") should now be a resource available to all families under stress, whatever the reason.'[24] This help ought to be 'open to all and available on demand,' to avoid distinguishing between the deserving and undeserving. 'This approach would normalise service delivery, recognise that all families are under stress from time to time and may need relief from the normal vicissitudes of parenting.'[25] After all, the Department of Health points out that parenting capacity may be 'limited temporarily or permanently by poverty, racism, poor housing or unemployment or by personal or marital problems, sensory or physical disability, mental illness or part-life experiences' [sic].[26] Respite care advocates are insistent that, if the concepts of parents as 'users' of services and the state's 'partnership' with children and parents 'have any real meaning' the issue of availability on demand:

> ... will have to be addressed. Otherwise, there will be no advance on the arrangements of the 1980s where gatekeeping prevented families from receiving help on their terms and when they required it.[27]

The idea is that children might enter the system without care orders or without even being formally accommodated, by developing 'partnership' arrangements under Section 17 of the Children Act 1989, dealing with the local authority's responsibilities to safeguard and promote the welfare of children who are in need.[28] Backed by other provisions, including those for cash assistance, these suggest much scope for creative social work, including ways in which families might be paid to look after their own children as foster carers.[29]

There is also Section 20, where a 'local authority may provide accommodation for any child within their area (even though the person who has parental responsibility for him is able to provide him with accommodation) if they consider that to do so would safeguard or promote the child's welfare'. Its use has already been sharply criticised in Sir William Utting's major report to government dealing with the childcare system. This highlighted the way in which 'exploitative adults'—who may have grudges against a family or families in general, ideological axes to grind about children's rights, or paedophile tendencies—are 'weaning children away from parents by telling them that they had a right to go into care, to do whatever they liked, and would be provided with ample cash'. (What tends to be downplayed or disregarded is that this is subject to parental permission.) Where educational or behavioural difficulties, or problems of physical of mental health, have been discovered or disclosed to 'malevolent external forces', intent on pushing families into the child protection and care system, this has only served to 'place relationships between parent and child—some of them already stressed—under intolerable strain'.[30] Expansion in this direction may offer further potential for both the abuse of children and persecution of parents.

Exponents of 'respite care' claim that they are reviving an old and well-attested form of care, where grandparents, aunts, uncles and other extended family provided relief for parents. It promises to provide a parent with: 'a sense of relief and support; more time for other children and partners; the ability to go out like an ordinary family... to go on holiday... get more sleep and catch up with the housework'. Respite care will be 'a permanent part of the ongoing services aimed at enhancing the quality of life for both child and parents'.[31] It will even 'encourage parents to use the time away from their children creatively as part of a self-realisation process'.[32]

Where social workers 'generate packages of services to suit each family', respite care would form part of a continuum running through: 'pre-school day care, out-of-school care, child minders, family centres, social work counselling and support, diversion schemes such as voluntary supervision, counselling, IT Programmes'.[33] Children will not just move into foster homes as and when the parents need relief, but respite carers will move in 'offering support for the family when the youngsters are living at home'.[34] Foster carers are also expected to take whole families into their own homes 'for long periods of time'.[35]

Alternatively, children and parents will go into residential care where 'they can all learn to live together as a family while parents have an opportunity to learn, in a supported and supervised setting, how to be good enough parents as well as fulfilled individuals'.[36] There is some worry that: 'The credibility of respite care is likely to be undermined if it becomes a trial run for full-time accommodation'.[37] Yet it is often difficult to see if, and where, any line is drawn, particularly when: 'the Children Act 1989 will lead to more parents being involved in partnership arrangements with the local authority providing accommodation for their children for quite long periods'.[38]

Indeed, we hear of 'models of permanence' which do not involve families, but appear to be no more than the group homes or institutions with whose dismal results we are all too familiar. It is naïvely imagined that 'such families [sic], or group care staff' should be 'willing, and enabled by their management structures, to play a continuing role in the youngsters' lives once they had reached eighteen',[39] when this is something that can hardly be expected from anyone but relatives.   The aspirations for 'respite care' are almost on a par with hopes for the 'therapeutic community' in the 1960s. It is unlikely that changing the labels will change the experience of the children who enter and endure the system. It is more likely to undermine adequate parents than to preserve negligent families.

Permanent Fostering: Permanent Insecurity?

Long-term fostering often arises by default from the problems which the workers involved have with taking definite, and perhaps hard, decisions about a child's future. It is also a way in which adoption is expressly avoided and the links to the original parent(s) are preserved, although they may never be able to rear their children, or even be in touch with them. As such, it may be seen to exist only 'because the natural parent is permitted... both to abandon the care of his child, and to prevent him [the child] from receiving stable permanent care in another family.'[40]

However, considering that 'one of the consequences of the Children Act may be an increased use of long-term foster care because of the provisions... which empower parents and make it more difficult for Social Services to decide children's futures unilaterally',[41] it is suggested we firm this up as 'permanent fostering' or use other 'limited' forms of adoption, as ways to recognise the interests of children in staying with the foster parents to whom they have become attached, without causing conflict with the original family. This has obvious attractions for 'hard-pressed childcare workers who find the present process of freeing and/or dispensing with consent stressful'.[42]

Forms of 'limited adoption' are also seen as more appropriate where contact of some kind is maintained with the original parent(s) or other relatives. They are being equated—intentionally or otherwise—with open adoption. Given this, it is understandable that suspicion of open adoption centres on the way that it binds the adoptive parents to the birth parents as well as to their adoptive child, with obligations to facilitate a continuing relationship.[43] Indeed, the Consultative Review of Adoption Law in 1992 was not only favourably disposed towards 'permanent' foster care, and other alternatives to adoption, but also suggested a 'compromise' whereby the birth parents could even retain 'parental responsibility' after adoption.[44] As such, 'adoptive parents have nothing to gain from open adoption. The next question to ask is whether too much is being asked of the adoptive parents, almost to adopt the whole birth family'.[45]

Claims that permanent fostering will be as good as adoption, because it is the 'sense of permanence', not the legal status, that is important, are very similar to those equating cohabitation with marriage.[46] Fostering also preserves professional control of child rearing, since the commitment and expertise of foster parents are only valued insofar as they agree with social workers. However, since the reasons for adoption may include the wish 'to acquire the normality of not being in care, having social work visits, medicals, etc.', some form of guardianship is proposed, for example by residence orders under the Children Act 1989.[47] This permits the child to be removed from care. The foster parents have more leeway to make decisions without 'back-seat driving' by social workers, while allowances continue to be paid. Again, this is seen as preferable to adoption where there may be conflict or contact with an original parent.[48]

Yet, while guardianship in various guises may transfer parental responsibilities to the carers, no ties are established with other members of the family. It also ceases at majority and the court which gives guardianship can take it away. The essence of guardianship is that it is *not* lifelong or permanent.

Claims that research shows that adoption and 'permanent fostering' are equally effective need to be treated with caution. In the study of 1,165 special-needs placements there were 49 cases where agency representatives considered that 'permanent fostering' was the appropriate placement, rather than adoption.[49] For nine of these, the children had severe disabilities and the foster parents did not want complete responsibility. Three-quarters of the other children were over ten years of age, some did not want to be adopted and virtually all had a strong sense of identity with birth parents. Clearly there are cases where, for example, older children may not be able to live with their mentally handicapped, chronically sick or otherwise disabled parents, due to the risks to themselves and others. This does not negate the meaningful relationship that continues to exist between parent and child.[50] Hence, there are children for whom adoption would not be very suitable, but who still needed long-term stability.[51]

Because long-term fostering may be appropriate in such cases, this does not make it as generally successful as adoption, nor should it become a justification for using it to replace adoption. There is evidence that children in long-term foster placements (for at least three years) do not do so well as adopted children, even when these placements remain stable.[52] High breakdown rates are also often recorded for children in long-term foster care. These are estimated to range from about 25-30 per cent during the first two years rising to around 40-50 per cent by the third year.[53]

If permanent fostering is extended, or open adoption effectively becomes synonymous with this, the successful record of adoption outcomes could be undermined.[54] Indeed, as none of the suggested alternatives to adoption provide 'real security or permanence for the child... their indiscriminate use could lead to a new drift in childcare arrangements'.[55]

June Thoburn and others tell us that, so long as it is seen as permanent, foster care status is acceptable to children.[56] Yet, when the views of young people have been solicited: 'The main complaint of those in foster care was to do with their status as foster children rather than "real" members of the family'.[57] In turn, the large majority of adoptees much prefer their adoptive status, even when they have been long-term foster children who were subsequently adopted.[58]

To be fostered is an embarrassment which the child experiences very young.[59] A child likes to pretend that he has 'real' parents, because he has a strong desire to have a 'proper family', with grandparents, uncles, aunts etc. This is not just a matter of living arrangements, as some suggest, or because he wants the same name, or does not want the paraphernalia of being 'in care', although this comes into it:

> In answer to the question as to what difference adoption made, Tim, who at the two-year stage had placed 'wanting to be adopted' at the top of his list of three wishes, said:
> 'Not a lot. They treated us as if we were adopted anyway. It's just a bit of paper, that's all. But I feel a lot better for it.'[60]

Most prominent amongst the valued features of adoption is security. However 'stable' the foster family, there is still the possibility of disruption. Fear that s/he would be subsequently lost is a barrier to the child's becoming part of the family. This is seen where there are protracted adoption proceedings:

> It was a long time after the children joined our family before the girls were seen as ours and not just 'that girl you look after'. I think it has been a hindrance to their acceptance by the extended family.[61]

While many of the later adoptees studied by M. Hill and John Triseliotis had experienced settled foster care for many years, they still saw it as impermanent. Like their parents, former foster children felt the main criterion centred on a guarantee that they could not be moved on or taken away:

> An eight-year-old girl, who still remembered her original mother, said adoption 'means that you canna go to stay with the other Mummy again, because you've got your own Mum now'. Several noted that adoption secured their position in the family not just now but permanently. 'You stay beside them forever' was one definition.[62]

In contrast:

> One boy summed up: '[f]ostering is about people who like children and take them into their home until they can find further parents for them or unless they want to adopt them themselves'. Another said: '[t]hey look after you till you go somewhere else'... One teenager described fostering as 'a part-time home'.[63]

As with marriage, people may have difficulty defining why adoption matters so much, when the 'piece of paper' indicates a publicly acknowledged and symbolic change in status which makes a profound difference to feelings and behaviour. It strengthens attachment and a sense of belonging, by expressing the adopters' commitment with an external sign of the child's place in the family. Adopted children are 'own children', to be distinguished from those who may be 'looked after' but are not inclusive to the family. Children in guardianship and long-term fostering remain, in important ways, outsiders.

Many of Hill's and Triseliotis's respondents were thrilled by the prospect of adoption: 'It's just like you're starting a new life... like when you're a baby'. (Carol, adopted by her houseparents after a difficult time in care.)[64] While a half rated their level of happiness the same before and after adoption, the other half registered an increase in happiness. Nearly all those adopted from long-term fostering regarded adoption positively; for some it was associated with significant emotional gains and for none was there an increase in discontent. In an earlier study of 40 young adults who had been fostered, many would have liked to have been adopted (and over a quarter of the foster parents would have adopted if they had been encouraged by their local authority).[65]

Moreover, is it reasonable to expect full parental involvement and investment without full parental possession?[66] While the idea might be repugnant to many social workers: 'it is a basic human instinct which cannot be wished away and which we are unwise to disparage entirely'.[67] The reality is that:

> Many people with excellent potentialities for substitute parenthood are unable and unwilling to make the necessary commitment to nurse a disturbed or deprived child back to health without the security of knowing that adoption can follow if the placement goes well. Older children going to substitute families also need to know how they stand... They cannot commit themselves to a new family if they are always wondering (fearing or perhaps half hoping), that their original parents will come and reclaim them. It is only when his past is settled that the child can move on to the future.[68]

Those who are willing to forego the security of adoption may not be offering permanence or commitment. Long-term foster parents often see their responsibilities as shared between themselves and the agency, with '...an escape route in the event of future difficulties'.[69] Some foster parents become adopters in the same way that some would-be adopters end up fostering, but the roles are essentially different.

Rather than there being a case for replacing adoption with more fostering, there are reasons to reverse the process. While fostering with a view to adoption can work out, and with some older or damaged children there may be reasons to avoid pressure, this is often: 'a roundabout way of achieving the security of a permanent relationship'. Lois Raynor found: 'nothing at all... to recommended this method over a more rapid, direct and less anxiety-provoking route when that is possible'.[70] Hence, even fostering with a view to adoption, or just ordinary fostering that might eventually develop into adoption, should be replaced with the goal of adoption, even if the placement does not ultimately progress to adoption.

15

Ending 'The Great Disjunction'

ADOPTION is 'widely believed to be of only marginal significance in social policy',[1] yet it is the childcare option most likely to be in the child's best interests. There are compelling reasons why it should be the primary means of dealing with children who cannot safely and securely live with their original families. It is time to bring an end to 'the great disjunction' (see p. 39) in the treatment of displaced children, so that they may become fully-fledged members of normal society. Even if some children have to board at specialist educational, medical or other therapeutic units, this does not obviate their need for a home base and a family for life. Where the parents may need expert post-adoption help, this should be available as part of everyday health and educational services for families—out of the way of social work practice and perspectives, governed by the 'care and protection' brief.

Given that a quarter of all children in care as at 31 March 1995 entered five or more years before, this suggests that approximately 12,200 children, or a goodly proportion of these, may be adoptable. (More than 16,000 children in care for a year or more have backgrounds of neglect or abuse.)

From the time of a child's birth, or at least from early childhood, it may simply have been unrealistic to expect the natural parent(s) to care for the child. If adoption were an option from the start, or the interest of prospective or new mothers in adoption were taken seriously, fewer young lives would be so disrupted. There are reasons to question why a decision to keep a baby must always be regarded as somehow more informed or more valid than other options. In the study by Michael Rutter and colleagues of ex-institutional women, the fact 'that they did not seek an abortion or adoption... may have involved a lack of decision rather than any considered choice'.[2]

Early adoptions do not have to be on the rigid, closed model prevailing in the 1950s, which owed much to the shame surrounding adoption, and it is time that this bogeyman was laid to rest.[3] Adoption now offers a real choice to women who do not feel up to the responsibilities of motherhood, yet who may not want to lose touch with how their child is faring, or may want some say in choosing the prospective adopters.[4] This can be a very positive decision, which helps both mother and child.[5]

A Change of Emphasis

A child welfare system must place children first. After safety, secure attachment is paramount. Hence, the:

> ...aim should be to keep children *in a family where they are wanted*. If that is not possible, the child's time in care should not be prolonged in keeping open the possibility of eventual restoration, but a decision should be reached swiftly ... to place the child for adoption.[6] (emphasis added)

Proper permanency planning would need systemic change, with a different outlook and different practices to those which have pertained since the Curtis Report of 1946. International experience suggests that, despite the best of intentions, permanence is unlikely to be achieved within open ended 'family preservation' guidelines, despite any amount of periodic reviews and individual care plans.

Detailed government guidance to the Children Act 1989 has spelt out a system for planning, decision making, contact arrangements and reviewing to be undertaken in partnership with parents to prevent drift in care and the weakening of family links, but with little success on either front. It avoids finding the best long-term living situation: the 'criterion for compliance is the existence of paperwork rather than some outcome for children'.[7]

This is not to deny that families should be preserved. But there is an argument against family preservation as the only or overriding goal when this locks too many children into the care system, while others are pushed back home only to be neglected or abused again. 'Family preservation' itself must become subject to considerations of permanence and safety, with controls to overcome the inertia and discretion of local authorities. Only with this fundamental change of perspective are we likely to get the 'clear strategic commitment to adoption, based on good information' sought by the Social Services Inspectorate.[8]

It goes almost without saying that any grounds for intervention in families must be narrowly and strictly defined; the discretion of decision makers must be limited; and there must be accepted legal safeguards. When the removal of a child from home is recommended, the programme(s) to be used to effect family rehabilitation must be specified, or it must be demonstrated that the parents are unlikely to reform or benefit from services.

When the child is not immediately put on the adoption track on removal from home, we might consider making one of two alternatives: either returning the child to his natural parent(s), or permanent placement in a new home, both to be operational within a specific time.[9] It has been suggested that a deadline—of perhaps 12 months—be set for the parents to establish their fitness to resume care of their children by, for example, getting off drugs or drink, with case reviews for progress checks. There could be exceptions to 24 months, granted on a case-by-case basis.

For children under three and for those involved in serious abuse, a shorter period might apply. There needs to be early identification of clear risks to the child's interests, and every effort should be made to ensure that children have a safe and settled environment by the age of three. 'Adoption delayed is adoption denied. Although children of all ages can be adopted, children with the best chance of getting and staying adopted are young children.'[10]

There are strong grounds for treating children who have been in voluntary accommodation for over six months as effectively, if not actually, abandoned. If the child is not freed for adoption at this point, it should be because of a time-limited plan for the resumption of parental care. Attention is drawn especially to the position of handicapped children in 'voluntary' accommodation who have less chance of a family life through adoption than those who are definitely 'in care' (where the social services have assumed parental responsibilities).[11] There also needs to be a limit to the number of care episodes or other interventions experienced by a child. We must be cautious about anything which might add new layers of bureaucracy, or which does not set definite schedules and final time limits.

The effort begun in the 1970s to place children out of institutional and foster care needs more than a renewed impetus. We also need to develop special strategies for the children who have already been in the care system for a long time.

Causing Unpleasantness?

A principal objection to permanency planning is that it militates against the no-conflict ideal, where parents and social workers are meant to co-operate harmoniously for the family's welfare. However, conflict is ubiquitous in human affairs. Like it or not, much intervention by statutory social services in families is compulsory and was instituted for the protection of children and others. As Jane Rowe and Lydia Lambert insisted long ago in *Children Who Wait*, the first aim should be 'to avoid indefinite care', and to achieve this it is better to face the possibility of conflict than to sacrifice the child. If 'parents do not co-operate there must be a confrontation and, if necessary, legal action must be taken to free the child for adoption'.[12]

Improvements are unlikely to be made at home unless it is certain that the parent(s) want the child, admit that there is a problem and are willing to work towards specified goals.[13] The realisation that the court 'will review their conduct, and possibly terminate parental rights, may induce parents to show greater interest in their children'. It will also give an incentive to social workers to focus their efforts, and attend properly to the family situation.[14] There is an urgent need to develop and use risk-assessment tools and other measures to identify children who can be safely reunified with birth parents, and those parents who are likely to benefit from support services. 'This would minimise the continuing problem of providing massive resources for a family that is unable or unwilling to change its behaviour'.[15] It would also act as a curb on all manner of therapeutic fashions and ideological predilections to which those in social services are so prone.

There will be cases where a court would not order termination even if the conditions for this were met. A close parent/child relationship may exist, despite the incapacity of the parent(s) to care for the child on a day-to-day basis. However, definite arrangements must still be made for the long-term care of the child within permanency planning, where guardianship may be appropriate in circumstances in which adoption is not a viable option.

The purposes of children's homes or foster carers must be framed in terms of this revolutionised childcare strategy.[16] Group or foster care is satisfactory if it is used briefly, because of an emergency, or as part of rehabilitative plan, not to rear or warehouse 'children who wait'. Specialist residential accommodation may still be needed for cases where a family placement is quite inappropriate, for medical or security reasons, for example.

Speeding up the Process

To ensure appropriate decisiveness with minimum delay, we need sanctions at various points against bureaucratic inertia. As schools must now make public their performance tables, perhaps local authorities should also make publicly available, within 30 days of each fiscal year, the number of children in care, the time that they have been there, and the number free to be adopted, but not in pre-adoptive placements.

Given the increasing court time taken up by child protection and adoption cases, the 'culture of delay' in family justice has to be tackled. Time limits may have to be built into the legislation to enable adoption proceedings to be expedited, with possible 'fast track' procedures. The aim should be to complete an adoption application in three months, subject to the natural parents' consent. In a genuinely contested case this three-month limit could be extended. This is part of a continuing argument for separating children's cases from the generality of court work, but not necessarily in a separate family court, where it could easily become isolated from the judicial mainstream and simply an arm of the welfare services.[17]

As the freeing system is a lengthy process riddled with delays (and, in many cases, the child is placed before or during the application), it is often suggested that it could be eliminated by making the placing agency party to the adoption application on behalf of would-be adopters. This would provide the forum for dealing with contested cases. However, the chief advantage of freeing is that this takes the worry out of the adoption process for prospective adopters.[18] It was proposed in the 1996 draft adoption bill (which never got to parliament) that placement orders should be available for children who were the subject of care orders, or where parents opposed adoptive placement. These would authorise an agency to place a child for adoption where this was considered to be in the child's best interests.

To dispense with parental consent to an adoption, it now has to be proven that the parents are unreasonably withholding consent, and that it is not possible to rehabilitate the child in the family. Proposals in the 1996 draft bill would have removed legal obstacles to adoption by allowing consent to be dispensed with where the parent cannot be found or is incapable of giving consent (for example, by reason of insanity), or that 'the court is satisfied that the welfare of the child requires consent to be dispensed with', according to a rigorous checklist.

Bringing in the Specialists

Too often, social services departments have emerged from reports and investigations as extremely inefficient, confused over roles, with a lack of openness and accountability, with inexperienced and unqualified staff at both ground and supervisory levels, and problems about prioritising adoption work.[19] In contrast, it is noted how workers from voluntary agencies are likely to have specialist training in child placement, small caseloads and good supervision.

Being 'seriously worried by the evidence, particularly from local authority social work practitioners',[20] the Review of Adoption Law for the Department of Health and Law Commission questioned: 'whether local authorities should continue in their present form to have primary responsibility for adoption agency practice'. By 1996 the Social Services Inspectorate also questioned whether the nature and volume of adoption work justified local authorities using an in-house service.[21] Everything points:

> to a need for a better managed and properly resourced network of adoption agencies. They possibly indicate the need to remove adoption work from individual local authorities altogether—an option which should at least be considered. Whether improved management could best be achieved by a consortium of local authorities say on a regional basis, or by voluntary agencies acting on behalf of the local authorities, or even entirely separate from them, is not for us to say.[22]

Unfortunately, the 1996 draft adoption bill reiterated the 1976 requirement for each local authority to provide an adoption service in its area.[23] However, if '[i]t's a difficult enough task arranging adoption without the weight and cumbersomeness of the department behind you',[24] the answer is to remove the department. There are no good reasons for social services departments to hang on to adoption, when so many are uninterested or even antagonistic, as well as unequipped for the task.[25] Albeit often late and reluctantly, local authorities have in any case found themselves continuing to refer children with special needs to voluntary societies with specialist staffs.

There needs to be a complete separation of adoption work from child protection services. Once an adoption panel has made a recommendation that a child should be freed or placed for adoption, the case should be immediately taken over by agencies specialising in the recruitment and preparation of adoptive families, the placement of children and the provision of professional post-adoption help and support. These agencies, perhaps operating within a franchise system, would be financed by direct grants from central government. So that neither children nor prospective adopters are kept waiting for placements, agencies need to be able to look as widely as they can for suitable adopters, which suggests mutual access to a national pool of available adoptive parents. Agencies which match and prepare the parents and children are probably in the best position to arrange post-adoption services.

The concentration of adoption work in specialist agencies would give more chance for the accumulation of expertise. Placement outcomes should be monitored according to key variables like the characteristics of adopters, selection methods, preparatory methods, timing, attitudes and so forth. With vigorous standards of accountability, contracts could specify the outcomes which the agency is expected to achieve in terms, for example, of non-disrupted adoptions, and well-being after placement.

Overlapping membership between adoption agencies or local authority decision-making systems and adoption panels may not be desirable. Panels should have an independent chairman, as well as members who are adoptees and adopters, staff from other adoption agencies and others with experience outside social services departments.

While it might be preferable for the child to be placed with those of his own racial or ethnic group, this should not delay permanent placement. In the USA, new laws signed in 1994 and 1995 prohibit adoption agencies from denying or delaying placement of a waiting child on the basis of race, colour, or national origin. Similarly, any contact arrangements with the original family should serve the interests of the adopted child and must offer no threat to a successful placement.

These and other measures should take us some way to realise the aim of a permanent home for every child as the centre of a child welfare system for the twenty-first century. Adoption would not be at the end of the line and no child should have to be written off before reaching it. Instead it would have the priority it deserves as a touchstone of concern for children, and an embodiment of good childcare practice.

Notes

Chapter 1: What's Wrong With Adoption?

1　Else, A., *A Question of Adoption*, Wellington, NZ: Bridget Williams Books, 1991, p. 200.

2　Dance, C., *Focus on Adoption: A Snapshot of Adoption Patterns in England-1995*, London: British Agencies for Adoption and Fostering, 1997. Estimates were based on a survey of 45 per cent of English local authorities.

3　*For Children's Sake: An SSI Inspection of Local Authority Adoption Services Social Services*, Social Services Inspectorate, Department of Health 1996.

4　Dance, *Focus on Adoption, op. cit.*, p. 12.

5　Olasky, M., 'Forgotten Choice', *National Review*, 10 March 1997, p. 43.

6　'Forgotten Mothers', ITV, 14 January 1997.

7　Lansdown, G,. 'The welfare of the child in contested proceedings', in Ryburn, M., *Contested Adoptions*, Aldershot: Arena, 1994, p. 63.

8　Howe, D., Sawbridge, P. and Hinings, D., *Half a Million Women*, Harmondsworth: Penguin, 1992, p. 154.

9　Mallows, M., 'Trans-racial Adoption: the most open adoption', in Mullender, A. (ed.), *Open Adoption*, London: British Agencies for Adoption and Fostering, 1991, p. 88.

10　See, for example, Schorr, A., *Children and Decent People*, London: Allen and Unwin, 1975.

11　Benet, M.K., *The Character of Adoption*, London: Jonathan Cape, 1976, p. 20.

12　See Benet, *ibid.*

13　Shawyer, J., *Death by Adoption*, Auckland, NZ: Cicada Press, 1979.

14　Howe, Sawbridge and Hinings, *Half a Million Women, op. cit.*, p. 151.

15　Mech, E.V., paper on 'Orientations of pregnancy counsellors toward adoption', University of Illinois, 1984, quoted in Fagan, P.F., 'Why serious welfare reform must include serious adoption reform', Washington: The Heritage Foundation, *Backgrounder*, No.1045, 27 July 1995.

The USA Congress's efforts to require adoption information and counselling in one federally funded programme providing services to pregnant women met with resistance from family planning professions. The Adolescent Family Life Act, passed in the early 1980s, added a modest budget for more 'pro-life', adoption-friendly additions to the pregnancy counselling provided under Title X and Title XIX family planning services. Evaluation of the programme's effectiveness revealed that 7 per cent of grantees provided no information on adoption to their clients at all, and most failed to give either adequate adoption information or counselling. 'Why Won't the Public Health Service Talk About Adoption?', *National Adoption Reports*, Washington DC: National Council for Adoption, October 1994.

16 Musick, J.S., Handlet, A. and Waddill, K.D., 'Teens and adoption: a pregnancy resolution alternative', *Children Today*, November/ December 1984, p. 26.

17 Howe, D., Sawbridge, P. and Hinings, D., *op. cit.*, p. 101.

18 Fratter, J. *et al.*, *Permanent Family Placement*, London: British Agencies for Adoption and Fostering, 1991, p. 10.

19 Department of Health, 'Adoption services in three London Local Authorities', *Adoption: In the Child's Best Interest*, London: HMSO, 1991, p. 14.

20 Mallows, M., 'Trans-racial Adoption: the most open adoption' in Mullender, A. (ed.), *Open Adoption*, London: British Agencies for Adoption and Fostering, 1991, p. 82.

21 Day, D., *The Adoption of Black Children*, Lexington Books, 1979, p. 97, quoted in Dale, D., *Denying Homes to Black Children*, London: Social Affairs Unit, Research Report No. 8, undated, p. 5.

22 Simon, R. and Alstein, H., *Trans-racial Adoption*, New York: Wiley, p.45, quoted in Dale, *Denying Homes to Black Children*, *op. cit.*,1977, p. 9.

23 Black children made up only 11 per cent of adoptions in 1975, and trans-racial adoptions 0.08 per cent. In 1977 the US Supreme Court declared in favour of the opposition by Georgia County's Department of Family and Children's Services to a white couple wishing to adopt a boy they had fostered from one month old. This judgement decreed that race was allowed to enter into the decision, not as 'an automatic type of thing or of placement, that is, that all blacks go to black families, all whites go to white families', but when it 'was properly directed to the best interests of the child'. It referred to professional literature on trans-racial placements, which purportedly showed how 'a couple has no right to adopt a child it is not equipped to rear'. *Drummond v. Fulton County* quoted in Simon, R. and Altstein, H., *Trans-racial Adoption: A Follow-Up*, Lexington: Lexington Books, 1982, pp. 81-82.

24 National Association of Black Social Workers and Allied Professions (ABSWAP) *Founding Statement*, 1982.

25 Dance, C., *Focus on Adoption, op. cit.*

26 Dale, *Denying Homes to Black Children, op. cit.*; also Bagley, C., Young, L. and Scully, A., *International and Trans-racial Adoptions*, Aldershot: Avebury, 1993.

27 *Be My Parent*, No. 42, October 1997. See also *About Adoption and Fostering*, London: British Agencies for Adoption and Fostering, 1996 for examples of children helped to find new families through its Exchange Service.

28 Hall, C., 'Fostered black and white half-sisters face separation', *Daily Telegraph*, 9 November 1996.

29 Barn, R., 'Black and White Care Careers: a different reality' in Marsh, P. and Triseliotis, J. (eds.), *Prevention and Reunification*, London: Batsford, 1993, p. 55.

30 Dance, *Focus on Adoption, op. cit.*, p. 33.

31 Children Act 1989, Part III, 22, 5c.

32 Department of Health, *The Family Placement of Children*, Circular letter. London: HMSO 1992

33 Akerlof, G.A, Yellen, J.L. and Katz, M.L., 'An analysis of out-of-wedlock childbearing in the United States', *Quarterly Journal of Economics*, Vol. CXI, May 1996, pp. 277-315.

34 Lone parents acquired the higher rate of social assistance (previously restricted to the old or disabled), and one-parent benefit as well as any tax allowances and benefits available to the married. Legislation gave preference in public housing to both pregnant women and vulnerable groups. To help lone parents, Family Credit for the low paid, was extended to part time work in the 1990s, followed up by earnings disregards for childcare expenses.

35 Macintyre, S., *Single and Pregnant*, London: Croom Helm, 1977. And ditto for the US: a study by the Child Welfare League of America reported that only one-fifth of adolescent mothers had ever considered adoption by the 1980s. Miller, S.H., 'Childbearing and child rearing among the very young', *Children Today*, May-June 1984, p. 27.

36 Medoff, M., 'An empirical analysis of adoption', *Economic Inquiry*, Vol. 31, No.1, January 1993, p. 59. By 1986 in the US 66 per cent of unintended pregnancies ended in abortion and 33 per cent ended with a woman choosing to be a single parent: only one per cent ended in adoption. (National Committee for Adoption, *Adoption Factbook*, June 1989.)

37 See Parton, N., *Governing the Family: Childcare, Child Protection, and the State*, London: MacMillan Education Ltd, 1991.

38 Triseliotis, J., Shireman, J. and Hundelby, M., *Adoption, Theory and Practice*, London: Cassell, 1997, p. 103.

39 'The Nature and Effect of Adoption', Discussion Paper Number 1, Inter-departmental Review of Adoption Law, Department of Health, September 1990 p. 65.

40 These fell into 4 main groups:
1. The large children's organisations, such as Barnardo's, the National Children's Home, and the Catholic Rescue Societies. They provided a range of services for children of which adoption was only one.
2. The large national adoption societies who brought together the prospective adopters and adoptees. Some placed large numbers of babies a year, with a small staff and volunteers.
3. Small societies set up by local councils of social service. While national placing agencies largely served a middle class clientele, these served a wider social spectrum. These were only placing agencies and provided no other services for children. However, the local authority or one of the large children's organisations with had residential nurseries dealt with babies with any health or developmental problems, or difficult family circumstances.
4. The Church of England and Catholic moral welfare societies, who had developed adoption programmes as part of their services for unmarried mothers.
    See Rowe, J., 'An historical perspective on adoption and the role of the voluntary agencies', in Fratter, J. *et al.*, *Permanent Family Placement*, British Agencies for Adoption and Fostering 1991.

41 *For Children's Sake: An SSI Inspection of Local Authority Adoption Services*, Social Services Inspectorate, Department of Health 1996.

42 *Ibid*, p. 19.

43 *Ibid*, p. 19

44 *Ibid*, pp. 3-4.

45 Murch, M., *et al.*, *Pathways to Adoption: Research Project*, Socio-Legal Centre for Family Studies University of Bristol, London: HMSO, 1993.

46 *For Children's Sake: An SSI Inspection of Local Authority Adoption Services*, *op. cit.*, Social Services Inspectorate.

47 'In an already over-stretched service, the burden on more experienced social workers of having to rewrite reports which will already have taken up much time... may be unjustifiable and suggests inefficient use of resources... ', *ibid*, p. 132.

48 *Ibid*, p. 124.

49 Rowe, J., Hundleby, M. and Garnett, L., *Childcare Now: A Survey of Placement Patterns*, London: British Agencies for Adoption and Fostering, 1989.

50 Murch, *et al.*, *Pathways to Adoption: Research Project*, *op. cit.*

51 See, for example, Raynor, L., *The Adopted Child Comes of Age*, London: Allen and Unwin, 1980; and more recently, Thoburn, J., *Review of Research Relating to Adoption*, Inter-departmental review of adoption law: background paper No 2, Department of Health, 1990.

52 *For Children's Sake: An SSI Inspection of Local Authority Adoption Services*, *op. cit.*, Social Services Inspectorate, p. 25.

53 *Ibid.*, p. 25.

Chapter 2: Getting Adopted

1 Lambert, L., Buisr, M., Triseliotis, J. and Hill, M., *Freeing Children for Adoption*, London: British Agencies for Fostering and Adoption, 1990. Three-quarters of the 67 freeing applications considered required dispensation with consent, but only two-fifths of these were actively contested.

2 *Children Looked After by Local Authorities: Year Ending 31 March 1995, England*, Department of Health, Government Statistical Service, 1996.

3 Murch, M., *et al.*, *Pathways to Adoption: Research Project*, Socio-Legal Centre for Family Studies, University of Bristol, London: HMSO, 1993.

4 Legally they seem to be in limbo. Freeing vests parental rights and duties in the adoption agency, so that at the adoption hearing the court has only to decide whether or not to make the adoption order on the basis of whether or not it is in the child's best interests to be adopted by the particular applicant(s). But, before adoption:
> 'Is the child therefore to be treated as still related to his parents and other birth relatives for other purposes? What happens if she or he reaches 18 and has not been adopted? Now too old... does the freed adult remain a member of his family of birth?' (*Agreement and Freeing*, Discussion Paper No. 2, Inter-Departmental Review of Adoption Law, London: Department of Health, September 1991, p.84).

See also: Thoburn, J., *Review of Research Relating to Adoption*, Background paper No. 2, Inter-departmental review of adoption law, London: Department of Health, 1990; National Children's Bureau, *Parents for Children: Some Findings from a Research Project*, London, 1985; and Thoburn, J., *Child Placement: Principles and Practice*, Aldershot: Gower/Wildwood, 1988.

5 Murch, *et al.*, *Pathways to Adoption: Research Project*, *op. cit.*

6 *Agreement and Freeing*, Discussion Paper Number 2, *op. cit.*, p. 103.

7   Murch, M., Lowe, N.V., Borkowski, M., Copner, R. and Griew, K. *Pathways to Adoption Research project: Report of the Research into the use and Practice of the Freeing for Adoption Provisions*, Socio-Legal Centre for Family Studies, University of Bristol, 1991.

8   *Ibid.*, p. 58.

9   Other sample years provide us with 1,172 in 1988, out of a total of 64,352 for England, 1,583 out of 60,532 in 1990, 2,700 out of 54,500 in 1992, and 1,900 out of 50,00 in 1994.

10 Berridge, D. and Cleaver, H., *Foster Home Breakdown*, Oxford: Blackwell, 1987.

11 *For Children's Sake: An SSI Inspection of Local Authority Adoption Services*, Social Services Inspectorate, Department of Health 1996.

12 Fitzgerald, J., *Understanding Disruption*, 2nd edition, London: British Agencies for Adoption and Fostering, 1990.

13 Triseliotis, J., and Hill, M., *Adoption Allowances in Scotland; the First Five Years*, Edinburgh: Social Work Services Group, 1986,

14 Craig, C. and Herbert, D., *The State of the Children: an Examination of Government-Run Foster Care*, Dallas, TX: National Center for Policy Analysis, August 1997.

15 Barth, R.P., Berrick, J.D., Courtney, M. and Albert, V., *From Child Abuse to Permanency Planning*, New York: Aldine de Gruyter, 1994.

16 Murch, *et al.*, *Pathways to Adoption: Research Project, op. cit.*

17 Letter from Jim Richards, Director, The Catholic Children's Society, Westminster to Institute of Economic Affairs, 16 December 1996.

18 The gap averaged over 17 months (and was three and a half years in one authority) in Murch, *et al.*, *Pathways to Adoption: Research Project, op. cit.* Not unsurprisingly, when the child is definitely freed for adoption, recommendation of the current placement—should s/he be in one *and* it is suitable—as potentially adoptive, is swifter.

19 Fratter, J., Rowe, J., Sapsford, D. and Thoburn, J., *Permanent Family Placement*, London: British Agencies for Adoption and Fostering, 1991.

20 *For Children's Sake: Part II: An Inspection of Local Authority Post-Placement and Post Adoption Services*, Social Services Inspectorate Department of Health 1997, p. 29. In the study for the Department of Health and the Law Commission, 36 per cent of cases in one area took three years or more from the time of placement to the date of final order. *(Pathways to Adoption, op. cit.)*

21 Murch, *et al.*, *Pathways to Adoption: Research Project, op. cit.*, p. 207.

22 *Ibid.*, p. 149.

23 See *Agreement and Freeing*, Discussion Paper Number 2, Inter-Departmental Review of Adoption Law, Department of Health, September 1991.

24 *For Children's Sake: An SSI Inspection of Local Authority Adoption Services, op. cit.*, Social Services Inspectorate.

25 Kelly, G., 'Foster parents and long-term placements: key findings from a Northern Ireland study', *Children and Society*, Vol. 9, No. 2, pp. 19-29, 1995.

26 Raynor, L., *The Adopted Child Comes of Age*, London: Allen and Unwin, 1980, p. 16.

27 Fitzgerald, *Understanding Disruption, op. cit.*, p. 22.

28 Lambert *et al.*, *Freeing Children for Adoption, op. cit.*

29 Triseliotis, J., Shireman, J. and Hundleby, M., *Adoption, Theory and Practice*, London: Cassell, 1997, p. 109.

30 *For Children's Sake: An SSI Inspection of Local Authority Adoption Services, op. cit.*, Social Services Inspectorate, p. 37.

31 *Ibid.*, pp. 42-43.

32 *Ibid.*, pp. 94-95.

33 Triseliotis, J., 'Open adoption', in Mullender, A. (ed.), *Open Adoption*, London: British Agencies for Adoption and Fostering, 1991.

34 Murch, *et al.*, *Pathways to Adoption: Research Project, op. cit.*, p. 223.

35 'Adoption services in three London Local Authorities', *Adoption: In the Child's Best Interest*, Department of Health, London: HMSO, 1991; also Dance, C., *Focus on Adoption: A Snapshot of Adoption Patterns in England-1995*, London: British Agencies for Adoption and Fostering, 1997. Here voluntarily relinquished infants were more likely to be placed in their first year of life if this was arranged by a voluntary agency, rather than the local authority.

36 Fein, E. and Maluccio, A., 'Permanency planning: another remedy in jeopardy?', *Social Service Review*, Vol. 66, pp. 335-48, 1992; and also Chambers, C., 'Cutting through the dogma', *Social Work Today*, Vol. 21, No. 6, pp. 14-15, 1989.

37 Fratter, J., Rowe, J., Sapsford, D. and Thoburn, J., *Permanent Family Placement*, London: British Agencies for Adoption and Fostering, 1991, p. 89.

38 In 1979, a survey of social services departments showed that in some areas as many as 50 per cent of children in care were already from these groups. Lindsay-Smith, C., 'Black children who wait', *Adoption and Fostering*, No.1, 1979.

39 Dance, *Focus on Adoption: A Snapshot of Adoption Patterns in England-1995, op. cit.*

40 *For Children's Sake: Part II: An Inspection of Local Authority Post-Placement and Post Adoption Services, op. cit.*, p. 27.

Chapter 3: The Children 'in Care'

1 Only two per cent of the whole population in care in 1991 were there on a care order made as a result of a criminal offence (or five per cent of children in residential homes). The proportion of children in community homes with education subject to criminal care orders declined from 55 per cent in 1980 to 15 per cent in 1990. The criminal care order expired with the introduction of the Children Act, to be replaced with a residence requirement in a supervision order.

2 *Children in the Public Care; A Review of Residential Childcare*, London: HMSO, 1991.

3 Hunt, J. and Mcleod, A., forthcoming, quoted in Murch, M. and Thorpe, Rt. Hon. Lord Justice, 'The development of the family justice system in England and Wales: past, present, and future', in Salgo, L. (ed.), *The Family Justice System*, Collegium Budapest Workshop, series No. 3, 1997, p. 23.

4 Hunt, J., 'Child protection, the Court and the Children Act', *Children's Services News*, Department of Health, April 1997.

5 Murch, and Thorpe, 'The development of the family justice system in England and Wales: past, present, and future', *op. cit.*, p. 24.

6 Packman, J. with Randall, J. and Jacques, N., *Who Needs Care? Social Work Decisions about Children*, Oxford: Basil Blackwell, 1986.

7 Barth, R.P., Courtney, M., Berrick, J.D. and Albert, V., *From Child Abuse to Permanency Planning*, New York: Aldine de Gruyter, 1994. In the US schools and daycare centres each refer 17 per cent of children, the police, medical profession and relatives refer about 12 per cent each.

8 In *ibid.* Here concerns about parenting were running at two-thirds of cases for referrals and the child's behaviour was an issue in a third of cases. For care admissions, the priorities changed significantly. However, in S. Millham and colleagues' study, the main reasons were the need to care for the child in 69 per cent of cases and the child's behaviour in 25 per cent of cases. (Millham, S. *et al.*, *Lost in Care*, Aldershot: Gower, 1986; see also Kelly, G., 'Patterns of care; the first twelve months', in Hudson, J. and Galaway, B., *The State as Parent*, London: Kluwer Academic Press, 1989.) Welfare concerns may provide a 'back door' into the system for delinquents who it would be more cumbersome or impossible to process through the juvenile justice gateway. In 24 per cent of cases in Packman *et*

al's study, the child was outright delinquent, while not one child was brought directly to court under care proceedings as the result of an offence, and only two offenders came in via prosecution.

Under the Children Act 1989, implemented in 1991, there are no criminal care orders. However, this does not obviate use of the welfare grounds for difficult and unattended children. The 'beyond parental control' ground can be used in combination with the ground of significant harm or the likelihood of such harm. It has also been made more difficult for the police or education authorities to seek orders for difficult children. It is suggested that they might also be dealt with by strengthened supervision orders which can now contain specific directions in relation to residence, or perhaps—in agreement with the parent(s)—by the use of voluntary 'accommodation'.

9 Packman, Randall and Jacques, *Who Needs Care?*, *op. cit.*, p. 32.

10 Bebbington, A. and Miles, J., 'The Background of Children who Enter Local Authority Care', *British Journal of Social Work*, Vol. 19, 1989, pp. 349-68.

11 Packman, Randall and Jacques, *Who Needs Care?*, *op. cit.*, p. 34.

12 Millham, S., *et al.*, *Lost in Care*, Aldershot: Gower, 1986, similarly found that only 27 per cent of children admitted to care were living with both natural parents.

13 Packman, Randall and Jacques, *Who Needs Care?*, *op. cit.*, p. 34

14 Millham, *et al.*, *Lost in Care, op. cit.*

15 Rowe, J., Hundleby, M. and Garnett, L., *Childcare Now: A Survey of Placement Patterns* London: British Agencies for Adoption and Fostering, Research Series 6, 1989.

16 *Ibid.*

17 Stevenson, O. and Smith, J., 'Report of the Implementation of Section 56 of the Children Act, 1975', Keele: University of Keele, Department of Social Policy and Social Work, 1983, found that 23 per cent of the 167 children discharged from voluntary care after at least six months, returned to care.

18 Research in six local authorities in the late 1980s showed how two out of five children admitted to care were placed first in an institution. Rowe, J., Hundleby, M. and Garnett, L., *Childcare Now, op. cit.*

19 Social Services Inspectorate, *Inspection of Community Homes, September 1985*, Department of Health and Social Security, London; see also Berridge, D., *Children's Homes*, Oxford: Blackwell, 1985.

20 *Review of Residential Services for Children in Care: Richmond*, Social Services Inspectorate, London Region, 1989.

21 Knapp, M., *Evidence to the House of Commons Committee on Childcare*, Personal Social Services Research Unit, 1983.

22 *Children in the Public Care: A Review of Residential Childcare*, London: HMSO, 1991; and *Personal Social Services: A Historical Profile of Reported Current and Capital Expenditure 1983-84 to 1993-94 England*, Department of Health, 1996.

The sharp growth in care costs is a reason why a Support Force was set up by the Department of Health in 1993, with the aim of helping them make the best use of resources in terms of the children who enter their care. However, before anyone can determine priorities and assess value for money, a framework for relating costs to care needs has first to be established—as this does not exist. *Partners in Caring*, the Fourth Annual Report of the Chief Inspector, Social Services Inspectorate 1994/5, Department of Health, 1995.

23 A third of the Leicestershire and Fife children were still in care after a year and 38 per cent of the Dartington cohort were still in care after two years. Rowe, Hundleby and Garnett, *Childcare Now: A Survey of Placement Patterns, op. cit.*

24 *Children Looked After by Local Authorities: Year Ending 31 March 1995, England*, Department of Health, 1997.

25 Kelly, G., 'Foster parents and long-term placements: key findings from a Northern Ireland study', *Children and Society*, Vol. 9, No. 2, 1995, pp. 19-29.

26 Three out of five of the study children were no longer in care after six months, typically leaving 27 per cent of the voluntary group and a half of the compulsory admissions. Packman, Randall and Jacques, *Who Needs Care? Social Work Decisions about Children, op. cit.*

27 For example: Millham, *et al., Lost in Care, op. cit.* Of 450 children who came into the care of five local authorities in the early 1980s, 36 per cent left care within six weeks, while 24 per cent were still in care and away from home at the two year stage (rising to 34 per cent for those aged six to eleven on entering care).

28 Barth, R.P., Courtney, M., Berrick, J.D. and Albert, V., *From Child Abuse to Permanency Planning*, New York: Aldine de Gruyter, 1994.

29 Vernon, J. and Fruin, D., *In Care: A Study of Social Work Decision Making*, London: National Children's Bureau, 1986; and Millham, *et al., Lost in Care, op. cit.*

30 Farmer, E., 'Going Home: what makes reunification work?', in Marsh, P. and Triseliotis, J., *Prevention and Reunification in Childcare*, London: Batsford, 1993; and Farmer, E. and Parker, R., *Trials and Tribulations: Returning Children from Local Authority Care to their Families*, London: HMSO, 1991.

31 Rowe, Hundleby and Garnett, *Childcare Now, op. cit.*

32 Farmer, 'Going Home: what makes reunification work?' *op. cit.*, p. 154.

33 *Ibid.*, p. 152.

34 *Ibid.*, p. 153.

35 *Ibid.*, p. 160.

36 Rowe, Hundleby and Garnett, *Childcare Now, op. cit.*

37 Farmer, 'Going Home: what makes reunification work?' *op. cit.*, p. 160.

38 *For Children's Sake: An SSI Inspection of Local Authority Adoption Services*, Social Services Inspectorate, Department of Health, 1996, p. 42; see also, *Children in Need: Report of an SSI Inspection of SSDs Family Support Services 1993-5*, Social Services Inspectorate, Department of Health, 1996; see also *Inspection of the Supervision of Social Workers in the Assessment and Monitoring of Cases of Child Abuse*, Department of Health and Social Security, London: HMSO, 1986.

39 Smith, G., 'Do children have the right to leave their pasts behind them?', in Argent, H., *See You Soon: Contact with Looked After Children*, London: British Agencies for Adoption and Fostering, 1996, p. 90.

40 *Adoption: The Future* London: HMSO, November 1993, p. 5.

41 *The NCH Factfile: Children in Britain*, National Children's Homes, 1992, p. 60.

42 Farmer, 'Going home: what makes reunification work?', *op. cit.*, p. 154.

43 *Ibid.* and Millham *et al.*, *Lost in Care, op. cit.* The same applies to the US: see Barth, Courtney, Berrick, and Albert, *From Child Abuse to Permanency Planning, op. cit.*

44 Fisher, M., Marsh, P. and Phillips, D., *In and Out of Care: The Experiences of Children, Parents and Social Workers*, London: Batsford, 1986.

45 Millham *et al.*, *Lost in Care, op. cit.*

46 Farmer, 'Going home: what makes reunification work?', *op. cit.*

47 In Millham *et al.*, *Lost in Care, op. cit.*, ten per cent of the children left care to join a completely different household. In Elaine Farmer's work this was 16 per cent.

48 Packman, Randall, and Jacques, *Who Needs Care?, op. cit.*, p. 175.

49 Maas, H.S. and Engler, R.E., *Children in Need of Parents*, New York: Columbia University Press, 1959.

Chapter 4: A Short History of Adoption

1 Boswell, J., *The Kindness of Strangers*, Allen Lane: The Penguin Press, 1988, p. 195.

2 Exodus 2: 6.

3 Circa 1,100 BC. Iversen, E., *Papyrus Carlsberg No. VIII, with some remarks on the Egyptian Origin of some Popular Birth Prognoses*, Copenhagan, 1939, quoted in Robins, G., *Women in Ancient Egypt*, British Museum Press, 1993, pp. 77-78.

4 Boswell, *The Kindness of Strangers, op. cit.*, p. 137.

5 *Ibid.*, p. 121.

6 *Ibid.*, p. 137.

7 Seneca in the *Controveriae*, quoted in Boswell, *The Kindness of Strangers, op. cit.*, p. 116.

8 It offered 'irresistible opportunities for hilarious misprisions of identity, titillating near misses of incest, and joyful turns of plot when slave girls turn out to be nubile aristocrats or long lost children'. [Boswell, *The Kindness of Strangers, op. cit.*, p. 7.]

9 Boswell, *The Kindness of Strangers, op. cit.*, p. 431.

10 *Ibid.*, pp. 431-32.

11 *Ibid.*, p. 433. However, Thomas Coram's Foundling Hospital, opened in London in 1739, was an exception to the generally grim nature of these institutions.

12 Else, A., *A Question of Adoption*, Wellington, NZ: Bridget Williams Books, 1991, p. xi.

13 Shaw, M., 'Growing up adopted', in Bean, P. (ed.), *Adoption: Essays in Social Policy, Law, and Sociology*, London: Tavistock, 1984, p. 113.

14 Triseliotis, J., 'Open adoption', in Mullender, A. (ed.), *Open Adoption*, London: British Agencies for Adoption and Fostering, 1991.

15 Else, *A Question of Adoption, op. cit.*, p. 24.

16 Kedgley, S., *Mum's the Word*, Auckland: Random House New Zealand Ltd, 1996, p. 23.

17 Quoted in, 'Discussion paper no.1: The nature and effect of adoption', Inter-departmental Review of Adoption Law, Department of Health, September 1990, quoted p. 4.

18 See Hapgood, M., 'Older child adoption and the knowledge base of adoption practice', in Bean, P. (ed.), *Adoption: Essays in Social Policy, Law, and Sociology*, London: Tavistock, 1984,

19 Rowe, J. and Lambert , L., *Children Who Wait*, London: Association of British Adoption Agencies, 1973, p. 37.

20 Tizard, B., *Adoption: A Second Chance*, London: Open Books, 1977, p. 12.

21 Else, *A Question of Adoption, op. cit.,* p. 106.

22 Tizard, *Adoption: A Second Chance, op. cit.,* p. 22.

23 *Ibid.,* p. 47.

24 Triseliotis, J. and Russell, J., *Hard to Place*, London: Heineman, 1984.

25 Tizard, *Adoption: A Second Chance, op. cit.,* p. 47.

26 Rowe and Lambert, *Children Who Wait, op. cit.,* p. 14.

27 Tizard, *Adoption: A Second Chance, op. cit.,* p. 46.

28 Rowe and Lambert, *Children Who Wait, op. cit.*

29 Raynor, L., *The Adopted Child Comes of Age*, London: Allen and Unwin, 1980, p. 42.

30 *Ibid.,* p. 45.

31 Rowe, J., Cain, H., Hundleby, M. and Keane A., *Long-term Fostering and the Children Act: A Study of Foster Parents Who Went on to Adopt*, London: British Agencies for Adoption and Fostering, 1984, p. 23.

32 See *Agreement and Freeing*, Discussion Paper Number 2, Inter-Departmental Review of Adoption Law Department of Health, September 1991.

33 *Ibid.,* p. 29.

34 Tizard, *Adoption: A Second Chance, op. cit.,* p. 12.

35 Bowlby, J., *Maternal Care and Mental Health*, 2nd edn., Geneva: WHO, 1952, p. 11. Evidence cited by Bowlby included a series of early American studies of children who had been fostered from the institutions in which they spent their early years, and, at adolescence, were said to be extremely backward, fearful, unable to concentrate and with an excessive craving for affection. In contrast, those fostered from birth were of nearly average intelligence, and had much less disturbed behaviour. As Tizard remarks, few people noticed that the institutions described in the early studies were exceptionally depriving, with babies in isolated cubicles, rarely touched or spoken too. There was also the lack of information on the

foster homes to which institutionalised children who 'failed' were sent, and plenty of suggestions that these were often unsatisfactory.

36 Skodak, M. and Skeels, H.M., 'A final follow-up of a hundred adopted children', *Journal of Genetic Psychology*, Vol. 75, 1949, pp. 85-125.

37 Rathbun, C., Di Virgilio, L. and Waldfogel, S., 'The restitutive process in children following radical separation from family and culture', *American Journal of Orthopsychiatry*, Vol. 28, 1958, pp. 408-15.

38 Kudashin, A., *Adopting Older Children*, New York: Columbia University Press, 1970.

39 Clarke, A.M. and Clarke, A.D.B., *Early Experience: Myth and Evidence*, London: Open Books, 1976; Semeroff, A.J. and Chandler, M.J., 'Reproductive risk and the continuum of caretaking casualty' in Hetherington, E.M. *et al.*, *Child Development Research*, Chicago: University of Chicago, 1975.

40 Dennis, W. and Najarian, P, 'Infant development under environmental handicap', *Psychology Monograph*, Vol. 71, 1957, pp. 1-13; and Pringle, M.K. and Bossio, V., 'Early prolonged separations and emotional adjustment', *Journal of Child Psychology and Psychiatry*, Vol. 1, 1960, pp. 37-48; Dinnage, R. and Pringle, M.K., *Residential Childcare: Facts and Fallacies*, London: Longman, 1967.

41 Report in *The Guardian*, 16th January 1970, mentioned in Howells, J.G., *Remember Maria*, London: Butterworths, 1974, p. 66.

42 In the last nine months of her life, 30 complaints were made by 17 people about the way she was being treated; to the NSPCC, the local authority, the housing authority and the police. Investigations and routine supervision led to 56 visits to the home by a number of people. Psychiatrist John. G. Howells spoke of how: 'Sadly, very sadly, because of the misconceptions... children at risk in their own homes are seldom rescued. The whole machine set up by our goodwill to care for our children has served to increase the danger to them, because of wrong notions. Our service unwittingly supports damaging forces by binding children to the natural family, whatever the circumstances. Hence the child has been placed in a defenceless position.' [Howells, *Remember Maria, op. cit.*, p. viii.]

43 Maas, H.S. and Engler, R.E., *Children in Need of Parents*, New York: Columbia University Press, 1959.

44 Rowe and Lambert, *Children Who Wait, op. cit.*, p. 13.

45 *Ibid.*, p. 100.

46 *Ibid.*, p. 104.

47 *Ibid.*, p. 46.

48 Bacon, B. and Rowe, J., *The Use and Misuse of Resources*, London: ABAFA, 1978.

49 *Ibid.*, p. 5.

50 Philip Bean, Professor of Criminology, Loughborough University, personal communication.

Chapter 5: New Excuses for Old

1 Rowe, J., Hindleby, M. and Garnett, L., *Childcare Now: A Survey of Placement Patterns*, London: British Agencies for Adoption and Fostering, No. 6, 1989.

2 Farmer, E. and Parker, R., *Trials and Tribulations: Returning Children from Local Authority Care to their Families*, London: HMSO, 1991.

3 Teague, A., *Social Change, Social Work and the Adoption of Children*, Aldershot: Avebury, 1989, p. 58.

4 Rowe, J., 'An historical perspective on adoption and the role of the voluntary agencies', in Fratter, J. *et al.*, *Permanent Family Placement*, London: British Agencies for Adoption and Fostering, 1991, pp. 11-12.

5 Smith, C., 'Restoring children from foster care to their parents', in Marsh, P. and Triseliotis, J., *Prevention and Reunification in Childcare*, London: Batsford, 1993, p. 167. Claims that the 1976 Adoption Act went too far are curious considering that the Houghton Committee in 1972 expressed its concern that adoption applications were already being made in what it considered inappropriate circumstances, or where the child had some links with his or her birth family, and favoured 'guardianship'. [Report of the Departmental Committee on the Adoption of Children, Cmnd. 5107, London: HMSO, 1972.]

6 Barth, R.P., Courtney, M., Berrick, J.D. and Albert, V., *From Child Abuse to Permanency Planning*, New York: Aldine de Gruyter, 1994, p. ix.

7 Fanshel, D. and Shinn, E., *Children in Foster Care: A Longitudinal Investigation*, New York: Columbia University Press, 1978; Emlen, A. *et al.*, *Overcoming Barriers to Planning for Children in Foster Care*, Portland, OR: Regional Research Institute for Human Services, Portland State University, 1977; Pike, V., 'Permanent planning for foster children: The Oregon Project', *Children Today*, Vol. 5. 1976, pp. 22-25; see also Lindsey, D., *The Welfare of Children*, New York: Oxford University Press, 1994.

8 Schuerman, J.R., Rzepnicki, T.L. and Littell, J.H., *Putting Families First*, New York: Aldine de Gruyter, 1994, p. 7.

9   *A Blueprint for Fostering Infants, Children and Youths in the 1990s*, Washington DC: Child Welfare League of America, 1991, p. 6.

10 *Ibid.*, p. 154.

11 Gelles, R.J., *The Book of David*, New York: Basic Books, 1996.

12 Barth, *et al.*, *From Child Abuse to Permanency Planning, op. cit.*

13 Toynbee, P., 'Care and be damned', *The Times Saturday Review*, 19 October 1991.

14 Tizard, B., *Adoption: A Second Chance*, London: Open Books, 1977, p. 238.

15 Dutter, B., 'If anything happens to him, be it on your heads... don't say I haven't warned you', *The Daily Telegraph*, 31 October 1996.

16 Gelles, R., *The Book of David, op. cit.*, pp. 116-20.

17 Fratter, J., Rowe, J., Sapsford, D. and Thoburn, J., *Permanent Family Placement*, London: British Agencies for Adoption and Fostering, 1991, p. 44.

18 Hill, M., *A Follow-up Study of Harder-to-Place Children*, Edinburgh: University of Edinburgh, 1986. In this study 60 per cent of the children awaiting placements were in touch with a member of the birth family other than a sibling with whom they were to be placed.

19 Festiger, T., *Necessary Risk: A Study of Adoptions and Disrupted Adoptive Placements*, New York: Child Welfare League of America, 1986; see also Rushdon, A., Treseder, J. and Quinton, D., *New Parents for Older Children*, London: British Agencies for Adoption and Fostering, 1988.

20 Fratter, Rowe, Sapsford and Thoburn, *Permanent Family Placement, op. cit.*, pp. 93-94.

21 Tizard, B., *Adoption; A Second Chance, op. cit.*, p. 239. This process is seen in a study of 779 children in foster care for at least two years in Connecticut on 1 January 1985. Most received visits from family members, while fewer than 10% were expected to return home. In some cases 'the child's behaviour after a visit with biological parents deteriorated to a point of concern for the foster parents'. Maluccio, A.N. and Fein, E., 'An examination of long-term foster-family care for children and youth', in Hudson, J. and Galaway, B. (eds.), *The State As Parent*, London: Kluwer Academic Press, 1989, p. 395.

22 Rowe, J. and Lambert, L., *Children Who Wait*, London: Association of British Adoption Agencies, 1973, p. 107.

23 Fratter, Rowe, Sapsford and Thoburn, *Permanent Family Placement, op. cit.*, p. 64.

24 Barth, R. and Berry, M., *Adoption and Disruption: Rates, Risks and Responses* New York: Aldine de Gruyter, 1988.

25 Barth, Courtney, Berrick, and Albert, *From Child Abuse to Permanency Planning, op. cit.,* p. 272, quoting O'Brien, P. 'Youth homelessness and the lack of adoption planning for older foster children: Are they related?', *Adoptalk,* No. 6, Spring 1993.

26 If, in the USA, some counties have categorised 100 per cent of their care caseload as special needs, the suggestion is that this is encouraged by Title IV-E funds to states for special-needs foster care. By 1993, all but three were using race or race plus age as a trigger for special-needs categorisation.

27 See Rowe and Lambert, *Children Who Wait, op. cit.;* also Murch, M. *et al., Pathways to Adoption: Research Project,* Socio-Legal Centre for Family Studies University of Bristol, London: HMSO, 1993 which documents high rates of emotional and behavioural problems, as well as learning difficulties, for children involved in freeing procedures.

28 Adcock, M., 'Assessing parenting: the context', in Adcock, M. and White, R., *Good Enough Parenting,* London: British Agencies for Adoption and Fostering, 1985, 1994 edn., p. 19. An illustration is provided by the case of three sisters.

> 'The family history of these three girls has been one long round of parental separation, changes of address, homelessness, living with relatives, and change of school. During the ten years of the parents' marriage, they have separated six times. The mother has had three prison sentences for prostitution. The children have been in care on three occasions; first following a place of safety order when the children were found unattended and badly neglected in the house; second, following allegations that the eldest daughter was being used for prostitution; and third, when they were received into care after their father had deserted the family and the mother had been sent to prison. The children have had no consistent routine in their lives and due to their unusual and unkempt appearance they have been frequently excluded and teased by other children. The eldest girl (aged 12) is already quite precocious sexually. She frequently talks to herself in unintelligible language and needs a psychiatric assessment. It is anticipated that she may present some difficulties for the children's home in the future.

29 Irving, K., 'The lost children', *The Times,* 26 November 1996.

30 Collier, F., Director of British Agencies for Adoption and Fostering personal communication, June 1997.

31 Triseliotis, J., Shireman. J. and Hundelby, M. *Adoption: Theory, Policy and Practice,* London: Cassell, 1997.

32 Archer, C., 'Families living with domestic violence', *Adoption and Fostering*, Vol. 20, Winter 1996/97, p. 17.

33 Fitzgerald, J., *Understanding Disruption*, 2nd edn., London: British Agencies for Adoption and Fostering, 1990, p. 5.

34 Fratter, *et al.*, *Permanent Family Placement, op. cit.*, p. 54.

35 Fitzgerald, *Understanding Disruption, op. cit.*, p. 5.

36 Fratter, *et al.*, *Permanent Family Placement, op. cit.*

37 See Hapgood, M., 'Older child adoption and the knowledge base of adoption practice', in Bean, P. (ed.), *Adoption: Essays in Social Policy, Law, and Sociology*, London: Tavistock, 1984.

38 The architects of Seebohm were determined to establish generic social work for reasons that owed more to the producers' demands for prestige, status and power than to any desire for a high quality service, or the need to protect vulnerable members of the community. Gledhill, A. *et al.*, *'Who Cares?' Children at Risk and Social Services*, London: Centre for Policy Studies, Policy Study No. 111, 1989.

39 *For Children's Sake: An SSI Inspection of Local Authority Adoption Services*, Social Services Inspectorate, Department of Health, 1996, p. 18.

40 Murch, *et al.*, *Pathways to Adoption: Research Project, op. cit.*, p. 119.

41 See Hapgood, 'Older child adoption and the knowledge base of adoption practice', *op. cit.*, p. 68.

42 Murch, *et al.*, *Pathways to Adoption: Research Project, op. cit.*, pp. 118-19.

43 Fratter, *et al.*, *Permanent Family Placement, op. cit.*

44 Shaw, M. and Lebens, K., *What Shall We Do With the Children?*, London: ABAFA, 1978, p. 22.

45 Raynor, L., *The Adopted Child Comes of Age, op. cit.*, p. 151.

46 Craig, C., 'What I Need is a Mom', *Policy Review*, Summer 1995, p. 41.

47 Irving, K ., director of Parents for Children, personal communication, June 1997.

48 The report, *Social Services: Achievement and Challenge*, candidly admitted: 'the management arrangements for children's services have not developed to the same degree as those for adult services and the quality of information to underpin decision-making about costs and priorities in many authorities is poor'. [Department of Health, Welsh Office, 1997, p. 25.]

49 Thoburn, J., *Success and Failure in Permanent Family Placement*, Aldershot: Avebury, 1990.

50 *The Guardian*, 18 April 1996.

Chapter 6: The Adopted Infant in Childhood

1 Kadushin, A., *Adopting Older Children*, New York: Columbia University Press, 1970, p. 231.

2 Benson, P.L., Sharma, A.R. and Roehlkepartain, E.C., *Growing Up Adopted*, Minneapolis: Search Institute, 1994, p. 78.

3 Raynor, L., *The Adopted Child Comes of Age*, London: Allen and Unwin, 1980, p. 35.

4 Ferguson, D.M., Lynskey, M. and Horwood, L.J., 'The adolescent outcomes of adoption: A 16-year longitudinal study', *Journal of Child Psychology and Psychiatry*, Vol. 36, No. 4, 1995, p. 597.

5 Brodzinsky, D.M., 'Long-term outcomes in adoption', in Behrman, R.E. (ed.), *The Future of Children: Adoption*, Los Altos, CA: Centre for the Future of Children, the Davis and Lucile Packard Foundation, 1993.

6 Brodzinsky, D.M., 'A stress and coping model of adoption adjustment', in Brodzinsky, D.M. and Schechter, M.D. (eds.), *The Psychology of Adoption*, New York: Oxford University Press, 1990, p. 23.

7 Fitzgerald, J., *Understanding Disruption*, London: British Agencies for Adoption and Fostering, 2nd edn., 1990.

8 Lambert, L. and Streather, J., *Children in Changing Families*, London: Macmillan, 1980. Ninety-three per cent of the children in the National Child Development Study who were adopted as babies were still with their adoptive families at 11.

9 Thoburn, J. and Rowe, J., 'A snapshot of permanent family placement for children', *Adoption and Fostering*, Vol. 12, No. 3, 1988; also Fratter, J., Rowe, J., Sapsford, D. and Thoburn, J., *Permanent Family Placement*, London: British Agencies for Adoption and Fostering, 1991.

10 The Essex Specialist Family Placement Service found that approximately one in five children had left placements two and a half years later. Wedge P., 'Family finding in Essex', in Wedge, P. and Thoburn, J. (eds.), *Finding Families for 'Hard-to-place' Children: Evidence from Research*, London: British Agencies for Adoption and Fostering, 1986. A lower disruption rate of 11.3 per cent for 335 'special-needs' children from care has been recorded for the Lothian home-finding teams (or 4.6 per cent for those aged under ten at placement, and 21.7 per cent for those ten or over). O'Hara, J. and

Hoggan, P., 'Permanent substitute family care in Lothian: placement outcomes', *Adoption and Fostering*, Vol. 12, No. 3, 1988. However, a follow-up study on 194 of the children reported that 20.6 per cent had disrupted by five years. Borland, M., Triseliotis, J. and O'Hara, G., *Permanency Planning for Children in Lothian Region*, University of Edinburgh, 1990.

11 Kaye, E. and Tipton, M., *Evaluations of State Activities with Regard to Adoption Disruption*, Washington: Office of Human Development Services, 1985. Defining disruption as the termination of placements before legal adoption, they came to a 13 per cent overall disruption rate. Reasons for disruption were the child's behaviour, lack of attachment between child and adoptive parents and the child's inability to meet parental expectations.

12 Wolkind, S. and Kozarek, A., 'The adoption of children with medical handicap', *Adoption and Fostering*, Vol. 7, No. 1, 1983.

13 Unsurprisingly perhaps, a special analysis of broken placements showed that nearly three-quarters of the children involved had experienced three or more placements in care. All experienced changes of staff and 'at best erratic parenting prior to reception into care'. [Fitzgerald, J., *Understanding Disruption*, London: British Agencies for Adoption and Fostering, 2nd edn., 1990, p. 11.]

14 The rates of breakdown were, respectively, 53 per cent compared with 13 per cent and 27 per cent within the group of 1,165 special needs placements. Fratter, J., Rowe, J., Sapsford, D. and Thoburn, J., *Permanent Family Placement*, London: British Agencies for Adoption and Fostering, 1991.

15 Proch, K., 'Differences between foster care and adoption: Perceptions of adopted foster children and adoptive foster parents', *Child Welfare*, Vol. 6, No. 5, 1982.

16 Festiger T., *Necessary Risk: A Study of Adoptions and Disrupted Adoptive Placements*, New York: Child Welfare League of America, 1986; also found in Westhues, A., and Cohen, J.S., 'Preventing disruption of special-needs adoptions', *Child Welfare*, Vol. 69, No. 2, 1990, pp. 141-56.

17 See Triseliotis, J., Shireman, J. and Hundelby, M., *Adoption, Theory and Practice*, London: Cassell, 1997.

18 Hornby, H.C., 'Why adoptions disrupt', *Children Today*, New York, 1986.

19 Irving, K., Director, Parents for Children, personal communication July 1997.

20 For example: Witmer, H.L., Herzog, E., Weinstein, E.A. and Sullivan, M.E., *Independent Adoptions: A Follow-up Study*, Beverley Hills: Russell Sage Foundation, 1963. This involved 484 children about

nine years after placement, and data from the adoptive parents, teachers and psychological testers. This described the outcomes for two-thirds of the children as 'excellent to fair', and a quarter as 'definitely unsatisfactory'.

21 Crellin, E., Pringle M.K. and West, P., *Born Illegitimate: Social and Economic Implications*, Windsor, England: NFER, 1971; and Seglow, J., Pringle, M.K. and Wedge, P., *Growing Up Adopted*, Slough: National Foundation for Educational Research in England and Wales, 1972.

22 Ferguson, D.M., Lynskey, M. and Horwood, L.J., 'The adolescent outcomes of adoption: A 16-year longitudinal study', *Journal of Child Psychology and Psychiatry, op. cit.*, pp. 597-615.

23 Ferguson, D.M., Horwood, L.J. and Shannon, F.T., 'Birth placement and childhood disadvantage', *Social Science and Medicine*, Vol. 15, 1981, pp. 315-26.

24 Lambert, L., and Streather, J., *Children in Changing Families*, London: Macmillan, 1980. The sample now included 294 children who had been born illegitimate and not adopted and 115 adopted children. A problem with longitudinal studies are the losses over time, due to death, emigration, refusals and inability to trace earlier respondents. While a third of the adopted children were lost to the Study, analysis showed that the results were unlikely to be biased through non-response.

25 *Ibid.*, p. 131.

26 St. Claire, L. and Osborn, A.F., 'The ability and behaviour of children who have been "in care" or separated from their parents', *Early Child Development and Care*, Vol. 28, No. 3, 1987.

27 Hoopes, J.L., *Prediction in Child Development*, New York: Child Welfare League of America, 1982.

28 Brodzinsky, D.M., Radice, C., Huffman, L. and Meckler, K., 'Prevalence of clinically significant symptomatology in a non-clinical sample of adopted and non-adopted children', *Journal of Clinical Child Psychology*, Vol. 16, 1987, pp. 350-56.

29 Lindholm, B.W., and Touliatos, J., 'Psychological adjustment of adopted and non-adopted children', *Psychological Reports*, Vol. 46, pp. 307-10, 1980; see also results from the Colorado Adoption Project, Coon, H., Carey, G., Corley, R. and Fulker, D., 'Identifying children in the Colorado Adoption Project at risk for conduct disorder', *Journal of the American Academy of Child and Adolescent Psychiatry*, Vol. 31, pp. 503-11, 1992.

30 See bibliography and discussion in Benson, P. L., Sharma, A.R. and Roehlkepartain, E.C., *Growing Up Adopted*, Minneapolis: Search Institute, 1994, p. 63.

31 Zill, N., Caoiro, M.J., Bloom, B., 'Health of our nation's children', *Vital and Health Statistics*, Series 10, No. 191, Public Health Service, 1994; and Zill, N., 'Adopted children in the United States: a profile based on a national survey of child health', testimony before the House Ways and Means Subcommittee on Human Resources, May 1995.

Chapter 7: The Adopted Infant at Adolescence and Adulthood

1   Benson, P.L., Sharma, A.R. and Roehlkepartain, E.C., *Growing Up Adopted*, Minneapolis: Search Institute, 1994.

2   Twelve per cent were highly attached to the father only; 18 per cent were highly attached to the mother only. On some measures, attachment rates were slightly lower than for non-adopted siblings, but nowhere did this exceed 10 per cent lower, and there was no statistical significance.

3   Based on a national USA sample of 47,000 adolescents from the public school system, Benson, P., *The Troubled Journey: A Portrait of 6th-12th Grade Youth*, Minneapolis: Search Institute, 1993.

4   *Ibid.*, p. 60.

5   Bohman, M., 'A comparative study of adopted children, foster children, and children in their biological environment born after undesired pregnancies', *Acta Pediatrica Scandinavica*, Supp. 221, 1971.

6   Bohman, M. and Sigvardson, S., 'A prospective longitudinal study of children registered for adoption: a follow-up', *Acta Psychiatrica Scandinavica*, Vol. 61, 1980, pp. 399-455.

7   Bohman, M. and Sigvardson, S., 'Outcome in adoption: lessons from longitudinal studies', in Brodzinsky, D.M. and Schechter, M.D. (eds.), *The Psychology of Adoption*, New York: Oxford University Press, 1990, pp. 93-106.

8   Warren, S.B., 'Lower threshold for referral for psychiatric treatment for adopted adolescents', *Journal of the American Academy of Child and Adolescent Psychiatry*, Vol. 31, 1992, pp. 512-17.

9   Cohen, N.J., Coyne, J. and Duvall, J., 'Adopted and biological children in the clinic: family, parental and child characteristics', *Journal of Child Psychology and Psychiatry*, Vol. 34, No. 4., 1993, pp. 545-62.

10 Ferguson, D.M., Lynskey, M. and Horwood, L.J., 'The adolescent outcomes of adoption: A 16-year longitudinal study', *Journal of Child Psychology and Psychiatry*, Vol. 36, No. 4, 1995, pp. 597-615.

11 Ferguson, D.M., Horwood, L.J. and Lloyd, M., 'The outcomes of adoption: A 12-year longitudinal study', Report prepared for the Adoption Practices Review Committee, Christchurch Health and Development Study, June 1990.

12 Maughan, B. and Pickles, A., 'Adopted and illegitimate children growing up', in Robins, L. and Rutter, M. (eds.), *Straight and Devious Pathways from Childhood to Adolescence*, Cambridge: Cambridge University Press, 1990, p. 41.

13 Raynor, L., *The Adopted Child Comes of Age*, London: Allen and Unwin, 1980.

14 They had fostered for the Thomas Coram Foundation, or adopted though the National Adoption Society. The original total of 288 families was reduced to 160 (56 per cent of the original sample) due to those who had died, emigrated, could not be found, or refused to take part. Background information suggested that those who were interviewed were much like the original overall group. Indeed, where one of a dyad refused, it seemed that is was the satisfied adopters, or adoptees from satisfied families, who were more likely not to want their children or themselves interviewed.

15 Raynor, *The Adopted Child Comes of Age, op. cit.*, p. 59.

16 *Ibid.*, p. 147.

17 *Ibid.*, p. 65.

18 *Ibid.*, p. 45.

19 *Ibid.*, p. 45.

20 *Ibid.*, p. 44.

21 *Ibid.*, p. 44.

22 *Ibid.*, p. 151.

23 *Ibid.*, p. 78.

24 Bohman and Sigvardsson, 'A prospective, longitudinal study of adoption', *op. cit.*; Bohman, M. and Von Knorring, A.L., 'Psychiatric illness among adults adopted as infants', *Acta Paediatrica Scandinavica*, Vol. 60, pp. 106-12, 1979.

25 Bohman, M., 'Nature and nurture: lessons from Swedish adoption surveys', *Adoption and Fostering*, Vol. 21, No. 2, 1997.

26 Maughan. B. and Pickles, A., 'Adopted and illegitimate children growing up', in Robins, L.N. and Rutter, M., (eds.), *Straight and Devious Pathways from Childhood to Adolescence*, Cambridge: Cambridge University Press, 1990.

27 *Ibid.*, p. 56.

28 Brodzinsky, D.M., 'A stress and coping model of adoption adjustment', in Brodzinsky, D.M. and Schechter, M.D. (eds.), *The Psychology of Adoption*, New York: Oxford University Press, 1990.

Chapter 8: Late Adoptions: New Families for Older Children

1 Hodges, J, and Tizard, B., 'IQ and behavioural adjustment of ex-institutional adolescents', *Journal of Child Psychology and Psychiatry* Vol. 30, No 1, 1989, p. 54.

2 Kadushin, A., *Adopting Older Children*, New York: Columbia University Press, 1970. The 91 families involved accepted a total of 117 children for adoption. The agency concerned had placed 150 children in the first instance, but 12 placements failed, leaving 138 cases and 112 families. Of these 112 families, 17 could not be contacted and 4 refused—a low rate for adoption follow-up research of 4.2%.

3 George, V., *Foster Care: Theory and Practice*, London: Routledge and Kegan Paul, 1970.

4 Lambert, L., 'Adopted from care by the age of seven', *Adoption and Fostering*, Vol. 105, No. 3, 1981.

5 Verhulst, F.C., Althaus, M. and Versluis-den Bieman, H., 'Damaging backgrounds: later adjustment of international adoptees', *Journal of the American Academy of Child and Adolescent Psychiatry*, Vol. 33, 1992, pp. 518-24; and Versluis-den Bieman, H. and Verhulst, F.C., 'Self-reported and parent-reported problems in adolescent international adoptees', *Journal of Child Psychology and Psychiatry*, Vol. 36, 1995, pp. 1411-28.

6 Hoksbergen, R.A.C., Juffer, F. and Waardenburg, B.C., *Adopted Children at Home and School*, Utrecht: Swets and Zeitlinger, 1987.

7 Cloninger, C.R, Svraric, D.M., Przybeck, T.R., 'A psycho-biological model of temperament and character', *Archives of General Psychiatry*, Vol. 50, 1993, pp. 975-89.

8 Groze, V., *Successful Adoptive Families: A Longitudinal Study of Special Needs Adoption*, Connecticut: Praeger Westport, 1996.

9 Berry, M. and Barth, R.P., 'Behaviour problems of children adopted when older', *Children and Youth Services Review*, Vol. 11, 1989, pp. 221-38. This study involved 900 cases of older-child, special-needs adoptions: 60 per cent had been physically abused, 80 per cent were neglected and 33 per cent sexually abused; also Reid, W.J., *et al.*, 'Adoptions of older insitutionalised youth', *Social Casework*, March 1987, pp. 140-49.

10 Nelson, K.A., *On the Frontier of Adoption: A Study of Special-Needs Adoptive Families*, Washington DC: Child Welfare League of America, 1985.

11 Irving, K., Director, *Parents for Children*, personal communication, July 1997.

12 Thoburn, J., *Success and Failure in Permanent Family Placement*, Aldershot: Avebury, 1990.

13 Tizard, B., *Adoption: A Second Chance*, London: Open Books Ltd., 1977; Tizard, B. and Rees, J., 'The effect of early institutional rearing on the behaviour problems and emotional relationships of four-year-old children', *Journal of Child Psychology and Psychiatry*, Vol. 16, 1975, pp. 61-73; Tizard, B. and Hodges, J., 'The effect of early institutional rearing on the development of eight-year-old children', *Journal of Child Psychology and Psychiatry*, Vol. 19,1978, pp. 99-118; Hodges, J. and Tizard, B., 'IQ and behavioural adjustment of ex-institutional adolescents', *Journal of Child Psychology and Psychiatry*, Vol. 30, No. 1, 1989, pp 53-75; Hodges, J. and Tizard, B., 'Social and family relationships of ex-institutional adolescents', *Journal of Child Psychology and Psychiatry*, Vol. 30, No. 1, 1989, pp. 77-97.

14 Hodges, and Tizard, 'Social and family relationships of ex-institutional adolescents', *op. cit.*, p. 78.

15 Tizard, *Adoption: A Second Chance, op. cit.*, p. 76.

16 *Ibid.*, p. 73.

17 Losses to the restored sample meant that their problems were underestimated (some had returned to care, been sent abroad, or mothers had refused to co-operate in cases where they intensely disliked the child).

18 *Ibid.*, p. 205.

19 Thoburn, *Success and Failure in Permanent Family Placement, op. cit.*

20 Hodges and Tizard, 'IQ and behavioural adjustment of ex-institutional adolescents', *op. cit.*, p. 70.

Chapter 9: The Late Adoptee as Adult

1 Triseliotis, J. and Russell, J., *Hard to Place: the Outcome of Adoption and Residential Care*, London: Heinemann Educational Books, 1984.

2 Just under a half of those identified were able to be traced and interviewed. Background comparisons by sex, socio-economic status, age at care, numbers of moves before placement, nature of original families, recorded problems etc., revealed no difference between those interviewed and those 'lost'. Those who did not want to take part may have done better, or worse, or the same as those interviewed. Obviously, those who underwent 'care' experiences may wish to put their unfortunate past this behind them, or the inadequate may lead the kind of marginal existence which makes them impossible to track.

3   Clarke, A.M., in *ibid.*, p. ix.

4   *Ibid.*, p. 33.

5   *Ibid.*, p. 90.

6   Wolkind, S.N. and Renton, G., 'Psychiatric disorders in children in long-term residential care: a follow-up study', *British Journal of Psychiatry*, Vol. 135, 1979, pp. 129-35. Also a survey of children from over 2,000 institutions in the USA, ten years before, found that three-quarters were thought to be emotionally disturbed. [Peppenfort, D.M. and Kilpatrick, D.M., 'Child rearing institutions, 1966; selected findings from the first national survey of children's residential institutions', *Social Service Review* Vol. 43, No. 4, pp. 448-59.]

7   Triseliotis and Russell, *Hard to Place, op. cit.*, p. 78.

8   Raynor, L., *The Adopted Child Comes of Age*, London: Allen and Unwin, 1980.

9   Triseliotis and Russell, *Hard to Place, op. cit.*, p. 157.

10   Tienari, P., *et al.*, 'Adopted-away offspring of schizophrenics and controls: The Finnish adoptive family study of schizophrenia', in Robins, L.N. and Rutter, M. *Straight and Devious Pathways from Childhood to Adolescence*, Cambridge: Cambridge University Press, 1990.

11   Rutter, M., Quinton, D. and Hill, J., 'Adult outcome of institution-reared children: males and females compared', in Robins and Rutter, *Straight and Devious Pathways from Childhood to Adolescence, op. cit.*

12   *Ibid.*

13   Kadushin, A., *Adopting Older Children*, New York: Columbia University Press, 1970.

14   Benson, P.L., Sharma, A.R. and Roehlkepartain, E.C., *Growing Up Adopted*, Minneapolis: Search Institute, 1994, p. 43.

15   Cohen, N.J., Coyne, J. and Duvall, J., 'Adopted and biological children in the clinic: family, parental and child characteristics', *Journal of Child Psychology and Psychiatry*, Vol. 34, No. 4., 1993, pp. 545-62.

16   Groze, V., *Successful Adoptive Families: A Longitudinal Study of Special-Needs Adoption*, Connecticut: Praeger Westport, 1996.

17   Raynor, *The Adopted Child Comes of Age, op. cit.*, p. 146.

18   Thoburn, J., *Success and Failure in Permanent Family Placement*, Aldershot: Avebury, 1990, p. 18.

19 Barth, R. *et al.*, 'Contributions to disruption and dissolution of older-child adoptions', *Child Welfare*, Vol. 65, 1986, pp. 359-71; and Festiger, T., *Necessary Risk: A Study of Adoption and Disrupted Adoption Placements*, New York; Child Welfare League of America, 1986.

20 Cohen, Coyne and Duvall, 'Adopted and biological children in the clinic: family, parental and child characteristics', *op. cit.*

21 Cadoret, R.J., *et al.*, 'Early life psychosocial events and adult affective symptoms', in Robins, and Rutter, *Straight and Devious Pathways from Childhood to Adolescence, op. cit.*; see also Brandon, S., Holland, A. and Murray, R., 'The genetics of schizophrenia and its implications', *Adoption and Fostering*, Vol. 9, No. 2, 1985, pp. 39-45.

22 Rowe, J. and Lambert, L., *Children Who Wait*, London: Association of British Adoption Agencies, 1973.

23 Benson, P. L., Sharma, A.R. and Roehlkepartain, E.C., *Growing Up Adopted*, Minneapolis: Search Institute, 1994, p. 42.

Chapter 10: Part of the Family?

1 Mallows, M., 'Trans-racial adoption: the most open adoption', in Mullender, A. (ed.), *Open Adoption*, London: British Agencies for Adoption and Fostering, 1991, p. 92.

2 *Ibid.*, p. 90.

3 Triseliotis, J. and Russell, J., *Hard to Place: The Outcome of Adoption and Residential Care*, London: Heinemann Educational Books, 1984.

4 Benson, P.L., Sharma, A.R. and Roehlkepartain, E.C., *Growing Up Adopted*, Minneapolis: Search Institute, 1994.

5 *Ibid.*, p. 24.

6 'One black person who grew up with the family's five children commented: "We all grew up together. They accepted me as part of the family... We were all very close"... The closeness of attachments between adoptees and the family's natural children continued into adult relationships. No adoptee experienced unfavourable discrimination in relation to the family's own or other adopted children. What appeared to have mattered was the atmosphere of the home and the quality of the parenting rather than the "status" of the child... With two exceptions, all the other adoptees said that they had been accepted by their parents' wider family. Some of them became very attached to grandparents or to uncles and aunts'. [Triseliotis, J. and Russell, J., *Hard to Place: The Outcome of Adoption and Residential Care, op. cit.*, p. 61.]

7 Benson, Sharma and Roehlkepartain, *Growing Up Adopted, op. cit.*, p. 57.

8 Triseliotis and Russell, *Hard to Place: The Outcome of Adoption and Residential Care, op. cit.*, p. 107.

9 Thoburn, J., *Success and Failure in Permanent Family Placement*, Aldershot: Avebury, 1990, p. 52.

10 See Groze, V., *Successful Adoptive Families: A Longitudinal Study of Special-Needs Adoption*, Connecticut: Praeger Westport, 1996.

11 Raynor, L., *The Adopted Child Comes of Age*, London: Allen and Unwin, 1980, p. 152.

12 Benson, Sharma and Roehlkepartain, *Growing Up Adopted, op. cit.*, p. 105.

13 *Ibid.*, 'People expect adopted kids to have problems', was mentioned by 30 per cent of adolescents, and 'society in general does not understand adoptive families' by 21 per cent of parents.

14 Triseliotis and Russell, *Hard to Place: the Outcome of Adoption and Residential Care, op. cit.*, p. 44.

15 See Triseliotis, J., Shireman, J. and Hundelby, M., *Adoption, Theory and Practice*, London: Cassell, 1997, p. 231.

16 Raynor, *The Adopted Child Comes of Age, op. cit.*, p. 38. She speaks of cases where 'a professional man felt dissatisfied with the adoption because his relationship with his son was not close and rewarding. This father was greatly disappointed because the boy had failed to carry on the family tradition for excellence in sport, and he had blinded himself to the fact that the boy was intellectually quite brilliant and was now making good use of his fine mind in another profession' (p. 37). Similarly: 'One father, a professional man, characterised as a plodder a son who is now in the same profession' (p. 38).

17 Raynor, *The Adopted Child Comes of Age, op. cit.*, p. 149. However, some youngsters turned out to be far more intelligent than their working-class adoptive parents and, although these were warm hearted and outgoing, they could not communicate properly and the children's talents were not encouraged.

18 Elonen, A.S. and Schwarz, E.M., 'A longitudinal study of emotional, social, and academic functioning of adopted children', *Child Welfare*, Vol. 47, No. 2, 1977, pp. 72-78.

19 Raynor, *The Adopted Child Comes of Age, op. cit.*, p. 52.

20 In the 1960s 'The emphasis on environment had a profound effect on the public perception of adoption, especially among well-educated middle-class couples. If environment was so much more important than heredity, what mattered was not who gave birth to you, but who brought you up.' Else, A., *A Question of Adoption*, Wellington, NZ: Bridget Williams Books, 1991, p. 54.

21 Groze, *Successful Adoptive Families: A Longitudinal Study of Special Needs Adoption, op. cit.*, p. 11.

22 Bentavim, A. and Gilmour, L., 'A family therapy inter-actional approach to decision making in childcare, access and custody cases', *Journal of Family Therapy*, Vol. 3, 1981, pp. 65-77.

23 Tizard, B., *Adoption: A Second Chance*, London: Open Books, 1977.

24 Jacka, A.A., *Adoption in Brief*, Slough: National Foundation for Educational Research, 1973.

25 Triseliotis and Russell, *Hard to Place, op. cit.*, p. 89.

26 *Ibid.*, p. 91.

27 Hill, M. and Triseliotis, J., 'The transition from long-term care to adoption', in Hudson, J. and Galaway, B., *The State as Parent*, London: Kluwer Academic Press, 1989.

28 *Ibid.*, p. 102.

29 *Ibid.*, p. 62.

30 Triseliotis and Russell, *Hard to Place, op. cit.*, p. 137.

31 *Ibid.*, p. 181.

32 Barth, R.P., Courtney, M., Berrick, J.D. and Albert, V., *From Child Abuse to Permanency Planning*, New York: Aldine de Gruyter, 1994, p. 264.

33 Triseliotis and Russell (p. 147) are referring to Miller, E.J and Gwynne, G.V., *A Life Apart*, London: Tavistock, 1972: 'the lack of any actual or potential role that confers a positive status in the wider society is tantamount to being socially dead'. The foremost work on institutions is that of Goodman, E., *Asylums: Essays on the Social Situation of Mental Patients and Other Inmates*, New York: Doubleday Anchor Books, 1961.

34 Triseliotis and Russell, *Hard To Place, op. cit.*, p. 143.

35 Quoted *ibid.*, p. 69.

36 Fletcher, B., *Not Just a Name: The Views of Young People in Foster and Residential Care*, London: National Consumer Council, 1993.

37 Kadushin, A., *Adopting Older Children*, New York: Columbia University Press, 1970, p. 222.

38 Hill and Triseliotis, 'The transition from long-term care to adoption', *op. cit.*

39 *Ibid.*, and Triseliotis and Russell, *Hard to Place: The Outcome of Adoption and Residential Care, op. cit.*

40 Triseliotis, J.P., 'Obtaining birth certificates', in Bean, P. (ed.), *Adoption: Essays in Social Policy, Law, and Sociology,* London: Tavistock, 1984.

41 Raynor, *The Adopted Child Comes of Age, op. cit.,* p. 148.

42 Triseliotis and Russell, *Hard to Place, op. cit.*

43 Raynor, *The Adopted Child Comes of Age, op. cit.*

44 Benson, Sharmar and Roehlkepartain, *Growing Up Adopted, op. cit.*

45 Letter to Herbert Laming, Department of Health from J.M. Richards, Director, The Catholic Children's Society, Westminster, 19 February 1996.

46 In the study of 1,156 'special-needs' placements, sixteen per cent of those needing a family able to cope with a contested adoption were also said to need contact with birth parents after placement, but only nine per cent remained in contact. Only 14 per cent of the whole sample were still in touch with parents after placement (including five per cent of the adopted).

47 Smith, G., 'Do children have a right to leave their pasts behind them?', Argent, H., *See You Soon: Contact with Children Looked After by Local Authorities,* London: British Agencies for Adoption and Fostering, 1995, p. 86.

48 *Ibid.,* p. 84.

49 Kaniuk, J., 'Openness in adoption', in Alcock, M., Kaniuk, J. and White, R. (eds.), *Adoption and Fostering,* Vol. 15, No. 1, 1993, p. 22.

50 Hughes, B., 'Openness and contact in adoption: a child-centred perspective', *British Journal of Social Work,* Vol. 25, 1995, pp. 729-47.

Chapter 11: Colour Blind?

1 *Be My Parent,* Issue 42, October 1997, British Agencies for Adoption Fostering.

2 Mallows, M., 'Trans-racial adoption: the most open adoption', in Mullender, A. (ed.), *Open Adoption,* British Agencies for Adoption Fostering, 1991, p. 90.

3 Leigh Chambers from British Agencies for Adoption Fostering quoted by Carlisle, D., in 'Tugging at heart strings', in *Community Care,* 14-20 November 1996, p. 11.

4 Chennells, P., *Explaining Adoption,* A Guide for Adoptive Parents, British Agencies for Adoption Fostering, 1987, p. 14.

5   Simon, R.J., 'Adoption of black children by white parents in the USA', in Bean, P., *Adoption: Essays in Social Policy, Law and Sociology*, London: Tavistock, 1984, p. 232.

6   Barn, R., 'Black and white care careers: a different reality', in Marsh, P. and Triseliotis, J. (eds.), *Prevention and Reunification*, London: Batsford, 1993, p. 64.

7   See summary of research in Thoburn, J., *Success and Failure in Permanent Family Placement*, Aldershot: Avebury, 1990, p. 57.

8   Zastrow, C.H., *Outcome of Black Children—White Parents Trans-racial Adoptions*, San Francisco: R.&.E Research Associates, inc., 1997. See also Kadushin, A., *Child Welfare Services*, New York: Macmillan, 1972 .

9   Grow, L. and Shapiro, D., 'Adoption of black children by white parents', *Child Welfare*, January 1975.

10 For example: One such in Britain was C. Bagley and L. Young's involving 51 trans-racial adoptions. One to four years after the placement, 94 per cent of the children and 75 per cent of the adoptive parents were assessed as having made a good or satisfactory adjustment to their changed family status. Forty-four of the 51 sets of parents were interviewed when the children were aged 12 to 16, when 83 per cent of the trans-racial placements were assessed as a success. ['The identity, adjustment and achievement of trans-racially adopted children: a review and empirical report', in Verma, G. and Bagley, L. (eds.), *Race, Education and Identity*, London: Macmillan, 1979.] Also see; Shireman, J. and Johnson, P., 'A longitudinal study of black adoptions', *Social Work*, May-June 1986. This study of 118 black children placed for adoption when under the age of three, with black or white parents, followed-up at four and eight. No placements were disrupted. On the basis of standardised tests, parents' reports and researchers observations, the adjustment of 56 of the 71 who agreed to take part was rated as excellent or good, at 79 per cent.

11 Silverman, A. and Feigelman, W., 'The long term effects of trans-racial adoption', *Social Services Review*, December 1984.

12 Gill, D. and Jackson, B., *Adoption and Race*, London: Batsford, 1983.

13 Tizard, B., *Adoption: A Second Chance*, London: Open Books, 1977. p. 185.

14 Day, D., *The Adoption of Black Children*, Lexington: Lexington Books, 1979; also see Simon, R.J., 'Adoption of black children by white parents in the USA', in Bean, *Adoption: Essays in Social Policy, Law and Sociology, op. cit.*

15 Bagley and Young, 'The identity, adjustment and achievement of trans-racially adopted childen: a review and empirical report', *op. cit.*

16 Ladner, J., *Mixed Families*, New York: Doubleday, 1997.

17 Simon, R.J., 'An assessment of racial awareness, preference and self-identity among white and adopted non-white children', *Social Problems*, October 1974; also Simon, R.J. and Altstein, H., *Trans-racial Adoption*, New York: John Wiley & Sons, 1977.

18 Simon, 'Adoption of black children by white parents in the USA', *op. cit.*, p. 238.

19 Simon, R.J. and Alstein, H., *Trans-racial Adoption: A Follow-Up*, Lexington: Lexington Books, 1981.

20 Simon, 'Adoption of black children by white parents in the USA', *op. cit.*, p. 239.

21 *Ibid.*, p. 240.

22 Shireman, J. and Johnson, P., 'A longitudinal study of black adoptions', *Social Work*, May-June 1986.

23 McRoy, R.G. *et al.*, 'Self-esteem and racial identity in trans-racial and in-racial adoptees', *Social Work*, Vol. 27, No. 6, 1982, pp. 522-26. Rather atypically, in this study of 30 black and 30 white adoptive families of ten year old black and mixed-parentage children, the trans-racially adopted children were more likely to refer to their race and to their adoptive status. However, no difference was found for self-esteem scores between the two groups, or between the adopted children and the general population of non-adopted children.

24 Hodges, J. and Tizard, B., letter to the Editor, *New Society*, 14 July 1983.

25 Tizard, *Adoption: A Second Chance*, *op. cit.*, p. 185.

26 Craig, C., 'What I need is a Mom', *Policy Review*, Summer 1995, p. 43.

27 Gill, D. and Jackson, B., *Adoption and Race*, London: Batsford 1983.

28 Triseliotis, J., Shireman, J. and Hundelby, M., *Adoption, Theory and Practice*, London: Cassell, 1997, p. 173.

29 Mallows, M., 'Trans-racial adoption: the most open adoption', in Mullender, A. (ed.), *Open Adoption*, London: British Agencies for Adoption and Fostering, 1991, p. 84.

30 Or 62 per cent compared to 52 per cent.

31 Fiegelman, W. and Silverman, A.R., *Chosen Children; New Patterns of Adoptive Relationships*, New York: Praeger, 1983.

32 Thoburn, J., *Review of Research Relating to Adoption*, Inter-departmental review of adoption law: background paper No 2, Department of Health, 1990, p. 55.

33 Howes, D. and Hinings, D., 'Adopted children referred to a child and family centre', *Adoption and Fostering*, 11 March 1987.

34 Dale, D., *Denying Homes to Black Children*, London: Social Affairs Unit, Research Report No. 8, undated, p. 9.

35 *Ibid.*, p. 17.

36 Mallows, M., Trans-racial Adoption: the most open adoption, *op. cit.*, pp.84-85.

37 Benson, P. L., Sharma, A.R. and Roehlkepartain, E.C., *Growing Up Adopted*, Minneapolis: Search Institute, 1994, pp. 109-10.

38 Triseliotis, Shireman and Hundleby, *Adoption, Theory and Practice*, *op. cit.*, p. 179.

39 Gill and Jackson, *Adoption and Race*, *op. cit.*

40 *Ibid.*, p. 130.

41 Dale, D., *Denying Homes to Black Children*, *op. cit.*, p. 32.

42 Mallows, Trans-racial Adoption: the most open adoption, *op. cit.*, p. 82.

43 *Ibid.*, p. 84.

44 Barn, 'Black and white care careers: a different reality', *op. cit.*

45 So that 47 per cent of the mothers were in white collar and skilled occupations, compared to only 22 per cent for white children.

46 The picture is similar in the US, where white children are more likely to be referred for sexual or physical abuse, and black children for neglect or caretaker incapacity. [Barth, R.P., Courtney, M., Berrick, J.D. and Albert, V., *From Child Abuse to Permanency Planning'*, New York: Aldine de Gruyter, 1994.]

47 *Ibid.*, pp. 67-68.

48 *Ibid.*, pp. 60-61.

49 *Ibid.*, p. 58.

50 *Ibid.*, p. 59.

51 A case is quoted involving a boy and girl, aged eight and seven, admitted to care following allegations of sexual abuse (both had been in voluntary care before). The stepfather is sentenced to three years imprisonment, but released on parole after 18 months, and the children placed at Home on Trial. The stepfather is again charged with having intercourse with the girl, and sent to prison for 4 years,

with both children re-admitted to care. The stepfather is released from prison with social worker arguing that, as he had received group therapy and other psychiatric help, the children should be returned home. [Barn, R. 'Black and white care careers: a different reality', *op. cit.*]

52 Cheetham, J., Ahmed, S. and Small, J. (eds.), *Social Work with Black Children and their Families*, London: Batsford, 1986.

53 One black boy had been fostered by a white couple for 14 years. Wanting security, he asked the local social services if the family could adopt him. The social workers tried to find him a black home: 'the suggested adoptive black family lived in homeless accomodation, the father had convictions for violence. They were supposed to be the 'best' of three—I don't know what the other two were like, I didn't like to ask'. [Professor Philip Bean, personal communication.]

54 See Owen, M., 'Single person adoption', in *Adoption and Fostering*, Vol. 21, No. 1, 1997, pp. 50-53. One-third of single-parent adoptions involved blacks. See also Dance, C., *Focus on Adoption, A Snapshot of Adoption Patterns in England-1995*, London: British Agencies for Adoption and Fostering, 1997, where there were more single adopters than married couples among ethnic minority families.

55 *Inspection of Local Authority Fostering 1994-5 National Summary Report*, Social Services Inspectorate, South and West Inspection Group, Department of Health, August 1995, pp. 7-8.

56 Tizard, *Adoption: A Second Chance, op. cit.*, p. 185.

Chapter 12: From Pillar to Post

1 Kudashin, A., *Adopting Older Children*, New York: Columbia University Press, 1970, p. 224.

2 Department of Health, 'The care of children: principles and practice in regulations and guidance', Consultant Jane Rowe, London: HMSO, 1990.

3 Packman, J. with Randall, J. and Jacques, N., *Who Needs Care? Social Work Decisions about Children*, Oxford: Basil Blackwell, 1986, p.179

4 Rowe, J. and Lambert, L., *Children Who Wait*, London: Association of British Adoption Agencies, 1973, p.37

5 Adcock. M., 'Contact: an overview', in Argent, H., *See You Soon: Contact with Children Looked After by Local Authorities*, London: British Agencies for Adoption and Fostering, 1996.

6 Triseliotis, J.P., 'Identity and security in adoption and long-term fostering', *Adoption and Fostering*, Vol. 7, No. 1, 1983, p. 26.

7   Thoburn, J., *Success and Failure in Permanent Family Placement*, Aldershot: Avebury, 1990, p. 23.

8   Derek Warren of the National Foster Care Association quoted by Carlise, D., 'Tugging at heart strings', *Community Care*, 14-20 November 1996, p. 11.

9   Craig, C. and Herbert, D., 'The state of child welfare today', from McKenzie, R., *Rethinking Orphanages for the 21st century*, Thousand Oaks, CA: Sage Publications, 1998, in press.

10 SSI, Department of Health and Social Security, 'Inspection of community homes, September 1985', London: HMSO, 1991.

11 Packman, Randall and Jacques, *Who Needs Care? Social Work Decisions about Children*, op. cit., p. 147.

12 Department of Health and Social Security, 'Social work decisions in childcare', (Pink Book) Consultant - Jane Rowe, London: HMSO, 1985.

13 Packman, Randall and Jacques, *Who Needs Care? Social Work Decisions about Children*, op. cit., p. 147.

14 *Children in the Public Care: A Review of Residential Childcare*, Department of Health, London: HMSO, 1991, p. 45.

15 SSI, Department of Health and Social Security, 'Inspection of community homes, September 1985', op. cit.

16 Para 17.21. of the 'Pindown Experience' report (Staffordshire County Council) quoted in *Children in the Public Care: A Review of Residential Childcare*, op. cit., p. 44.

17 Trasler, G., *In Place of Parents: A Study of Foster Care*, London: Routledge and Kegan Paul, 1960; George, V., *Foster Care: Theory and Practice*, London: Routledge and Kegan Paul, 1970 and Parker, R.A., *Decisions in Childcare*, London: Allen and Unwin, 1966.

18 The White Paper to the Children and Young Persons Act was *Children in Trouble*, Cmnd. 3065, London: HMSO, 1966.

19 Children and Young Persons Act, London: HMSO, 1969. Similarly, the children's hearings established by the Social Work (Scotland) Act had the remit to promote social welfare where, as well as searching out and meeting all 'need', there was the injunction to 'improve the life of the community'. The background to the Social Work (Scotland) Act is provided in the *Report of the Committee on Children and Young Persons, Scotland*, Cmnd. 2306, London: HMSO 1964; also *Social Work and the Community*, Cmnd. 3065, White Paper, London: HMSO, 1966. See Morris, A. and McIsaac, M., *Juvenile Justice*, London: Heinemann, 1978, for the background, principles and operation of the Social Work (Scotland) Act and Morgan, P., *Delinquent Fantasies*, London: Temple Smith, 1978.

20 Becoming the Local Authority Social Services Act of 1970. This reorganisation was inseparable from the advancement of the members and ideology of professional social work; coinciding with the establishment of the British Association of Social Workers.

21 These 'experts in living', employing Anthony Crosland's 'science in the service of the community', were supposed to be able to make a contribution to social regeneration on a par with the role which the physical sciences were expected to make to technological advancement. [Crosland, A., *The Future of Socialism*, London: Jonathan Cape, 1962.]

22 The newly created children's regional planning committees similarly concentrated on providing institutions. The particular demand for 'intensive care' or 'secure' provision grew as the youngsters referred got younger, less delinquent, and came from less disturbed backgrounds. The growth in the number of places itself appeared to be the predominant factor which increased the pressure for more. Because children were being referred and admitted, this seemed to demonstrate a growing need for more children to have 'intensive care'.

23 *Care and Treatment in a Planned Environment*, A report for the Community Home Project by the Home Office Advisory Council for Childcare, London: HMSO, 1970.

24 Triseliotis, J. and Russell, J., *Hard to Place: The Outcome of Adoption and Residential Care*, London: Heinemann Educational Books, 1984.

25 Ferguson, T., *Children in Care and After*, Oxford: Oxford University Press, for the Nuffield Foundation, 1966.

26 Cornish, D.B. and Clarke, R.V.G., *Residential Treatment and Its Effects on Delinquency*, Home Office Research Study No. 32, London: HMSO, 1975; see also Clarke, R.V.G. and Sinclair, L., 'Towards more effective treatment evaluation', European Committee on Crime Problems, *Collected Studies in Criminological Research*, Vol. XII, Strasbourg, Council of Europe, 1974; Martinson, R., 'What works?: questions and answers about prison reform', *The Public Interest*, Spring 1974, pp. 22-54. Lipton, D., Martinson, R. and Wilks, J., *The Effectiveness of Correctional Treatment: A Survey of Evaluation Studies*, New York: Praeger, 1975.

27 Cawson, P. and Martell, M., *Children Referred to Closed Units*, DHSS Research Report No. 5, London: HMSO, 1979. A report on the show piece St Charles Youth Treatment Centre, Brentwood, Essex (where a place cost £33,280 p.a in April 1981), spoke of bored, inactive youngsters, left without education, care or anything which might have given some shape or purpose to their lives. Staff (who outnumbered inmates) were 'remarkably unclear about their treatment aims, using vague and grandiose terms' and resorting to

a pot pouri of therapies, without comprehension of the rationale, however bogus, behind any of them, whether role-playing, bio-feedback, Gestalt, 'time-out', encounter therapy, doses of Largactil, etc.,

One of the inspection team remarked that the 'prevailing philosophy is to let a thousand flowers bloom' and how: '...there appeared to be a lack of common concepts and language, which would have helped us to form a clearer picture of what the Centre was trying to do and how ...some staff tried to express what they were doing in psychodynamic [Freudian or psychoanalytic] terms. But there seemed little grasp of what a psychodynamic approach implied in either theory or practice'. [*Report of the St Charles Youth Treatment Centre Evaluation Team*, DHSS, undated.]

28 *Children in the Public Care: A Review of Residential Childcare*, London: HMSO, 1991, p. 7, a review commissioned by the Secretary of State following the publication of the 'Pindown Experience' Report (Staffordshire County Council 1991).

29 Utting, W., *People Like Us: The Report of the Review of the Safeguards for Children Living Away from Home*, Department of Health and Welsh Office, 1997, p. 22.

30 *Ibid.*, p. 54.

31 The Review asked local authorities as a matter of priority to, at least, get all officers in charge suitably qualified. 'I consider [said Sir William Utting] that the Department of Health, the Local Authorities Associations and CCETSW should formulate an action plan, within the strategy for social services training, for securing the number of qualified staff needed within five years. They should also appoint an expert group to report, within 6 months, on the residential childcare content of qualifying courses' [p. 55].

A residential Childcare Initiative was launched by the Department of Health in 1992/3, designed to ensure that all heads of residential homes were minimally qualified.

32 Utting, *People Like Us: The Report of the Review of the Safeguards for Children Living Away from Home*, op. cit., p. 24.

33 *Children in the Public Care*, op. cit., p. 13. Barry O'Neill, then Director of Social Services during the tenure of Tony Latham in Staffordshire children's homes, admitted that there had been a policy in the department up to 1986 'to let him get on with it and not to interfere as long as he "produced the goods" '. [Graves, D., 'Pindown was violation of human rights', *The Daily Telegraph*, 31 May 1991.]

34 *Small Unregistered Children's Homes*, Social Services Inspectorate, Department of Health, 1995, p. 2.

The conduct of these units are not covered by the Children's Homes regulations, nor the Foster Placement (Children) Regulations, and they are not required to undergo regular inspection. Instead, they are meant to be regulated by other Children Act Regulations, the Arrangements for the Placement of Children (General) Regulations 1991 and the Review of Children's Cases Regulations 1991. These cover the placement of children by 'other arrangements' as described in Section 23(2)(f) of the Children Act 1989 and they simply place a general duty on each local authority using any placement to ensure that: (i) it is suitable (ii) the children are being properly supervised (iii) their welfare is being promoted.

35 *Ibid.*, p. 15; also *Partners in Caring*, the Fourth Annual Report of the Chief Inspector, Social Services Inspectorate, 1994/5, Department of Health, 1995. This speaks of 'such homes... growing quite quickly. This has the potential for leaving some of the most vulnerable and emotionally damaged young people insufficiently supervised by placing authorities' [p. 21].

36 *Small Unregistered Children's Homes, op. cit.*, p. 2.

37 *Ibid.*, p. 7.

38 *Ibid.*, p. 8. One agency charged £3,000 per week, plus extra for education and therapy. Some local authorities ignorantly believed that they were placing youngsters in foster homes or registered homes. Social workers failed to make accurate assessments of the placements, often because they could not see past the glossy publicity material and bogus claims put out by proprietors. Playing on the language of therapy and concern, these might offer a 'psychotherapeutic environment using psychodynamic counselling' or 'outward-bound focused activities, generally land-based but sometimes operating in a boat' or 'semi-secure' accommodation (when proper secure accommodation is formally designated and approved as such).

39 *Ibid.*, p. 11.

40 *Ibid.*, p. 11.

41 See 'Children's Homes at 31 March 1996, England', Department of Health, Government Statistical Service, 1996.

42 Singleton, R., Senior Director, Barnardo's, letter to *The Times*, 7 January 1997 in response to Barker, P., 'Finding homes for our lost children', *The Times*, 30 December 1996.

43 Utting, *People Like Us, op. cit.*, pp. 1-3; see also Taylor, A., 'Hostages to fortune: the abuse of children in care', unpublished paper, 1996.

44 Widespread abuse is also alleged for South Glamorgan, where Geoffrey Morris was jailed for indecent assaults against teenage boys. Another worker committed suicide and a third man has been convicted of offences elsewhere.

45 Bunyan N., 'Boys abused on "unimaginable scale" in home', *The Daily Telegraph*, 23 January 1997.

46 The boys are described as being '...neglected, ill-fed and clothed, dirty and often infested, and little attention was paid to signs of distress or addiction to solvents. Bryn Estyn seemed little better than a human warehouse, dominated by a malaise and unease which probably arose from the conflict between fickle conscience and failure to act'. [Taylor, A., 'Hostages to fortune: the abuse of children in care', *op. cit.*]

47 Alan Langshaw, care worker, pleaded guilty to 30 counts of serious sexual assaults and indecent assaults against boys aged under 16 at homes in Cheshire and Liverpool. Jailed for 10 years.

Colin Dick, care worker guilty of nine serious sexual offences and indecent assaults against children at one home in Cheshire. Jailed for four years.

Dennis Grain, care worker, pleaded guilty to 19 cases of serious sexual offences and indecent assault at homes in Cheshire and Yorkshire. Jailed for seven years.

Terrence Hoskin, guilty of 22 counts of indecent assault and physical assault and serious sexual offences at home where he was head. Jailed for eight years.

John Clarke, convicted of indecent and physical assault at a care home in Cheshire. Jailed for three and a half years.

Roy Shuttleworth, care worker, found guilty of 11 counts of serious sexual offences and indecent assaults on boys in a care home in Cheshire. Jailed for 10 years.

John Clarke, convicted of five indecent assaults at children's homes. Jailed for three and a half years.

James Traynor, convicted of five indecent assaults and one serious sexual assault. Jailed for eight years.

Keith Laverack, convicted of 20 serious sexual assaults and indecent assaults. Jailed for 18 years.

In turn, two men (Philip Savage and Edward Stanton) have been respectively jailed for 13 and 15 years in Liverpool in prosecutions arising from the Cheshire enquiry

48 Report 'The Hackney scandal', *Evening Standard*, 4 September 1996.

49 See review in Utting, *People Like Us: The Report of the Review of the Safeguards for Children Living Away from Home, op. cit.*, and Crosse, S.B., Kaye, E. and Ratnofsky, A.C., *A Report on the Maltreatment of Children with Disabilities*, Washington DC: National Center on Child Abuse and Neglect, 1993.

50 Utting, *People Like Us, op. cit.*, p. 121.

51 Alison Taylor, quoted in Grice, E., 'The suffering I could not condone', *The Daily Telegraph*, 9 April 1996.

52 Triseliotis, Russell and James, *Hard to Place, op. cit.*

53 *Ibid.*, p. 71.

54 *Ibid.*, p. 66.

55 *Ibid.*, p. 67.

56 Quoted in *ibid.*, pp. 71-72.

57 If necessary, assaults and injuries can be explained as mishaps, or the accidental outcome of restraint.

58 Jardine, C., 'The world of Tony Latham, where childcare is just a poor relation', *The Daily Telegraph*, 31 May 1991.

59 Utting, *People Like Us: The Report of the Review of the Safeguards for Children Living Away from Home, op. cit.*

60 A 20 year old is suing Durham Council, the Aycliffe Centre and five individuals for personal injuries. Claiming that he worked as a rent boy at 14, and that those looking after him failed in their duty of care, Carl August maintains that he was '...systematically abused for three years and allowed to visit the gay scene'. ['Aycliffe at centre of new abuse allegations', *Community Care*, 14-20 November 1996.]

61 Rogers, T., 'Lost children of the night', *The Sunday Telegraph*, 18 August 1996.

62 Survey of clients, APA Community Drug and Alcohol Initiatives, London, 1996.

63 *Children in the Public Care: A Review of Residential Childcare, op. cit.*, p. 42. Similar reasons are reported by the Children's Society from their refuges.

64 Checks on nearly 3,000 files of children in care in Gloucestershire between 1970 and 1994 found that files on almost 400 young people were missing and the whereabouts of 97 were not recorded or recorded as 'unknown' after they had left care. *In Care Contacts: the West Case: The Report of a Review of over 2,000 files of Young People in Residential Care*, The Bridge Consultancy, 1996; and 'Report reveals scale of missing runaways', *Community Care*, 14-20 November 1996, p. 1.

65 *Children in the Public Care: A Review of Residential Childcare, op. cit.*, p. 89.

66 'Lost children', *Community Care*, 14-20 November 1996.

67 *Children in the Public Care: A Review of Residential Childcare, op. cit.*, pp. 99 and 105.

68 It is also possible to see support for a *laissez-faire* approach in the Criteria and Guidelines for services for children and families issued by the Social Services Inspectorate, which stress how these must 'ensure that the child's self-esteem is promoted with respect to race, religion, language, culture, gender, *sexuality* and disability' (emphasis added). [Appendix B, Standard 4, in *Inspection of Local Authority Fostering 1994-5*, National Summary Report.] However, this was intended to be read in the context of concern at the way in which local authorities were not bothering to find out which religion a child was affiliated to and ignoring their sexual development in such a way as left them open to exploitation.

69 Laming, H., *The Control of Children In the Public Care: Interpretation of the Children Act 1989*, Department of Health, 20 February 1997. There was concern that 'the Children Act may have gone too far in stressing the rights of children at the expense of upholding the rights and responsibilities of parents and professionals in supervising them'.

70 Guidance on Permissible Forms of Control for Children in Residential Care (LAC(93) 13). This emphasized how it was 'quite explicit' that, under a care order, 'the local authority shares parental responsibility with the parents and legal authority with respect to the care and control of the child'.

71 Because the child was not in secure accommodation did not 'disempower staff' or 'oblige them to agree to the child's preferences or wishes where doing so would be likely to prejudice its welfare'. It was reasonable to bolt doors, and use physical restraint and limit a child's mobility, and every effort should be used to secure the presence of other staff to ensure that any action taken was safe and successful. It was emphasised that 'although physical restraint cannot be used as a punishment' it should be regarded as a disciplinary measure within the meaning of Regulation 8(4) of the Children's Homes Regulations 1991 and recorded in this way.

72 *Children in the Public Care, op. cit.*, p. 23.

73 *The Foster Care Market: A National Perspective*, Association of Directors of Social Services, 1997; see also report by Cathy Cooper 'Councils rely on agency fosterers', *Community Care*, 12-18 December 1996.

74 *Inspection of Local Authority Fostering 1995-6*, Department of Health London: HMSO, 1997.

75 *The Organisation of Fostering Services: A Study of the Arrangements for Delivery of Fostering Services in England*, London: National Foster Care Association, 1997.

76 Kelly, G., 'Foster parents and long-term placements: key findings from a Northern Ireland study', *Children and Society*, Vol. 9, No. 2, 1995, pp. 19-29.

77 Triseliotis, J., Sellick, C. and Short, R., *Foster Care: Theory and Practice*, London: British Agencies for Adoption and Fostering, 1995.

78 *Small Unregistered Children's Homes*, Social Services Inspectorate, Department of Health, 1995.

79 Johnson, V., 'Children in need', letter to *Guardian*, 16 December 1996.

80 *Small Unregistered Children's Homes, op. cit.*, p. 13. Hence we get cases like that of Julie:

'Her mother suffered bouts of mental illness and Julie had gone from one placement to another... at the age of 11, her previous placements by now too numerous to count, Julie was proposed for long-term admission to a specialist community home... she was said to be presenting uncontrollable and wholly inappropriate sexual behaviour, such that she constituted a danger to male and female adults, and required 24 hour supervision.

'She did indeed exhibit an inappropriate sexuality, which was wholly consistent with her having been abused. Her social worker eventually admitted... that three or four years earlier, Julie had made allegations of sexual assault against an adult male in the foster family... Social workers continued to place children with this family, and never disclosed the allegation because the department could not 'afford' to lose the resource... We later learned from her of the physical, sexual and psychological abuses she endured in several of the other placements for whose failure she was blamed.' [Taylor, 'Hostages to fortune: the abuse of children in care', *op. cit.*]

81 See, for example, *Inspection of Local Authority Fostering*, Social Services Inspectorate, London: Department of Health, 1996.

82 Rowe, J., Hundleby, M. and Garnett, L., *Childcare Now: A Survey of Placement Patterns*, London: British Agencies for Adoption and Fostering, 1989.

83 'Children in care', Barnardos Scottish division, report 1997.

84 Evidence to the Review, *Children in the Public Care, op. cit.*

85 Redgrave, K., letter to *The Independent*, 18 November 1996. The principal officer at the National Children's Bureau also claimed that children may have as many as 10, 12 or 14 placements in the space of two years. [Youdan, P., quoted in Stone, K., 'Moving stories', *Community Care*, 30 January 1997.]

86 Packman, Randall and Jacques, *Who Needs Care? Social Work Decisions about Children, op. cit.*

87 Millham, S. *et al.*, *Lost in Care*, Aldershot: Gower, 1986.

Chapter 13: Children with the Odds Against Them

1   Or one in six according to Wolkind, S.N., 'Children who have been "in care"; an epidemiological study', *Journal of Child Psychology and Psychiatry*, Vol. 14, 1973, pp. 97-105.

2   Fanshel, D. and Shinn, E.B., *Children in Foster Care: A Longitudinal Study*, New York: Columbia University Press, 1978. In welfare families, 36 per cent had suffered some developmental impairment and 20 per cent had serious behavioural difficulties.

3   Rutter, M., Quinton, D. and Hill, J., 'Adult outcome of institution-reared children: males and females compared', in Robins, L.N. and Rutter, M., *Straight and Devious Pathways from Childhood to Adolescence*, Cambridge: Cambridge University Press, 1990, p. 143.

4   Thorpe, R., 'The experience of parents and children living apart', in Triseliotis, J.P. (ed.), *New Developments in Foster Care and Adoption*, London: Routledge and Kegan Paul, 1980.

5   Rowe, J., Cain, H., Hundleby, M. and Keane, A., *Long-Term Foster Care*, London: Batsford, 1984.

6   Fletcher, B., *Not Just a Name: The Views of Young People in Foster and Residential Care*, National Consumer Council, 1993.

7   Utting, W., *People Like Us: The Report of the Review of the Safeguards for Children Living Away from Home*, Department of Health and Welsh Office, 1997, p. 26.

8   Butler, I. and Payne, H., 'The health of children looked after by the local authority', *Adoption and Fostering*, Vol. 21, No. 2, Summer 1997, p. 29.

9   Hill, M. and Triseliotis, J., 'The transition from long-term care to adoption', in Hudson, J. and Galaway, B. (eds.), *The State as Parent*, London: Kluwer Academic Press, 1989.

10 Dinnage, R. and Kellmer Pringle, M., *Residential Care: Facts and Fallacies*, London: Longman, 1967.

11 Prosser, R., *Perspectives on Residential Care: An Annotated Bibliography*, Slough: National Foundation for Educational Research, 1976.

12 Packman, J. with Randall, J. and Jacques, N., *Who Needs Care? Social Work Decisions about Children*, Oxford: Basil Blackwell, 1986. pp.193-94.

13 Heath, A., Colton, M. and Aldgate, J., 'Failure to escape: a longitudinal study of foster children's educational attainment', *British Journal of Social Work*, Vol. 24, 1989, pp. 241-60.

14 Garnett, L., *Leaving Care and After*, London: National Children's Bureau 1992; and Stein, M. and Carey, K., *Leaving Care*, Oxford: Blackwell, 1986.

15 Prison Reform Trust, *The Identikit Prisoner*, 1991; see also the National Prison Survey, Home Office, 1991.

16 ' "One of the major residential placements for kids who age out of the system is jail", says Nancy Nazaroff, clinical director at Project Rap, in Beverly, which deals with homeless youths. "In jail, they're warm, they get food and a roof over their head, they can get education and substance abuse help, and there's TV." Some girls have a different career strategy: early pregnancy. Then they can get a monthly welfare check, food stamps, Medicaid, and even day care.' [English, B., 'Nobody's children: too old for foster care, too young for independence', *The Boston Globe*, 16 October 1994, p. 39.]

17 Rosen, A.C., 'The social and emotional development of children in long-term residential care', *Therapeutic Education*, Spring 1971.

18 Rutter, M., Quinton, D. and Hill, J., 'Adult outcome of institution-reared children: males and females compared', in Robins, L.N. and Rutter, M., *Straight and Devious Pathways from Childhood to Adolescence*, Cambridge: Cambridge University Press, 1990.

19 Buchanan, A. and Ten Brinke, J. *What Happened When They Were Grown Up?*, York: Joseph Rowntree Foundation, 1997.

20 *Ibid.*

21 Triseliotis, J. and Russell, J., *Hard to Place: The Outcome of Adoption and Residential Care*, London: Heinemann Educational Books, 1984, p. 150.

22 Quoted in *Too Much, Too Young: The Failure of Social Policy in Meeting the Needs of Care Leavers*, Action on After Care Consortium, Barnardos, 1996, p. 1.

23 Francis, J., 'Still waiting', *Community Care*, 22-28 August 1996.

24 Biehal, N., Clayden, J., Stein, M. and Wade, J., *Prepared for Living? A Survey of Young People leaving the Care of Three Local Authorities*, London: National Children's Bureau, 1992.

25 Buchanan and Ten Brinke, *What Happened When They Were Grown Up?, op. cit.*

26 Triseliotis and Russell, *Hard to Place: The Outcome of Adoption and Residential Care, op. cit.*, p. 190.

27 *Ibid.*, p. 154.

28 *Ibid.*, p. 154.

29 *Ibid.*

30 Packman, Randall and Jacques, *Who Needs Care?*, *op. cit.*

31 *Ibid.*, p. 119.

32 Rowe, J. and Lambert, L., *Children Who Wait*, London: Association of British Adoption Agencies, 1973 p. 114-15.

33 *Children in the Public Care: A Review of Residential Childcare*, London: HMSO, 1991.

34 *Ibid.*, p. 26.

Chapter 14: New Ways to go Backwards

1 White, R., 'Standards of parenting and the law', in Adcock, M. and White, R., *Good Enough Parenting*, London: British Agencies for Adoption and Fostering, 1985, reprint 1994, p. 38; see also Wald, M., 'State intervention on behalf of endangered children: a proposed legal response', *International Journal of Child Abuse and Neglect*, Vol. 16, No. 1, pp. 3-45.

2 'The way ahead', *Community Care*, 19 December 1996 - 8 January 1997.

3 Triseliotis, J. and Russell, J., *Hard to Place: The Outcome of Adoption and Residential Care*, London: Heinemann Education, 1984, p. 195.

4 *Ibid.*, p. 196.

5 Mayer, S.E., *What Money Can't Buy*, Cambridge, Massachusetts and London: Harvard, 1997, p. 49.

6 Economic and cultural factors which were quite closely related to differences in adult homicide rates between American states did not explain variations in infant homicides. [Straus, M.A., 'State and regional differences in US infant homicide rates in relation to sociocultural characteristics of the states', *Behavioural Sciences and the Law*, Vol. 5, 1987, pp. 61-75.]

7 *Partners in Caring*, the Fourth Annual Report of the Chief Inspector, Social Services Inspectorate, 1994/5, Department of Health, 1995; and *Social Services: Achievement and Challenge*, Department of Health and the Welsh Office, 1997.

8 Triseliotis and Russell, *Hard to Place, op. cit.*, p. 194.

9 Barth, R.P., Courtney, M., Berrick, J.D. and Albert, V., *From Child Abuse to Permanency Planning*, New York: Aldine de Gruyter, 1994, p. 265.

10 *Ibid.*, p. 132. Family preservation originated with David Haapal and Jill Kinney in 1974 when they put a programme to the National Institute of Mental Health for Homebuilders for intensive, short-term intervention in the client's own home. As it snowballed, family

preservation appealed to a broad political spectrum in the US. Conservatives supported it because it was consistent with supporting the sanctity of the family, or limiting state intervention in the private sphere of life. Liberals saw it as consistent with the tradition of a caring government that supports needy families and children. With growing numbers of children entering the care system in the 1980s, and its costs rising, there was concern for where the new funding was going to come from. Clearly: 'In a climate where spending for social programs was becoming more and more constrained while the demand for such programs was growing, a program that could be supported on both sides of the political aisle was an almost irresistible opportunity'.

11 Heneghan, A.M., Horwitz, S.H. and Leventhal, J.M., 'Evaluating intensive family preservation programs: a methodological review', paper presented at the Ambulatory Pediatrics Association meeting, Seattle, May 1994.

12 Gelles, R., 'The doctrine of family reunification: child protection or risk?', Paper presented at the Boys Town conference on Child Protection: Old Problem, New Paradigm, May 20-22, 1994, p. 127.

13 Schuerman, J.R., Rzepnicki, T.L. and Littell, J.H., *Putting Families First*, New York: Aldine de Gruyter, 1995.

14 'Some original supporters of the Illinois family preservation program have admitted to us that they did not really think that the program would have major placement prevention effects but that the claims had been made in order to get the program passed by the Illinois legislature. For others, the claims of benefits appears to have been simply an excess of zeal'. *Ibid.*, pp. 239-40.

15 Matlick, J., 'Fifteen years of failure: an assessment of California's foster care system', Pacific Research Institute 1997. The California Senate Bill 14, 1982 was intended to solve the problems that plagued California's child welfare system in the 1970s, 'when foster children spent their formative years moving from home to home in a system that had lost sight of their need for a stable and loving family'. Between 1988-89 and 1995-96 the overall funding of Child Welfare Services rose 80 per cent. The amount spent on families considered to have children at risk of ending up in care rose from $1m to $45m. The amount allocated, per case, increased by 32 per cent. During this time, there was a rapid rise in the care population, as elsewhere in the USA. While services were faced with an initial crisis caused by the increase in case loads, resources largely kept pace. After more than a decade, the system should have been realising its goals of healing families and achieving permanency for children.

However, 80 per cent of care children came from families that had received at least one type of family preservation service. Indeed;

'whenever the family maintenance [services to help children stay at home] caseload grew, the foster care caseload grew at an even faster rate'. [Barth, *et al.*, *From Child Abuse to Permanency Planning, op. cit.*] Reunification had not improved since 1986-7, so that 51 per cent of children would not be reunited with their families. The average foster child had been in two homes, and ten per cent in five or more homes, with 40 per cent of children in care having been in the system for at least three years and one in ten for five or more. In 1995 37 per cent of care children had been in the system at least three times; up from 27 per cent in 1985. One in five infants reunified with his/her parents was re-abused.

16　*Ibid.*, p. 112.

17　Gelles, 'The doctrine of family reunification: child protection or risk?', *op. cit.*

18　Gelles, R.J., *The Book of David*, New York: Basic Books, 1996, p. 127.

19　*A Nation's Shame: Fatal Child Abuse and Neglect in the United States, A Report of the US Advisory Board on Child Abuse and Neglect*, US Advisory Board on Child Abuse and Neglect, Washington, DC: Department of Health and Human Services, Administration for Children and Families, 1995.

20　Barth, *et al.*, *From Child Abuse to Permanency Planning, op. cit.*, p. 249.

21　*Ibid.*, p. 246.

22　Marsh, P. and Triseliotis, J., *Prevention and Reunification in Childcare*, London: Batsford, 1993, p. 19.

23　*Ibid.*, p. 23.

24　Thoburn, J., *Child Placement: Principles and Practice*, second edn., Aldershot: Ashgate Publishers, 1995, p. 30.

25　Aldgate, 'Respite care for children: an old remedy in a new package', in Marsh and Triseliotis, *Prevention and Reunification in Childcare, op. cit.*, p. 90.

26　*The Care of Children, Principles and Practice in Regulations and Guidance*, Department of Health, London: HMSO, 1990, p. 8.

27　Aldgate, 'Respite care for children: an old remedy in a new package', *op. cit.*, p. 105.

28　The rather dubious reasoning is that it would be rare for a child found to be 'in need of protection' following a Section 47 investigation not to be a 'child in need' under Section 17. This is a slippery slope to go down, widening the catchment area for social services intervention. See Thoburn, J., *Child Placement: Principles and Practice*, Aldershot: Arena, 1994.

The Department of Health guide, *The Care of Children: Principles and Practice in regulations and Guidance* (DH, 1990) accompanying the new Children Act, gives a clear mandate to widen the scope of what have been traditionally called 'preventive services' to include short-term out-of-home placements as a viable option for any family under stress, not just those with disabled children.

Regulation 13 accompanying the Children Act 1989 allows for a series of pre-planned placements to be treated as a single placement. However, these must all occur within one year, with each single placement no longer than four weeks and with a total duration not exceeding 90 days. They must all be with one carer. Critics claim that too rigid an interpretation would create a new demarcation between respite and other care. [See Aldgate, 'Respite care for children: an old remedy in a new package', *op. cit.*]

29 As allowances exist for foster care, and are discretionary for foster carers adopting older or other special-needs children, 'why not do the same for own-family placement?' [Marsh and Triseliotis, *Prevention and Reunification in Childcare, op. cit.*, p. 18.] It has always been customary 'to address any problems of children's material needs by using financial support from Boarding Out allowances to purchase clothes, toys and equipment for children which become the permanent property of children at the end of the placement'. (Aldgate, 'Respite care for children: an old remedy in a new package', *op. cit.*, p. 103.) However, development of this cash-dispensing service (on a 'user-led' basis?) suggests that social services will become fully-fledged benefits agencies. They already have elsewhere. 'Kinship care' is one of the most striking trends in American welfare, swelling the foster care population. Typically, a relative of the parent, usually the grandmother or aunt, is paid to be the foster carer. Most 'kinship' carers are poor and single, and appear to be second generation welfare mothers. With the foster pay supplementing the family's benefits, the parallel is with the increase in recipients of disability payments. [Matlick, J., 'Fifteen years of failure: an assessment of California's foster care system', San Francisco: Pacific Research Institute, 1997.]

30 Utting, W., *People Like Us: The Report of the Review of the Safeguards for Children Living Away from Home*, Department of Health and Welsh Office, 1997, p. 90.

31 Aldgate, 'Respite care for children: an old remedy in a new package', *op. cit.*, p. 86.

32 *Ibid.*, p. 103.

33 Marsh and Triseliotis, *Prevention and Reunification in Childcare, op. cit.*, p. 12.

34 Thoburn, *Child Placement: Principles and Practice, op. cit.*, p. 30.

35 Atherton, C., 'Reunification: parallels between placement in new families and reunifying children with their families', in Marsh and Triseliotis, *Prevention and Reunification in Childcare, op. cit.,* p. 188.

36 *Ibid.*

37 Aldgate, 'Respite care for children: an old remedy in a new package', *op. cit.,* p. 105.

38 Thoburn, J., *Review of Research Relating to Adoption,* Inter-departmental review of adoption law: background paper No 2, Department of Health, 1990, p. 88.

39 Thoburn, J., *Success and Failure in Permanent Family Placement,* Aldershot: Avebury, 1990, p. 78.

40 Tizard, B., *Adoption: A Second Chance,* London: Open Books, 1977, p. 211.

41 Kelly, G., 'Foster parents and long-term placements: key findings from a Northern Ireland study', *Children and Society,* Vol. 9, No. 2, 1995, p. 20; see also Thoburn, *Inter-departmental Review of Adoption Law op. cit.*

42 Triseliotis, J., Shireman, J. and Hundelby, M., *Adoption, Theory and Practice,* London: Cassell, 1997, p. 111.

43 Fagan, P.F., 'Why serious welfare reform must include serious adoption reform', *Backgrounder,* No. 1045, Washington DC: Heritage Foundation, 27 July 1995.

44 Department of Health and Welsh Office, 'Review of Adoption Law: Report to the Ministers of an Independent Working Group: A Consultative Document', London: Department of Health, 1992; and Department of Health, *Adoption: The Future* (White Paper), London: HMSO, 1993.

45 Triseliotis, Shireman and Hundelby, *Adoption, Theory and Practice, op. cit.,* p. 83.

46 *Ibid.,* p. 35.

47 A residence order settles the arrangements as to the person with whom the child is to live, and gives them the authority that by law a parent has in relation to a child and his or her property.

48 As with June Thoburn's review for the Department of Health.

49 Thoburn, *Success and Failure in Permanent Family Placement, op. cit.;* and Fratter, J., Rowe, J., Sapsford, D. and Thoburn, J., *Permanent Family Placement,* London: British Agencies for Adoption and Fostering, 1991.

50 See, for example Booth, T. and Booth, W., *Exceptional Childhoods, Unexceptional Children: Growing Up with Parents who have Learning Difficulties*, London: Family Policy Studies Centre, 1997. Up to 50 per cent of children whose parents are mentally retarded are taken into care. The children are likely to be removed partly because of risks to their welfare and development and also because, as they get older, they pass out of parental control. Moreover, they suffer high levels of abuse, not from their mothers but from 'partners' and other 'normal' men who exploit handicapped women.

51 Triseliotis, J.P., 'Older children in care', in Wedge, P. and Thoburn, J., *Finding Families for 'Hard-to-Place' Children*, London: British Agencies for Adoption and Fostering, 1986.

52 Rowe, J., Cain, H., Hundleby, M. and Keane, A., *Long-Term Foster Care*, London: Batsford, 1984.

53 Triseliotis, J., 'Foster care outcomes', *Adoption and Fostering*, Vol. 13, No. 3, 1989 pp. 5-16. See also, Berridge, D. and Cleaver, H., *Foster Home Breakdown*, Oxford: Blackwell, 1987. For planned long-term foster care breakdowns ranged from 42 per cent of placements for one rural authority to 21 per cent for a London borough. [Rowe, J., Hundleby, M. and Garnett, L., *Childcare Now: A Survey of Placement Patterns*, London: British Agencies for Adoption and Fostering, 1989; Kelly, G., 'Foster parents and long-term placements: key findings from a Northern Ireland study, *Children and Society*, Vol. 9, No. 2, 1995, pp. 19-29.]

54 Fagan, 'Why serious welfare reform must include serious adoption reform', *op. cit.*, p. 16; also see Silber, K. and Martinez Dormer, P., *Children of Open Adoption*, San Antonio, Texas: Corona Publishing Co., 1989; and Berry, M., 'The effects of open adoption on biological and adoptive parents and the children: the arguments and the evidence', *Child Welfare*, Vol. 70, No. 6, November-December 1990.

55 Triseliotis, Shireman and Hundelby, *Adoption, Theory and Practice, op. cit.*, p. 111.

56 Thoburn, *Success and Failure in Permanent Family Placement, op. cit.*

57 Fletcher, *Not Just a Name: The Views of Young People in Foster and Residential Care, op. cit.*, p. 8.

58 Triseliotis and Russell, *Hard to Place: The Outcome of Adoption and Residential Care, op. cit.*; and Hill, M. and Triseliotis, J., 'The transition from long-term care to adoption', in Hudson, J. and Gallaway, B. (eds.), *The State as Parent*, London: Kluwer Academic Press, 1989.

59 Tizard, *Adoption: A Second Chance, op. cit.*

60 Thoburn, *Success and Failure in Permanent Family Placement, op. cit.*, p. 44.

61 Ryburn, M., 'Adoptive parents and contested adoptions', in Ryburn, M., *Contested Adoptions*, Aldershot: Arena, 1994 pp.150-52.

62 Hill and Triseliotis, 'The transition from long-term care to adoption', *op. cit.*, p. 423.

63 *Ibid.*, p. 420.

64 *Ibid.*, p. 425.

65 Treseliotis, J., 'Growing up in foster care and after', in Triseliotis, J. (ed.), *Developments in Foster Care and Adoption*, London: Routledge and Kegan Paul, 1980.

66 Rowe, J. and Lambert , L., *Children Who Wait*, London: Association of British Adoption Agencies, 1973.

67 *Ibid.*, p. 109.

68 *Ibid.*, p. 112.

69 Hapgood, M., 'Older child adoption and the knowledge base of adoption practice', in Bean P. (ed.), *Adoption: Essays in Social Policy, Law, and Sociology*, London: Tavistock, 1984, p. 63. Somewhat incongruously, considering her championship of 'permanent fostering', guardianship or 'limited adoption' as of equal utility with adoption proper, June Thoburn acknowledges that 'If such [committed] families are to continue to come forward to offer homes, especially for "special-needs" children, there will continue to be a need for adoption or some equally secure legal status'. Inter-departmental Review of Adoption Law, *op. cit.*, p. 85.

70 Raynor, L., *The Adopted Child Comes of Age*, London: Allen and Unwin, 1980, p. 152.

Chapter 15: Ending 'The Great Disjunction'

1 Tizard, B., *Adoption: A Second Chance*, London: Open Books, 1977, p. 234.

2 Rutter, M., Quinton, D. and Hill, J., 'Adult outcome of institution-reared children: males and females compared', in Robins, L.N. and Rutter, M. (eds.), *Straight and Devious Pathways from Childhood to Adolescence*, Cambridge: Cambridge University Press, 1990 p. 153.

3 Research on young unwed mothers suggests that those who are ambivalent about keeping the child will more willingly part with their babies if they can be assured of having news of their progress and some choice of family. [Barth, R., 'Adolescent mothers' beliefs about open adoption', *Social Casework*, June 1987, pp. 313-21.]

4 Lindsay, J.W., *Open Adoption: A Caring Option*, Morning Glory Press, 1987.

5 Lancette J. and McClure, B.A., 'Birth mothers: grieving the loss of a dream', *Journal of Mental Health Counselling*, Vol. 14, No. 1, 1992, pp 84-96.

6 Hodges, J. and Tizard, B., 'IQ and behavioural adjustment of ex-institutional adolescents', *Journal of Child Psychology and Psychiatry* Vol. 30, No. 1, 1989, p. 69.

7 Schuerman, J.R., Rzepnicki, T.L. and Littell, J.H., *Putting Families First*, New York: Aldine de Gruyter, 1995 p. 7.

8 *For Children's Sake: An SSI Inspection of Local Authority Adoption Services*, Social Services Inspectorate, Department of Health, 1996, p. 15.

9 See, White, R., 'Standards of parenting and the law', in Adcock, M., and White, R., *Good Enough Parenting*, London: British Agencies for Adoption and Fostering, 1985, reprint 1994. This draws heavily on Wald, M., 'State intervention on behalf of endangered children: a proposed legal response', *International Journal of Child Abuse and Neglect*, Vol. 16, No. 1, pp. 3-45.

10 Barth, R.P., Courtney, M., Berrick, J.D. and Albert, V., *From Child Abuse to Permanency Planning*, New York: Aldine de Gruyter, 1994, p. 258.

11 See Utting, W., *People Like Us: The Report of the Review of the Safeguards for Children Living Away from Home*, Department of Health and Welsh Office, 1997.

12 Rowe, J. and Lambert, L., *Children Who Wait*, London: Association of British Adoption Agencies, 1973. p. 106.

13 Stein, T.J., Gambrill, E.D. and Wiltse, K.T., *Children in Foster Care: Achieving Continuity of Care*, New York: Praeger Publications, 1978. The authors suggest that the parents enter into a contractual agreement which sets out the goals and what the parties must do to achieve these.

14 White, R., 'Standards of parenting and the law', in Adcock, M. and White, R., *Good Enough Parenting*, London: British Agencies for Adoption and Fostering, 1985, reprint 1994 p. 38, quoting Wald, M., p. 39.

15 Gelles, R.J., *The Book of David*, New York: Basic Books, 1996, p. 88.

16 *Children in the Public Care: A Review of Residential Childcare*, London: HMSO, 1991.

17 Murch, M. and Thorpe, Rt. Hon. Lord Justice, 'The development of the family justice system in England and Wales: past, present, and future', in Salgo, L. (ed.), *The Family Justice System*, Collegium Budapest Workshop, Series No. 3, 1997, pp. 3-34.

18 See *Agreement and Freeing*, Discussion Paper Number 2 Inter-Departmental Review of Adoption Law, Department of Health, September 1991.

19 Murch, M. Lowe, N., Borkowski, M., Copner, R. and Griew, K., *Pathways to Adoption*, Research Project Socio-Legal Centre for Family Studies, University of Bristol, London: HMSO, 1993.

20 *Ibid.*, pp. 243-44.

21 *For Children's Sake: An SSI Inspection of Local Authority Adoption Services*, Social Services Inspectorate, *op. cit.*

22 Murch, *et al.*, *Pathways to Adoption*, *op. cit.*, p. 224.

23 *Adoption: A Service for Children*, Adoption Bill: A Consultative Document, London: HMSO, March 1996.

24 *For Children's Sake*, Social Services Inspectorate, *op. cit.*, p. 119.

25 There is also, of course, the question of whether child welfare services should be disaggregated and turned over to non-profit agencies. Kansas has become the first state in the USA to privatise its adoption, foster-care, and family preservation services. Contractors must agree to serve each child for a fixed price, with incentives to work intensively with the parents to get the child back home or, if that is not possible, to proceed to the termination of parental rights. Competition has encouraged providers to create an array of partnerships and consortia to address their weaknesses. [Eggers, W.D., 'There's no place like home', *Policy Review*, May - June 1997, pp. 43-47.]

Index